Way Beyond PowerPoint: Making 21st - Century Presentations™

PERFORMING AND CREATING SPEECHES, DEMONSTRATIONS, AND COLLABORATIVE LEARNING EXPERIENCES

WITH COOL NEW DIGITAL TOOLS

SUSAN MEYER

rosen publishing's
rosen
central®

NEW YORK

Published in 2014 by The Rosen Publishing Group, Inc.
29 East 21st Street, New York, NY 10010

Library of Congress Cataloging-in-Publication Data

Meyer, Susan.
Performing and creating speeches, demonstrations, and collaborative learning experiences with cool new digital tools/by Susan Meyer.
  p. cm. — (Way beyond PowerPoint: making 21st-century presentations)
Includes bibliographic references and index.
ISBN 978-1-4777-1837-7 (library binding) — ISBN 978-1-4777-1851-3 (pbk.)
— ISBN 978-1-4777-1852-0 (6-pack)
1. Public speaking — Juvenile literature. 2. Speechwriting — Juvenile literature. I. Meyer, Susan, 1986–. II. Title.
PN4129.15 M49 2014
808.5—dc23

Manufactured in the United States of America

CPSIA Compliance Information: Batch #W14YA: For further information, contact Rosen Publishing, New York, New York, at 1-800-237-9932.

CONTENTS

Introduction   4

Chapter 1   Presentations Enter the
Twenty-First Century   7

Chapter 2   Tricked Out: Enhancing with Multimedia   17

Chapter 3   Setting It in Motion:
Screencasting and Animation   23

Chapter 4   Get the Word Out! Sharing Your Presentation   29

Glossary   39
For More Information   41
For Further Reading   44
Bibliography   45
Index   46

INTRODUCTION

Thomas Suarez is a whiz kid by anyone's definition. At ten years old, he persuaded his parents to loan him the 99 cents he needed to download the Apple app development kit. This kit helps people create applications like tools and games for mobile devices such as the iPhone and iPad. Before his parents knew it, Thomas had used his programming skills to create *Bustin Jieber*, a game app designed for the anti-Justin Bieber crowd at his middle school that pokes fun at the pop star. But awareness of Thomas's game didn't remain confined to only his group of friends at school.

One of the ways that Thomas was able to have his game reach a much larger audience was by giving a presentation about it. At the age of twelve, he introduced Bustin Jieber to the masses on an online platform called TED Talks. TED stands for "Technology, Entertainment, and Design," and its motto is "Ideas Worth Spreading." TED Talks started as presentations that were delivered during the annual TED Conference. Now these talks are available for download and streaming online.

Thomas has a passion not only for building apps, but also for sharing his interests with others. The key to a great presentation is a true interest in the content and the desire to teach it. Thanks to the power of digital tools and being able to use the platform of TED Talks, Thomas was able to spread his

Thomas Suarez won an award at the Tribeca Disruptive Innovation Awards for his app development, his popular TED talk, and his advocacy for app clubs in public schools. These awards are given out to people whose ideas have broken the mold to create something new and exciting.

message on the Internet. Based on the strength of the positive reaction to his talk, Thomas went on to found his own company, CarrotCorp.

The good news is you don't have to be a pre-teen programmer to use innovative technology and tools to make a great presentation. Many digital programs and software are very easy to use. They can help you find the best way to package and present the information that you want to share. New digital tools can also help you reach a larger audience with your message. They can help you tailor that message to a specific audience that might find the information relevant. New digital tools can also help you organize your material into key slides. You can even create and pre-record your own content to play later or upload to the Internet.

While the most important parts of any presentation are the content and the time that you put into writing and research, how you present the information can have a huge impact on how your audience receives it. With so many cool new Web sites, software, and tools designed just for creating, improving, and showcasing presentations, there's no end to what you can do. If you have an assignment for school or even just an idea that interests you and that you want to share and explore with others, you can create an amazing presentation or speech. All that is required is your imagination, creativity, and a little help from the latest digital technology.

PRESENTATIONS ENTER THE TWENTY-FIRST CENTURY

For many students, being assigned a speech, demonstration, or group project is a nightmare come true. But it doesn't have to be! A presentation can be an exciting chance to teach your classmates something new you've learned. If your teacher assigns a speech or demonstration, it can be scary at first. Whether you are presenting information you've researched or your own opinions, talking in front of an audience by yourself or with a group of students can inspire nervousness and high anxiety.

If you are allowed to include digital components, there are plenty of exciting tools that will kick your presentation up to the next level. Including visual and audio elements can take some of the nervousness out of presenting, as multimedia content can provide you with cues that will help you remember what to say next. Also, designing a really great multimedia presentation will make you that much more excited to share it with others, and that excitement will trump any lingering nervousness.

POWERPOINT

One of the earliest versions of presentation software ever created was Microsoft's PowerPoint. It remains one of the most popular. PowerPoint was first launched in 1990. It has now been installed on more than one billion computers. An estimated 350 PowerPoint presentations are given every single second worldwide.

At its most basic, PowerPoint allows users to make slides with photos, text, bulleted points, videos, charts and graphs, and animations in order to easily display information. A slide is basically a blank canvas

Interactive whiteboards are a new technology that have changed the way teachers and students present information in the classroom. Whiteboards allow users to project information on a board or screen while still interacting with both the material and the audience.

upon which you can project and display words and ideas. You can choose different templates based on what you want on the slide, such as a title, subtitle with text, or maybe text with a photo. This can make it easier to decide how to format the presentation.

During the presentation, a user can switch slides with just a click of a button. A user can also time the slideshow to advance automatically as he or she speaks. Adding photos, videos, and charts is a good way to include visual aids in your PowerPoint presentation. PowerPoint also allows users to create animated transitions between slides, such as having the words slide on and off or dissolve away. These special effects can be fun, but try not to overuse them. Make sure everything you add to your presentation truly enhances—rather than distracts from—the content. Long and elaborate transitions between slides don't always add to your presentation. In some cases, they just slow it down.

Having been around for over twenty years, PowerPoint has evolved with the changing technology. One of these advances is the ability to post your presentation online. This is made possible by cloud computing, which means storing and managing data over the Internet so that it can be accessed from anywhere.

Storing your presentation in the cloud also makes it available for viewing on many different computers. This means you can work on your presentation at home or at the library, and then access it in class to present it from your classroom computer, projection screen, or whiteboard. PowerPoint's cloud storage capability works particularly well with group projects and collaborative presentations. If your teacher needs to look at your presentation while you are working on it, you can grant access and your teacher can view it from school or home at his or her convenience. Or if you are working on a group project, the group members can all have access to the presentation, even if they are working from different computers. In fact, PowerPoint allows several collaborators to write and edit the same document from different computers at the exact same time. This feature is called coauthoring. During a coauthoring session, each user can see who else is updating the presentation and receive notification when changes are made.

Digital tools make collaborative projects far easier to organize and execute. Research can be saved in the cloud so that group members can access it when they're together or working separately on their home computers.

BEYOND POWERPOINT

While PowerPoint is among the first and most popular of available presentation software, it is far from the only option. Microsoft's competitor, Apple, introduced its own presentation software in 2003 called Keynote. Like PowerPoint, Keynote has gone through a number of versions over the years.

The key difference between the two presentation programs is that Keynote has a wider range of default themes. This means it has a number of themes that exist without you having to create or edit them. The theme you choose for your presentation includes the background and often the color or font of any text that appears. Keynote also makes it very easy to include media, such as photos and videos. The slides of a Keynote presentation are designed with media in mind and have placeholders ready to drop in these elements.

Other presentation software includes SoftMaker Presentations, ProPresenter, and Power Presentation. Many of these programs are similar, but you may find some easier to use than others. If you are considering purchasing any software, make sure you shop around, run free trials if you can, and figure out which program has the features that would best suit the needs of your presentation.

ONLINE OPTIONS

There are some limitations to presentation software. You either have to purchase it in order to use it, or, in some cases, you must subscribe to it and pay a monthly fee. If you're working with a group of people, all of them need access to the software. Luckily, there are many free Web sites that can help you make impressive presentations and visual aids for speeches.

One of these is Google Presentation. This Web site, powered by the search engine giant Google, provides several different templates that you can use for your presentation. You can also save templates that you have used in the past. In addition, you can create your own template and submit it so that others can use it. Google Presentation doesn't have as many functions as PowerPoint or Keynote, but it does have multimedia options. You can enhance your text with embedded photos, images, or videos.

Another Web site you may find useful is SlideRocket, which has merged with a second presentation site, ClearSlide. SlideRocket has many of the same features as Google Presentation, in that you can create presentations online, adjust the look and feel, foster group collaboration, and easily share presentations with others. SlideRocket, like Google Presentation, allows multiple users to view and edit it. SlideRocket keeps a record of who has edited what. This makes it easy to learn with your classmates as you work together toward the common goal of making the best possible presentation.

KEEP CALM AND SPEAK ON

The mark of a good public speaker is confidence. By being prepared and rehearsing your speech in front of others, you will be confident on the day that you present your work. At the same time, it's understandable to feel nervous. Public speaking is a skill that has to be learned and practiced. If you are new to it, public speaking can be scary. Here are some tips and tricks for overcoming nervousness when making a presentation:

- Remember that your audience is likely made up of people who must also deliver oral presentations. They are probably just as nervous as you are.
- Use visual aids to help give you something to focus on other than the audience. This is where digital presentation tools really come in handy.
- Practice your speech or demonstration in front of friends, parents, siblings, neighbors, or anyone else who will listen. Practicing in front of an audience will help you get used to having people stare back at you while you speak.
- Focus on the topic of your speech or demonstration. This will take your mind off the audience. If you are really interested in your topic and focus on that, your passion will come through in your delivery.

SlideRocket has a different look than Google Presentation. Some find it easier to navigate. The best way to decide what is right for you or your group is to try out the features and figure out which is easiest to use and which has the features that best suit your presentation.

Another tool that can be used both online and off is Prezi. Prezi markets itself as a way to make presentations not just with linear slides, but also through digital storytelling. Instead of having information on individual slides that follow each other in linear sequence, Prezi is more free-form. Think of it as an infinitely large chalkboard upon which you can jot ideas, all of which are visible simultaneously. Using Prezi's zooming software, you can draw the viewers' attention to one part or another of the board while discussing a particular point. The spatial movement of the presentation and the way information is placed in relation to other information on-screen will help the audience better remember it, according to Prezi's creators. This makes for a more dynamic and engaging presentation, one that holds viewers' attention.

With a basic membership, Prezi is free to use. However, you have limited storage space, and all the presentations, or "prezis," you create are shared publicly. To access advanced features, such as the ability to use Prezi offline on your desktop, decide with whom you share your prezis, and increase storage space, a monthly fee is required.

PRESENTATIONS 101: BACK TO THE BASICS

While digital tools can help improve your presentation and impress your audience, it's important to always remember the biggest part of a successful speech or demonstration: content. No matter how flashy or technologically advanced your presentation is, it won't get off the ground if your material isn't interesting, informative, and well organized.

The first step is to research your subject thoroughly. Whether your presentation is designed to persuade, inform, or demonstrate something, you must first learn whatever it is that you hope to teach your audience. Once you have fully researched your topic, you need to organize the information in a way that

Laptops and tablets make researching a presentation on-the-go very easy and convenient. However, if you don't own your own computer or other digital device, or don't have access to it at school or around town, most school and public libraries have computers and Internet access available for public use.

will make sense to your audience. Figure out what the main point of your presentation or speech will be. You will want to state this main point clearly in your introduction. The rest of the speech or presentation should contain facts that support this main point. Try to include interesting and colorful facts that might surprise your audience. This will help keep the audience engaged and wanting to hear more.

If you are working with other students on a group presentation, you should discuss the project before beginning. Make sure everyone is on the same page. While it might make sense to divide up the project's tasks based on everyone's personal interests, don't just assign each person a section of the presentation and stitch them all together at the last minute. To make a cohesive presentation or speech, all parts must have a similar tone and smooth transitions. Part of collaborative learning is being able to combine the ideas of a number of people into a single, unified work. Working together with a group toward one goal helps build critical thinking skills as you learn to solve problems and utilize each group member's strengths. This involves taking everyone's ideas and finding a way to logically piece them together. The group's speech or presentation will be much stronger for it.

Presentation software is particularly well suited to collaborative learning. It can be used to facilitate group projects and presentations. But it can also be employed for everything from study groups and student-run test prep to archived online lectures and student-produced labs and demonstrations. For example, students can use presentation software to help prepare for a big exam, creating slides for the main ideas and facts and figures. They can also embed useful diagrams, charts, and videos, including taped class lectures. In this way, studying is transformed from cramming and rote memorization into a creative, hands-on exercise that better teaches and imprints the knowledge upon which you will be tested.

TRICKED OUT: ENHANCING WITH MULTIMEDIA

Speeches and demonstrations don't just have to be accompanied by static visual aids and text on slides. For example, there are many digital tools that you can use to create and record your own dynamic digital content. Videos and recorded audio, whether created by you or downloaded from another source, can be added to a presentation to enhance it. There are software tools that you can use to both create and edit video content.

If you are using multimedia like photos or videos, make sure to check that the creator of the content is OK with you using or changing his or her work. Often when people post videos or photos online, they include copyright information and the circumstances in which they will allow use of their work. Many people are fine with the use of their work for noncommercial purposes (meaning you won't use their work to make money for yourself), but it's important to double-check before using or editing someone else's content. Also, make sure to cite the creators of the photos and videos that you use in the same way that you cite the sources of any research and facts that you use in your presentation.

Videos and photos can serve a number of purposes in a good presentation. For one, they provide a visual refreshment, breaking up the stream of text-only slides. In this way, the viewer's attention is re-engaged. In addition, visual aids often help people remember information better. This can be true both for the presenter—who can use photos and videos as cues to remember what to say next—and for the audience trying to absorb the information. Well-chosen videos can bring the material to life. Videos can also be used to record parts or all of the presentation in advance, assuming that's an option allowed by your teacher.

This person is filming protesters in Thailand on an iPad. Tools like this tablet make it easy for anyone to digitally film relevant footage to strengthen a speech, report, or presentation.

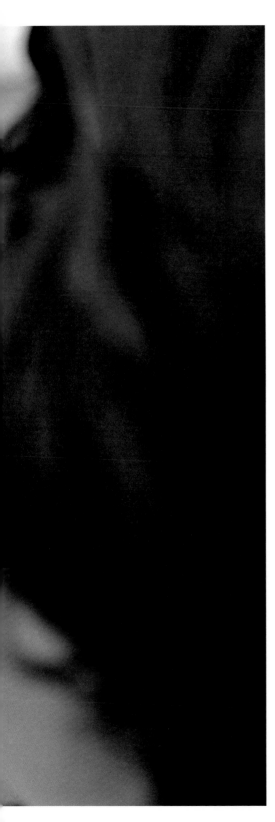

SOFTWARE TOOLS

There are a number of visual tools that can help you edit and create videos. These include software tools like iMovie and PhotoBooth. Both are programs designed for use on Apple devices, including computers, smartphones, and tablets. For Windows-based personal computers, there is the video-editing program MovieMaker. You can also use video-editing software like Blender, which is free to download.

All of these programs make it easy to edit video clips and add music, sound effects, and text. You can also record your own video to edit. Many computers and smartphones have cameras built in that you can use to record footage. If you don't have access to a computer, smartphone, or camera at home, ask a teacher or librarian if your school has any that it loans out to students.

Once you have recorded the video of your presentation or a video segment for your presentation, you can drop the file into video-editing software. Then it's easy to cut out parts you don't want and add any desired audio or visual effects to enhance the footage. You can include a title card to introduce your presentation. You can also include credits to detail for your audience who was involved in the video's production and whose work you

A HARD-HITTING EXPOSE

THE TRUTH IS... GROSS!

YUCK

A 4TH GRADER'S SHORT DOCUMENTARY ABOUT SCHOOL LUNCH

MAXWELL PROJECT PRESENTS
"YUCK: A 4TH GRADER'S SHORT DOCUMENTARY ABOUT SCHOOL LUNCH"
EDITED BY CJ MAXWELL
WRITTEN AND DIRECTED BY ZACHARY MAXWELL
WWW.YUCKMOVIE.COM

Zachary Maxwell, seen here on his movie poster, filmed seventy-five school lunches over the course of six months, with the help of a small handheld digital video camera.

Eleven-year-old Zachary Maxwell, a student at a New York City public school, didn't think the lunches that his school was serving were tasty or healthy. He did some research and determined that the lunches at his school didn't sound at all like the nutritious food the city's Department of Education claimed on its Web site to be serving. Zachary decided to make a movie about his findings. He recorded his lunch every day using a camera on his phone. He edited all of the footage into a movie and included the facts he learned through research.

The movie started out as a way to convince his parents to let him bring lunch from home instead of buying it at school. However, Zachary soon committed to the project and started teaching others what he had learned from his research and filming. Zachary's twenty-minute documentary, which he titled *Yuck! A 4th Grader's Short Documentary About School Lunch*, appeared at the 2013 Manhattan Film Festival.

used or cited, such as someone else's photos, video clips, text quotations, or music. You can add background music, sound effects, and visual transitions, like fading from one scene to the next.

Don't forget that the primary focus of the presentation is the content. All audiovisual enhancements should serve only to complement and highlight your content, not distract from or swamp it. Adding relevant music and visual effects can enhance a presentation, but sometimes a little goes a long way. Don't get caught up in making your videos too flashy, thus losing sight of the true focus of your project.

ONLINE VIDEO EDITING

Outside of software, there are online options for creating and editing video content. Animoto is a Web site that makes it easy to turn photos and videos into a professional video slideshow. The site is free to use if you select from a limited range of backgrounds and short presentations. For a monthly fee, users can access more advanced features and elaborate backgrounds and can create much longer presentations.

Stupeflix is another Web site that offers video-editing tools and options at a variety of price points. With Stupeflix, users can mix photos, videos, and music to tell a story or get a message across. The site also has a collection of transitions and sound effects that can easily be added.

If you find a video on the popular video-sharing social network YouTube, sites like TubeChop can help you download and use just the segment you want. Remember to always cite your sources and give credit to the creators of videos that you use.

USING VIDEO TO EXPAND YOUR AUDIENCE AND FOSTER COLLABORATIVE LEARNING

If recording your presentation is an option, you might want to share your work with an audience beyond the classroom by posting it online. The act of

Video-editing programs like Final Cut Pro, seen here, make editing digital videos quick and simple. Users can cut and move footage, add sounds, and otherwise alter the video content to tailor it specifically to the needs of their presentation or demonstration.

teaching others something, or even just trying to convince them of your opinion, is actually a way of learning content better yourself. Whether learning the material to present to a group of classmates, under the guidance of a teacher, or to a larger online audience, you are participating in collaborative learning. This means that by filling the role of researcher and presenter, you are both learning and teaching as you share what you have learned and discovered with others.

SETTING IT IN MOTION: SCREENCASTING AND ANIMATION

The core content of multimedia speeches, demonstrations, and collaborative projects can be enhanced with the use of photos, charts and other dynamic graphics, and video and audio clips. These types of multimedia presentations are designed for display on computers, whiteboards, tablets, and even phones. Any device that supports the software or Web site you're using to create your presentation will do. However, it is also possible to make the computer screen itself part of the presentation. This is called screencasting.

SHARING YOUR SCREEN

Screencasting involves making a live digital video of your computer screen so that an audience can view exactly what you are doing and seeing on your computer. Your computer screen can either be projected onto a whiteboard or the audience can view it on their laptops or other digital devices. A screencast is usually accompanied by audio narration, either in person or pre-recorded. For as long as the screencast lasts, everything on your screen is viewable to your audience, including open files, visited Web sites, and streaming video.

Screencasting is particularly well suited to presentations that involve demonstrating how to do something. It is especially useful when teaching computer skills or instructing users in a new software program or operating system. Your audience can watch your mouse movements and learn exactly what sequence of actions they need to take in order to achieve a certain task.

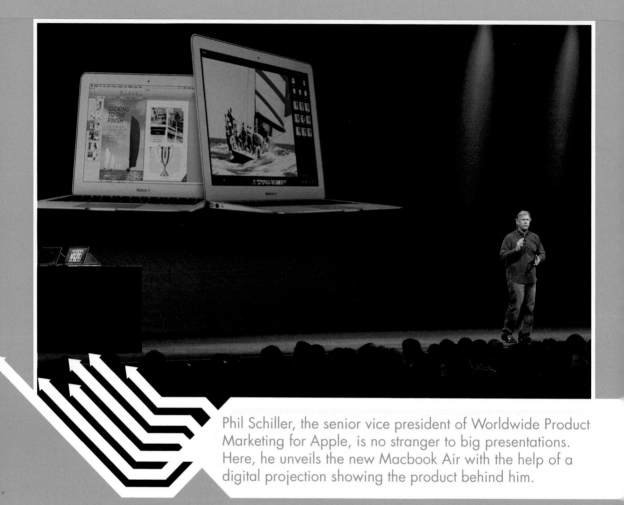

Phil Schiller, the senior vice president of Worldwide Product Marketing for Apple, is no stranger to big presentations. Here, he unveils the new Macbook Air with the help of a digital projection showing the product behind him.

AMAZING ANIMATION

Depending on the content of your speech, demonstration, or collaborative project, other types of digital tools to consider are animation sites and software. Animation tends to work better for storytelling and more creative presentations. But in the right circumstances, it can really make your presentation pop. Animation is a series of images displayed in quick succession to give the illusion of movement. Today, most animation is done on computers

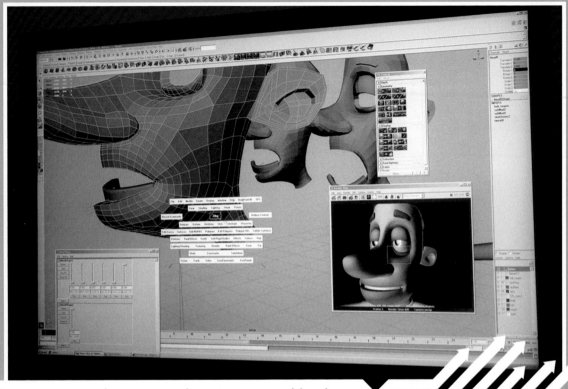

Creating unique characters and cartoons can add a dynamic and innovative new creative element to a presentation or demonstration. Special animation software and programs available online can help make anyone an animator in no time.

with the help of user-friendly programs like Flip Boom Cartoon, Animation-ish, and Comic Boom.

You can also turn to the Internet to find reliable animation tools. One tool that can help you animate your presentation is Scratch. Scratch is available both as a download and for use online. It allows you to choose from a library of animated characters or upload your own images. You can direct your character in a number of movements that are easily customizable. You can also add costumes, change colors, and add music and sound effects.

SCREENCASTING IN THE CLASSROOM

It isn't only students who can use screencasting in support of their speeches, demonstrations, or collaborative projects. Many teachers now use screencasts in their classrooms. In a world ever more dependent on constantly evolving technology, it is becoming more and more important to keep one's knowledge of the latest digital tools up-to-the-minute. Screencasting offers teachers a great way to quickly and easily show students exactly how to use the newest digital devices, operating systems, programs, and apps.

There are many advantages to screencasting, both for the teacher and for students, and for both in collaboration. The teacher is able to show step-by-step processes that make it easy for the students to follow along. For visual learners especially, this method is much more successful than explanation alone. The teacher also has the option of recording and archiving the lesson so that students can revisit it when they need to refresh their memory about how to do something. If archived online, students can review the lesson in school, at the library, at home, or even on the go with a tablet or smartphone. The ability to pause, go back, or advance past certain sections of content allows students to work at their own pace, which isn't as easy with traditional lessons.

Screencasts can even be broadcast to classrooms in small schools that might not have a dedicated technology program. Students who wouldn't have access to high-quality computer education otherwise can avoid falling behind, thanks to screencasting's ability to bridge geographic distances and educational gaps.

Another animation tool that can be used online or downloaded is FluxTime. It allows users to move objects around the screen and record those movements. Another animation tool is Stykz, which is a free download. With Stykz, a user can create animations using stick figures. He or she can customize the backgrounds and movements of each frame. Animated figures and objects created by these kinds of programs can be used to reenact historical scenes, demonstrate a step-by-step process, or illustrate certain concepts.

With so many digital tools that let your audience follow along with a screencast or be entranced by animation, there is no end to how creative your presentation can be. No longer do you have to scroll through color-free, text-only slides that list dreary dates, facts, and figures about the Civil War. Instead,

Sharing a screen, or screencasting, enables one student to show what is on his or her screen to students viewing from several different computers at once.

you can easily design an animated map showing Union and Confederate movements from battle to battle. Your dramatic delivery of the Gettysburg Address can feature screencasts streaming still photographs, video clips of battle reenactments, audio clips of Civil War–era military bands, and animated figures representing the war's heavy toll of casualties.

Presentations are a fun way to really think outside the box. While brainstorming ideas on your own or with your group, make sure to get guidance from your teacher. Creativity and excitement make for a great presentation, but make sure that what you have planned will meet your teacher's expectations and requirements.

GET THE WORD OUT! SHARING YOUR PRESENTATION

Digital tools aren't just useful for creating a fantastic presentation. They can also be a way to share your speech, demonstration, or collaborative learning project with a virtual audience, as well as those sitting right in front of you. The ability to share what one knows and has learned with a wide audience—whether that audience is physically before you or in cyberspace—gives the presentation format a distinct advantage over something like a research paper, where the audience tends to be a solitary reader.

THE LINK BETWEEN SHARING AND COLLABORATIVE LEARNING

Preparing and presenting a speech, demonstration, or group project gives you the opportunity to immerse yourself deeply in a subject, as well as share and teach what you have learned with your audience. The act of teaching others helps reinforce knowledge for both you the presenter and your audience. This is known as collaborative learning.

One important aspect of collaborative learning in a presentation context is the feedback you receive from members of your group as you research and design your project and from your audience after delivering it. This is one of the reasons why you rehearse your speech or demonstration in front of an actual audience—to invite comments and suggestions and make necessary improvements. Even after your final presentation, you can still accept advice on how to improve your

Sharing a presentation or demonstration with an audience helps others learn what the speaker has learned during the process of researching and designing the project. Audience feedback, in turn, helps the presenter learn how to improve the content of the presentation and its delivery.

approach to future projects. Accepting feedback is one of the main ways that you can become a better public speaker and presenter in the future.

Over the course of your project, you can take pride in sharing and teaching something that you are passionate about and have put a lot of work into. Whether it is delivering a speech in support of reducing carbon emissions to combat global warming, breaking down step-by-step a difficult guitar playing technique, or taking part in a group examination of the history, culture, economy, religion, and politics of Tibet, the free sharing of information in your presentation is of benefit to everyone.

SHARING MADE SIMPLE

Sharing your presentation with your teacher, classmates, friends, and family is one way to get your message out there. However, digital tools can make sharing your presentation with people around the globe much easier. There are Web sites devoted solely to posting presentations.

One of the largest dedicated presentation-sharing sites is SlideShare.

It attracts sixty million visitors each month, many of whom are educators and businesspeople. The site was voted one of the top ten tools for education and learning in a recent survey by the Center for Learning & Performance Technologies. Anyone can sign up for free and post a presentation online. Acceptable formats include PowerPoint, Word documents, PDFs, videos, and webinars.

In addition to posting your presentations, you can take advantage of the wealth of presentations that other people have posted to the site. Anyone can view and even download presentations on topics of interest. SlideShare is a great way to share ideas and connect with others. The site's content is often shared on other social media sites, including blogs, Twitter, Facebook, and LinkedIn. Once you post your presentation online, you can use social media to tell your friends—and their friends—to check it out.

Similar sites include SlideBoom and authorSTREAM. SlideBoom prides itself on being able to preserve all the original features and formatting of a presentation uploaded to the site. It supports a number of versions of PowerPoint, as well as other presentation and slideshow applications. It allows you to create Web-ready presentations from PowerPoint files and embed them in blogs and Web sites. You can collect and respond to feedback from online viewers and form discussion groups centered on particular subjects of interest.

The Web site authorSTREAM allows users to share PowerPoint presentations online, while retaining animations, audio, and videos. The presentations can be shared publically or privately for free. You can broadcast your presentation live or have it archived for viewing at any time. The site also allows you to convert PowerPoint to video. In addition, group members can communicate and collaborate in real time when using authorSTREAM.

Check out the features of each presentation-sharing site before deciding which is best for hosting your work online. It is also a good idea to read the user and privacy policies before signing up for any site. If you are working on the speech or presentation with collaborators, decide on the hosting site as a group. The good thing about hosting a presentation online is that most sites are easy to use collaboratively, allowing for multiple users to make changes to the presentation.

YOUTUBE GOES TO SCHOOL

As previously discussed, you can create original content by recording video and audio of your speech or demonstration in advance or by recording video and audio segments for use in your live presentation. This original content—either a video of your entire presentation or the prerecorded elements in it—can be posted on sites that aren't necessarily geared toward the sharing of presentations.

YouTube, for example, is the Web's largest video-sharing network. It's where you can upload video content for viewing by the general public or by a select group of people designated by you. Videos that you post can be

More than one billion people visit the video-sharing site YouTube each month. Video-sharing sites like this one can be a good place to post a presentation or demonstration in order to share it with a much larger and broader audience than that of your classmates.

kept totally private so that only you can watch them. In this case, you would be using YouTube basically as a personal storage site.

More than one billion people view YouTube each month. Seventy-two hours of video footage are added to the site every minute. The content on YouTube varies widely, but plenty of people do use the site to share presentations, speeches, and tutorials. It is free to use, although you do have to sign up and have an account in order to post content.

THE ONLINE ETIQUETTE OF GIVING AND RECEIVING FEEDBACK

The advantage of sharing your work online is that you can get immediate feedback from others. You can also comment on the presentations of your friends and even those of complete strangers. This can be a positive and constructive learning experience. Ideally, everyone on the Internet would use commenting only to offer positive feedback and useful criticism. Unfortunately, as anyone who has spent time online knows, it doesn't always work that way. People can say mean, hurtful things that don't provide helpful

From interactive whiteboards to smartphones, there's no end to the ways people can upload, download, view, and comment upon content both in the classroom and outside of it.

advice for your project. It's best to ignore these people. If they call you names or insult your work or appearance, don't call them names back. Delete their comments if you can, and if they continue to harass you, report them to site administrators.

PROTECTING YOURSELF AND YOUR WORK ONLINE

With the rise of social networking, people share more and more online. While this is a good thing if you want to get information to a large number of people, it can also be dangerous. It's easy to forget that when you post something for a particular audience, a much larger unintended audience might also see it. In your classroom, your teachers and fellow students already know you and your personal details, like your name, age, and where you go to school. However, these details don't need to be told to people who don't already know them. If your presentation includes any information that could identify you to a stranger, remove it before posting the work online.

It's also important to read through the privacy policy of any site that you want to post content on *before* posting it. Find out what happens to your work once you post it. Are you allowing the site's visitors to use your content without crediting you? Another important thing to remember about the Internet is that once something is posted, it's there to stay. Even if you delete something, someone else may have already downloaded it and reposted it elsewhere. It can be very difficult, if not impossible, to remove something once it's posted. So think twice before posting anything you aren't sure you want to

Not sinking to the level of online bullies and trolls (people whose comments are intended to start a fight) is only part of being a good online citizen. When offering feedback on the presentations of others, make sure to carefully consider how your words might be taken. If you have criticism that you really think might help the creator improve his or her work, you should definitely share it. However, try to say it in a courteous, gentle way. Think of something positive to say about the presentation, as well as something critical.

One of the problems with offering comments and criticism over the Internet, instead of face-to-face, is that it's hard to get the tone of the message across. In person, something that is said with a cheery voice and a smile might be taken for the well-meaning feedback that it is. But in a text comment, the

This presenter is teaching people about ocean reefs. Using a combination of digital presentation tools, photos, graphics, and good old-fashioned enthusiasm for her topic, she has captured the attention of her audience and made them eager and ready to learn more.

same words might accidentally offend. For this reason, it's very important to choose your words carefully when commenting on anyone's work.

SHOW THEM WHAT YOU'VE GOT!

By this point, you are probably very eager to get started on your presentation. With so many exciting technologies and new digital tools at your fingertips, presenting information isn't just easy—it can actually be a lot of fun. When you first think of presenting a speech, demonstration, or group project, it might sound like a scary thing. Consider it your chance to really teach your friends and classmates something exciting you've learned. It's also an opportunity to show off your digital know-how with a slick, dynamic, expertly crafted presentation.

By choosing to approach the assignment with confidence and excitement, you'll be amazed at what you can do. A good speech or demonstration is first and foremost about the content of the presentation and the enthusiasm of the presenter. With a few well-placed digital touches, however, a merely average presentation can be transformed into a truly educational, entertaining, and highly memorable one.

GLOSSARY

COAUTHORING A function that allows two users to work on the same document or project at the same time.

COLLABORATIVE LEARNING Two or more people learning together and working toward a shared learning goal.

DEMONSTRATION A type of presentation in which the speaker explains a process or how to do something, often by actually performing the task and adding commentary and helpful tips.

HYPERLINK A link, usually indicated by blue underlined text, that takes the user to another Web site or file when clicked on.

INFORMATIVE Describes a type of presentation in which the speaker seeks to provide factual information to the audience and teach them something they do not yet know.

MULTIMEDIA Mixed content that supplements straight text, including videos, audio, photos, and graphs and charts.

PERSUASIVE Describes a type of presentation in which the speaker tries to convince the audience to accept a certain idea, viewpoint, opinion, policy, or proposed course of action.

SCREENCAST A digital recording of computer screen output, also known as a video screen capture, often containing audio narration. It is essentially a movie of the changes over time that a user sees on a computer screen, enhanced with audio narration.

SCREENSHOT A snapshot showing everything that was on a computer screen at the time the shot was taken; a still picture of a computer screen at one specific moment in time.

SOCIAL NETWORK An online community where people connect and exchange personal news, views, and information based on shared interests, activities, backgrounds, or real-life connections.

SOFTWARE Programs that are run on a computer.

SPATIAL Describes how things are placed in relation to each other.

TEMPLATE A basic model to be copied and tailored to specific needs.

THEME A preset background and font color that gives foreground content, such as text, a certain look or feel.

TROLL A person who posts negative, antagonistic, mocking, or mean-spirited comments in online forums in order to start fights.

VISUAL AID A video, chart, graph, image, graphic design, or photo that is paired with, enhances, and helps illustrate text or spoken word.

WEBINAR A presentation conducted over the Internet. It can be viewed live or in recorded and archived form.

Digital Video Professionals Association (DVPA)
135 Interstate Boulevard, Suite One
Greenville, SC 29615
(888) 339-3872
Web site: http://www.dvpa.com
DVPA is the largest organization in the world devoted exclusively to helping
   those who use digital media and video editing. Its official Web site
   includes tips and advice for video editing at all skill levels.

Educational Computing Organization of Ontario (ECOO)
10 Morrow Avenue, Suite 202
Toronto, ON M6R 2J1
Canada
(416) 489-1713
Web site: http://www.ecoo.org
ECOO helps teachers and students incorporate computer learning into the
   educational process.

MediaSmarts
950 Gladstone Avenue, Suite 120
Ottawa, ON K1Y 3E6
Canada
(613) 224-7721
Web site: http://mediasmarts.ca
MediaSmarts is a Canadian not-for-profit charitable organization for digital
   and media literacy. Its mission is to provide children and youth with the

critical thinking skills necessary to engage with media as active and informed digital citizens.

National Communication Association (NCA)
1765 N Street NW
Washington, DC 20036
(202) 464-4622
Web site: http://www.natcom.org
NCA is devoted to advancing the art of communication in all its forms. The organization serves its members, such as scholars, teachers, and public speakers, through its research and teaching.

Public Relations Society of America (PRSA)
33 Maiden Lane, 11th Floor
New York, NY 10038-5150
(212) 460-1400
Web site: http://www.prsa.org
This nonprofit is made up of members of the communications and public relations industries. These men and women make speeches and presentations as part of their careers, and the organization provides articles, seminars, and webinars to help them improve their presentation skills.

Software & Information Industry Association (SIIA)
1090 Vermont Avenue NW, 6th Floor
Washington, DC 20005-4095
(202) 289-7442
Web site: http://www.siia.net
SIIA is the principle association for sellers of software and digital content. Its Web site offers articles, newsletters, and awards to keep readers current on the latest in digital technology, including those digital tools useful for creating presentations.

Toastmasters International
23182 Arroyo Vista
Rancho Santa Margarita, CA 92688
(949) 858-8255
Web site: http://www.toastmasters.org
This nonprofit organization provides education and resources to foster the art
of public speaking and presentation making.

World Debate Institute
85 South Prospect Street
Burlington, VT 05401
(802) 656-3131
Web site: http://debate.uvm.edu
The World Debate Institute helps train people in the art of public speaking
and debate. It offers resources, holds workshops, and trains educators
to help encourage organized debate in schools.

WEB SITES

Due to the changing nature of Internet links, Rosen Publishing has developed
an online list of Web sites related to the subject of this book. This site is
updated regularly. Please use this link to access the list:

http://www.rosenlinks.com/WBPP/Speec

FOR FURTHER READING

Berkun, Scott. *Confessions of a Public Speaker*. Cambridge, MA: O'Reilly Media, 2011.

Collins, Phillip. *The Art of Speeches and Presentations: The Secrets of Making People Remember What You Say*. Hoboken, NJ: Wiley, 2012.

Darkin, Christian. *The Really, Really, Really Easy Step-by-Step Guide to Creating & Editing Digital Videos Using Your Computer: For Absolute Beginners of All Ages*. London, England: New Holland Publishing, 2009.

Donovan, Jeremey. *How to Deliver a TED Talk: Secrets of the World's Most Inspiring Presentations*. Seattle, WA: CreateSpace, 2012.

Duarte, Nancy. *Slide:ology*. Cambridge, MA: O'Reilly Media, 2012.

Galloway, Ron. *Rethinking PowerPoint: Designing & Delivering Presentations That Engage the Mind*. New York, NY: Method Content, 2011.

Kapterev, Alexi. *Presentation Secrets*. Hoboken, NJ: Wiley, 2011.

Reynolds, Garr. *Presentation Zen: Simple Ideas on Presentation Design and Delivery*. New York, NY: New Riders, 2008.

Steele, William R. *Presentation Skills 201: How to Take It to the Next Level as a Confident, Engaging Presenter*. Parker, CO: Outskirts Press, 2009.

Sykes, Martin, and Nick Malik. *Stories That Move Mountains: Storytelling and Visual Design for Persuasive Presentations*. Hoboken, NJ: Wiley, 2012.

Waldo, Dixie. *Persuasive Speaking*. New York, NY: Rosen Publishing, 2007.

BIBLIOGRAPHY

Atkinson, Cliff. *Beyond Bullet Points: Using Microsoft PowerPoint to Create Presentations That Inform, Motivate, and Inspire.* Redmond, WA: Microsoft Press, 2011.

Chadra, Kieren. "PowerPoint vs. KeyNote: Let's Compare and Contrast." Bright Carbon, November 19, 2012. Retrieved April 2013 (http://www.brightcarbon.com/blog/powerpoint-vs-keynote).

Clark, Josh. *Creating Keynote Slideshows: The Mini Missing Manual.* Cambridge, MA: O'Reilly Media, 2010.

ConstructingKids.com. "Thomas Suarez: 12-Year-Old App Developer." November 28, 2012. Retrieved April 2013 (http://constructingkids .com/2012/11/28/thomas-suarez-12-year-old-app-developper).

Durate, Nancy. *Resonate: Present Visual Stories That Transform Audiences.* Hoboken, NJ: Wiley, 2010.

Gallo, Carmine. *The Presentation Secrets of Steve Jobs: How to Be Insanely Great in Front of Any Audience.* New York, NY: McGraw-Hill, 2009.

Kats, Yefim. *Learning Management Systems and Instructional Design: Best Practices in Online Education.* Hershey, PA: Information Science Reference, 2013.

Klein, Rebecca. "Zachary Maxwell, 11-Year-Old, Makes Documentary About 'Gross' New York City School Lunches." *Huffington Post*, May 13, 2013. Retrieved May 2013 (http://www.huffingtonpost.com /2013/05/13/zachary-maxwell-documentary-yuck-school-lunches _n_3268723.html?utm_hp_ref=new-york).

Reynolds, Garr. *Presentation Zen Design: Simple Design Principles and Techniques to Enhance Your Presentations.* Berkeley, CA: New Riders, 2010.

Ruffini, Michael F. "Screencasting to Engage Learning." Educause, November 1, 2012. Retrieved April 2013 (http://www.educause.edu /ero/article/screencasting-engage-learning).

INDEX

A

animation, 7, 9, 24–28, 32
Animation-ish, 25
Animoto, 21
Apple Inc., 4, 10, 19
apps, 4, 26
audio clips, 7, 17, 19, 21, 23, 25, 28, 32, 33
authorSTREAM, 32

B

Blender, 19
blogs, 32
Bustin Jieber, 4

C

CarrotCorp, 6
charts, 7, 9, 16, 23
ClearSlide, 11
cloud computing, 9
coauthoring, 9
Comic Boom, 25
copyright, 17
credits, 19, 21, 36

F

Facebook, 32
feedback, giving and receiving, 29–31, 32, 34, 36–38

Flip Boom Cartoon, 25
FluxTime, 27

G

game apps, 4
Google Presentation, 11, 13
group projects, 7, 9, 16, 29, 38

I

iMovie, 19
iPads, 4
iPhones, 4

K

Keynote, 10–11

L

LinkedIn, 32

M

Manhattan Film Festival, 20
Maxwell, Zachary, 20
Microsoft, 7, 10, 32
MovieMaker, 19
music, adding, 19, 21, 25

N

nervousness, coping with, 7, 12

O

online safety, tips for, 36
operating systems, 23, 26

P

PDFs, 32
PhotoBooth, 19
PowerPoint, 7, 9–11, 32
Power Presentation, 11
presentations
    animation, 24–28
    multimedia, 17–22
    online options, 11, 13, 21
    overview of, 4–6
    screencasting, 23
    sharing, 29–38
    in today's world, 7–16
Prezi, 13
privacy polices, 32, 36
ProPresenter, 11

S

Scratch, 25
screencasting, 23
SlideBoom, 32
SlideRocket, 11, 13
SlideShare, 31–32
social media, 21, 32, 36
SoftMaker Presentations, 11
sources, citing your, 17, 19, 21

Stupeflix, 21
Stykz, 27
Suarez, Thomas, 4–6

T

TED Talks, 4
templates, 9, 11
title cards, 19
TubeChop, 21
Twitter, 32

U

user polices, 32

V

videos, 7, 9, 11, 16, 17–22, 23, 28, 32, 33–34

W

webinars, 32
whiteboards, 9, 23
Windows, 19
Word documents, 32

Y

YouTube, 21, 33–34
Yuck! movie, 20

ABOUT THE AUTHOR

Susan Meyer is an editor and writer living in Queens, New York. While not a born public speaker, Meyer can attest to the fact that the art of presentation is a learned skill that can be improved upon with practice and experience. She is happy to see how much presentation technology has improved upon the humble poster board since her elementary school science fair days.

PHOTO CREDITS

Cover, pp. 8, 34–35 Photo and Co./The Image Bank/Getty Images; p. 5 Jemal Countess/Getty Images; p. 10 wavebreakmedia/Shutterstock.com; pp. 14–15 Ermolaev Alexander/Shutterstock.com; pp. 18–19 1000 Words /Shutterstock.com; p. 20 © Bill Aron/PhotoEdit; p. 22 Everett Collection; p. 24 Kimberly White/Getty Images; p. 25 Tampa Bay Times/ZUMA Press; p. 27 Jetta Productions/Lifesize/Thinkstock; pp. 30–31 Hill Street Studios /Blend Images/Getty Images; p. 33 Jochen Tack/imagebroker.net/SuperStock; p. 37 Paul Dymond/Lonely Planet Images/Getty Images; cover and interior graphics (arrows) © iStockphoto.com/artvea.

Designer: Michael Moy, Photo Researcher: Karen Huang

THE LITERATURE CONNECTION
A Read-Aloud Guide for Multicultural Classrooms

Betty Ansin Smallwood

▲▼ Addison-Wesley Publishing Company

Reading, Massachusetts • Menlo Park, California • New York
Don Mills, Ontario • Wokingham, England • Amsterdam • Bonn
Sydney • Singapore • Tokyo • Madrid • San Juan

A Publication of the World Language Division

Editorial: Kathleen Sands-Boehmer and Jennifer Bixby
Manufacturing/Production: James W. Gibbons
Design & Typesetting: The Sant Bani Press
Cover Design: Bonnie McGrath
Cover Art: Doron Ben-Ami

Library of Congress Cataloging-in-Publication Data

Smallwood, Betty Ansin.
    The literature connection : a read-aloud guide for multicultural
classrooms / Betty Ansin Smallwood.
        p.   cm.
    Includes bibliographical references.
    ISBN 0-201-51706-X
    1. English language—Textbooks for foreign speakers—Bibliography.
2. Pluralism (Social sciences) in literature—Bibliography.
3. Young adult literature, English—Bibliography.   4. Children's
literature, English—Bibliography.   5. Intercultural communication-
-Bibliography.   6. Readers—Bibliography.   7. Oral reading.
I. Title.
Z5818.E5S6   1990
[PE1128.A2]
016.428.2'4—dc20   89-48128
                                                        CIP

Pages 6–7, poem reprinted from *How to Grow a Young Reader: A Parent's Guide to Books for Kids,* © 1989 by John and Kathryn Lindskoog. Used by permission of Harold Shaw Publishers, Box 567, Wheaton, IL 60189.

Page 1, art by Doron Ben-Ami. **Page 51,** photo by Jim McGrath.

ISBN 0-201-51706-X
    3 4 5 6 7 8 9 10—AL—95 94 93

Contents

Preface   v

Acknowledgements   vii

Part I READ-ALOUD GUIDELINES

1. The Literature Connection: Introduction   3

2. The Theoretical Connection: Benefits of Reading Aloud   6

3. The Library Connection: Criteria for Selecting Read-Alouds   12

4. The Classroom Connection: Techniques for Reading Aloud   17

5. The Curriculum Connection: Follow-up Activities Generated from
   Literature   22
   Listening Activities   25
   Speaking Activities   28
   Reading Activities   33
   Writing Activities   38
   Creative Arts Activities   45

Part II READ-ALOUD LIBRARY

1. Introduction   53

   Organization of the Read-Aloud Library   54

   Listing of Books by Topics   58

2. Read-Aloud Library Annotations   65

   Family Relationships   65
   Life Passages   72
   House/Home   76
   Friendship   80
   Emotions/Values   85
   School/Learning   90
   Basic Academic Skills   95
   Clothing/Body   110
   Holidays   113
   Food/Nutrition   121
   Community   129
   Recreation/Sports   137
   Role Models   140
   History/Geography   146
   Immigration/Cross-cultural Adjustment   152
   Animals   157
   Seasons/Weather   173
   Science   179
   Imagination/Monsters/Magic   186
   Anthologies   191

   References   195

   Indexes   199

   Multicultural Index   199
   Literary Genre Index   203
   Book Title Index   209
   Author-Illustrator Index   213

Preface

I started to read a story.[1] Five-year-old bodies were squirming. Five-year-old faces of many cultures, many races faced in all directions. I told them it was a story from Africa about giants, pantomiming what a giant was for those new to English. Faces turned my way. I began to read. Bodies became still. The second time they heard the repeated refrain, "Abiyoyo, Abiyoyo," they began to join in. When the story ended, there was a moment of silence. Then a small, dark-haired boy implored, "Read it again!"

We had a match. The theme of overcoming a great obstacle (a giant!) had universal appeal to young children. The illustrations of a multiracial, multicultural community of people living in harmony and the theme of learning to accept and value differences among people gave the book special appeal to this group of children from many backgrounds.

I started to read another story.[2] The middle school students to whom I read had been in their new country for a year or two, a week or two, or some time in between. The illustrated book was about a crowded house. Most of the students knew a lot about crowded houses. They tuned in and listened raptly, some following the story line with the help of the pictures.

We had a match. The students fell in love with the book, returning to it often and exploring it in many ways. They retold the story with a picture-map; they compared and contrasted it to others they'd heard; they wrote and told stories from their homes and homelands that it brought to mind; they discussed the values and veracity of folk tales.

The author of *The Literature Connection* is the matchmaker who can help you find works for your students to love and learn from. Betty Smallwood clearly lays before you reasons to use literature with such classes, ways to choose literature, ways to use the literature you have chosen, and compact descriptions of carefully selected works. To help you with your selection, she provides a variety of indices for your easy access to works that will relate to your students' ages, interests, and cultures.

In recent years, we have not used literature and reading aloud frequently or well in teaching English to speakers of other languages (or native speakers, for that matter). Our reasons are varied: the popularity of grammar-based or audiolingual methodologies; our mistaken belief that students will not benefit from language they do not completely understand; our dependence on basals that have not included quality literature. It is time for change. *The Literature Connection* provides a much-needed, warmly written, deftly organized tool for the ever-increasing number of teachers who wish to share good books with their multilingual, multicultural students. My hope—and my prediction—are that this book will lead to many literary love affairs in your classroom.

Mary Lou McCloskey
Atlanta, Georgia

---

1. *Abiyoyo*, by Pete Seeger, illustrated by Michael Hays (annotation on p. 187)
2. *It Could Always be Worse*, written and illustrated by Margot Zemach (annotation on p. 88)

ACKNOWLEDGEMENTS

No man is an island
No man stands alone

These opening lines from a folk song (based on one of John Donne's 17th century devotions) capture my experience in writing this book, once I change "man" to the more inclusive "one." From the initial inspiration to the final writing, I worked independently, but I could have done it only with the generous help of many. I would like to thank them here.

Many public and school librarians helped me locate specific books or suggested ones for a content topic. I appreciate their efforts and enthusiasm about this book. Thank you Naomi Morse, Ann Newland, Susan Pardo, Cecily Pilzer, Eva Shankman and Michelle Schuster of Montgomery County Public Libraries and Barbara Geyger and Peggy Flynn of The District of Columbia's Public Libraries and Susan Keren of East Silver Spring Elementary School.

Throughout my sixteen years of teaching, my students have been a major source of inspiration for using literature. I remember especially fondly my first students—5th and 6th graders in Navukailagi District School in the Fiji Islands (where I was a Peace Corps Volunteer) and my most recent students—Kindergarten through 3rd grade ESL children at East Silver Spring Elementary in Silver Spring, Maryland. Together, we enjoyed many books. These times form some of my fondest memories.

My colleagues—from Montgomery County Public Schools, TESOL (Teachers of English to Speakers of Other Languages) and George Mason University—have offered professional support and motivation during the growth of this book. Their attendance at my conference presentations helped refine my ideas and their frequently expressed desire to see and use the book helped keep me plugging away. A special thanks to Alan and Lauri Coltri for their computer advice, to Dr. Dee Ann Holisky for the refinement of the grammatical categories and to Dr. Virginia Collier for her academic guidance.

My Addison-Wesley family has been just wonderful and very patient. Thank you Judie Bittinger, Jennifer Bixby, Elinor Chamas, and Kathy Sands-Boehmer.

And last, and very deeply, I want to thank my family. To my mother, the late Evelyn Rudnick Ansin, for reading me all those childhood stories and for instilling in me a lifelong love of reading; to my father, Harold Ansin, for listening and caring; to my in-laws, Rheta and Leon Smallwood for their bountiful family support; to my two sons, Jesse Tiko Smallwood and Jonah Evan Smallwood for listening to all those books, for their honest critiques and for their independence while mom was writing. And finally, to my husband, John Smallwood, for his steadfast encouragement and his strong belief in my potential.

Taking poetic liberty, with the song, "No Man is an Island," I would like to close with a modification of its final two lines:

Each one as my brother or sister
Each one as my friend

Betty Ansin Smallwood
Bethesda, Maryland

PART ONE
Read-Aloud Guidelines

CHAPTER ONE

The Literature Connection:
Introduction

> There is no substitute for a teacher who reads children good stories. It whets the appetite of children for reading, and provides a model of skillful oral reading. It is a practice that should continue throughout the grades. (*Becoming a Nation of Readers,* 1985: 51.)

The Literature Connection has evolved from my 16 years of teaching English as a Second Language (ESL). Over the years, I have found children's literature to be one of the most effective and readily available quality teaching materials for students of all ages. The idea of using it to teach language emerged gradually, with much trial and error. Educational research (Elley, 1989, 1983; Hancy, 1989; Feitelson, Kita and Goldstein, 1986; Chomsky, 1972) has confirmed what I and other classroom teachers and librarians have known for years:

- Reading aloud to STUDENTS OF ALL AGES is a positive learning experience in and of itself.
- When integrated into the curriculum of any subject area, it provides a natural springboard for reading and writing.
- It lends itself to creative and holistic lesson planning.
- And, on a steady diet, it enhances every aspect of the learning and school achievement cycle.
- In addition to all this, it is fairly easy to do!

Fortunately, some books already have been written to guide English speaking parents to good read-alouds (Trelease, 1985; Kimmel and Segal, 1983). These books are intended mainly for home use. Fortunately also, some teacher resources on using literature with mainstream students in elementary school settings have been developed (Monson, 1985; Moss, 1984). In addition, short articles on using children's literature with elementary ESL students are now beginning to appear in the professional education journals (Appleberry and Rodriguez, 1988; Radenich, 1985; Hough, 1986; Appolt, 1985). Teachers are using literature with their ESL students and are eagerly looking for literature suggestions and activity ideas. Unfortunately, very little comprehensive resource material on reading aloud with the multicultural population of elementary and middle/junior high schools has been written. *The Literature Connection* is intended to fill that gap.

This, then, is a resource book written primarily for teachers who work with limited English proficient (LEP) students, K-8. These students represent one of the fastest growing school-age populations in the United States. Oxford et al. (1981) estimate that by the year 2000, LEP students, 5-14 years old, will number 3.4 million or 10% of that age population. Originally, most of this group was serviced in schools by pull-out ESL or separate bilingual programs. With the growing numbers, however, educational needs will have to be met in mainstream, grade-level classes as well. *The Literature Connection* has been designed for use in any of these multicultural settings. In fact, one of its goals is to enhance cross-cultural awareness and sensitivity through the sharing of literature. In this way, literature becomes a connector among the students as well as a connection to the curriculum.

It is hoped that this book will be useful to other audiences as well. For years, ESL teachers have successfully used material designed primarily for special education students. It is therefore intended that this book will also be a resource for that population. Both groups benefit from enriched structured activities, such as literature read-aloud, and carefully sequenced, follow-up activities that enhance language development. Reading specialists who work with multicultural students will hopefully find that this book streamlines some of their work. Also, school and community librarians should discover this guide to be helpful in recommending literature for multicultural students and in preparing for their "book talks." And finally, parents will hope-fully find much useful information here too.

This book is more ambitious than just a compilation of annotations for reading aloud. Its goal is to help teachers use literature for language learning. Original children's literature, with its dramatic illustrations and elemental story lines, are natural material for the "comprehensible input" necessary for language acquisition (Krashen, 1985). No longer is reading aloud just for pre-schoolers and pre-readers! It can and should form an integral part of the entire educational program.

The process begins by teachers selecting books to meet their curriculum objectives from the thousands of books available in school and community libraries. Teachers then read the litera-ture aloud to their students and follow up with language-based activities that help develop both oral and written skills. Literature can be integrated into the elementary/middle school curricu-lum, especially language arts and ESL. This book shows you how!

In general, Part One, Read-Aloud Guidelines, suggests why and how teachers can do this themselves. More specifically, Chapter 2 addresses the benefits, Chapter 3 the criteria for book selection and Chapter 4 the techniques for reading aloud successfully. All these guidelines are written with a multicultural population in mind. Chapter 5 describes in detail over 25 classroom activities that develop language skills from literature sources. They provide concrete suggestions of how to use literature to meet specific curricular objectives, with literature recommended for each activity. These activities cover various language skills, age and proficiency levels. With these guidelines and activities, teachers can integrate literature into any ongoing curriculum.

Part Two, Read-Aloud Library recommends over 260 books, selected especially for limited English proficient students, but also appropriate, as explained above, for a broader, special needs population. The Introduction includes an explanation of how to use the collection and The Outline of Books, which lists all the books in the Read-Aloud Library, sequenced by topics. The annotations, which follow, are specifically organized with teachers in mind. Books are presented by teaching themes (e.g. family, school, U.S. History) and useful classroom information is provided (e.g. book length, ESL proficiency levels), in addition to the basic bibliographic data and book descriptions.

The book concludes with two other sections, intended to provide additional resources to the busy teacher. The first, References, lists all professional books and articles referred to in the text, plus major sources in the field. For easier usage, I have grouped the references by academic topics. For example, references on children's literature for second language learners and those more generally for native speakers are listed separately. The second section, Indexes, provides five different ways to access the 261 books annotated in the Read-Aloud Library. It identifies them by ethnic group, literary genre, book title, author and illustrator. All this information is included in each annotation, but if a teacher knows she definitely wants a book about Hispanics or a nursery rhyme, this is the place to start.

This then is a book by a teacher for a teacher. It is my way of sharing and returning—to my stimulating colleagues, my patient students, and my supportive family—what I have learned from all of them over the years. I hope you find it useful and a good read!

NOTES ABOUT LANGUAGE

As a language teacher, I am especially sensitive to language usage and its possible stereotypic effects. Regarding gender, I have tried to use the plural pronoun *they*, rather than the singular *he* or *she*, whenever possible. When this made the text too awkward, I have alternated the male and female pronouns, by chapter.

The terminology to refer to speakers of English who also speak other languages is more complex and usage has varied over the years. English as a Second Language, with its common acronym ESL, has been a fairly constant term, although it usually refers to students in special ESL classes. The term Limited English Proficient (LEP) or Limited English Speaker (LES) are widely used in the professional community and do describe a person's fluency in English. However, they are pejorative, especially in their acronym form, alluding to the fact that someone lacks something. Another popular term language minority (LM) is only somewhat less negative, especially when contrasted with language majority. These two terms also do not accurately describe the condition: that someone is learning a second language. I prefer the term second language (SL), with the assumption, for this book that English is the second language. This could be criticized as inaccurate, if English is the student's third, fourth or fifth language, but it seems the least pejorative of the available choices. I do, on occasion, use the other terms, but rely most heavily on second language learners.

I had been struggling with these terms even before I read *Integrating English*, by Scott Enright and Mary Lou McCloskey (1988). It was affirming that they shared the same discomforts as I expressed above. They settled upon "second language" as the best available choice, and I am following their lead. Maybe, together, we will start a new trend!

CHAPTER TWO

The Theoretical Connection:
Benefits of Reading Aloud

In today's educational atmosphere of testing, accountability and time management, everything that teachers do must be justified. School administrators want to see lesson plans and objectives. Parents want to be assured that teachers are not wasting time. Given the pressures of completing a long curriculum, how can teachers justify spending a leisurely 10-15 minutes a day reading to students? For English as Second Language (ESL) teachers in pull-out programs, this can take up one third of the instructional time.

Often I am asked, "What are the students actually learning during this time? Aren't they being passive, just like in watching TV?" Just what are the benefits of reading aloud? As an admirer of literature, my first response is to share a poem, written by Kathryn Lindskoog, as an introduction to her book, *How to Grow a Young Reader, A Parent's Guide to Books for Kids* (1989):

> Open books and open faces,
> Loving times and loving places.
>
> Loving words and loving looks,
> Precious voices, precious books.
>
> Open books for open eyes,
> Snuggly stories, snug and wise.
>
> Funny figures, funny rhymes,
> Sunny pictures, sunny times.
>
> Minds so drowsy, minds awake,
> Hearts that give and hearts that take.
>
> Questions new and questions old—
> Answers silver, answers gold.

Pictures touched and pages turned,
Lessons offered, lessons learned.

Happy smiles and happy laughter,
Happy memories ever after.

Through predictable patterns, repeated words and rhyming (key elements of successful children's literature), Lindskoog captures the essence of the reading aloud experience. Although written primarily about a parent-child interaction at home, these benefits apply equally to reading aloud at school.

To feel justified about reading aloud, one could almost stop here (and as a reader you are certainly entitled to). However, as an educator, I feel responsible to relate reading aloud to specific benefits, many of them based on research or current educational theories.

1. Reading Aloud Provides a Pleasurable Experience _____

It is often one of the things we remember most fondly about our own school days. The lucky among us can remember a special teacher reading a favorite book, one that we are still drawn to today when we peruse the library shelves.

Any school experience needs to be more than just fun and a warm memory, but that certainly is a good place to begin. Students learn more when they are relaxed. Few academic expectations are made during the initial read-aloud time. This lowers a listener's "affective filter" (Krashen, 1985), reducing the stress often associated with learning tasks. This allows the listener to psychologically remain more open to the input. (See Benefit #6 for how this ties in with overall language acquisition.)

2. Reading Aloud Bonds the Reader and Listener _____

Through a book, a class shares an experience together. For a short time, the teacher steps back from the responsibility of teaching something and the students are released from completing a task. Together they share something enriching, something that draws them closer as human beings. From this shared experience, meaningful dialogue often naturally occurs, either between teacher and student(s) or among the students themselves, possibly continuing even after class. This bonding can occur with something humorous, like the nonsense verses of *A Hunting We Will Go* or with a gripping drama like *Stone Fox*, a touching short novel about a boy who races against great odds to save his ailing grandfather's farm.

3. Reading Aloud Focuses on Listening Comprehension _____

A baby listens to language for at least a year before he is expected to speak. Psycholinguists recognize that this absorption time is an integral part of the normal language acquisition process. Second language learners seldom have the opportunity to just receive input planned specifically for them, without some output expected. Listening to literature read aloud provides that experience. For a short time, students can concentrate on just understanding a message.

Elley's two studies, a pilot one in the South Pacific (1983) with SL learners and a large one in New Zealand with native speakers (1989) provide evidence that reading stories aloud to elementary students at school on a regular basis (three days a week) significantly increases their vocabulary acquisition. His studies further found that

teachers' additional explanation of words as they read can more than double such gains, that the new learning is relatively permanent, and that students who score low on vocabulary at the outset can gain at least as much as students who score higher. (1989: 185)

An increase in oral vocabulary is extremely helpful for the subsequent skills of speaking, reading and writing. These skills can be developed later, ideally with the same book.

Reading aloud also helps develop attending skills. This is especially critical for K-3 students who are often unfamiliar to listening for extended periods of time. Since much information in academic settings is communicated orally, learning how to physically sit still and pay attention to oral stimuli is important training.

It is true that television also provides the opportunity to just listen, but the benefits can hardly be compared. When listening to literature, one receives direct human interaction. The material is selected with the listener in mind and is controlled for his language proficiency, age and attention span. The reader can also adjust the speed of the reading. Television is fast, flashy and difficult to really understand for SL students, except perhaps *Sesame Street*, *Mr. Rogers* or *Reading Rainbow*.

4. Reading Aloud Improves Reading and Writing Skills _____

Over the past twenty years, research has consistently shown that students who have been read to perform more successfully in their reading and language development at school (Elley, 1989, 1983; Chomsky, 1972; Cohen, 1968). In a review of much of this literature, McCormick (1977) concludes that

> hearing literature read is as important as any other element of the curriculum . . . In this age of accountability, the time spent reading to children can be justified since this activity does promote measurable growth in achievement. (p. 143)

The more recent national report, *Becoming a Nation of Readers* (1985) argues this even more forcefully, concluding that

> the single most important activity for building the knowledge required for eventual success in reading is reading aloud to children. (p. 23)

Hearing interesting literature stimulates the desire to read. It also presents models of adults reading and enjoying the experience. This helps to transform the one-time listener into a pleasure reader. This hopefully will evolve into a life long pursuit.

In a school setting, the motivation from reading aloud helps the child learn the skills necessary to enjoy reading independently. Reading and writing are integral processes, with the stimuli from self-motivated reading long acknowledged to improve writing. Reading provides writers with tacit knowledge of conventional prose and options that they can draw upon to organize and express their ideas. Numerous studies have confirmed this. Applebee (1978), for example, in a study of 481 good high school writers (winners of the NCTE achievement awards), concludes that "these successful writers were also successful readers." They reported having read an average of 14 books over their summer vacation. In another study, college freshmen at the University of Southern California (Kimberly et al., cited in Krashen, 1978) indicated a high correlation between students who read independently and better writing skills. Strength in both reading and writing are the pillars of overall academic achievement.

Students are never too late in the learning process to reap the benefits of being read to, although they are most open to the experience until about age 14. It can positively impact the cycle at any point and should be encouraged throughout.

5. Reading Aloud Introduces Books Beyond the Reader's Skill Level _____

Reading independently at one's skill level is certainly important. Yet for beginning readers and students whose reading ability lags behind their interest level this can be stultifying as a steady diet. The problem escalates for LEP students and other limited readers in grades three and above. Publishers, recognizing this market, have produced watered down versions of literary classics. These books do serve a valuable function, but limited readers should not be denied the benefits of hearing quality literature. Their ability to understand exceeds their ability to read.

A teacher can stimulate students by reading aloud literature beyond their own reading level. This motivates the students' desire to continue developing their reading skills in order to read more challenging literature themselves. It also serves the important function of introducing more content-based information through non-fiction.

6. Reading Aloud Enhances Overall Language Acquisition

Current psycholinguistic theory distinguishes second language acquisition (SLA) from second language learning (SLL). Language learning, a conscious process associated with the explicit teaching of rules, is generally viewed as less powerful and less important than language acquisition. SLA is a subconscious process that functions similarly to a child's natural acquisition of his first language. It is responsible for overall language comprehension and production. For this output, both "comprehensible input" and "a low socio-affective filter" (Krashen, 1985) are needed.

"Comprehensible input" (CI) involves language which is natural, meaningful and interesting to the student. It focuses on what is said, rather than analyzing how it is said. It is what Urzua (1985) calls "real" language. This "comprehensible input" should also include language that is a step beyond the student's present level of competence. A "low socio-affective filter" is also necessary to allow the student to be open to the input. This involves a low stress environment with high motivation that encourages self-confidence.

In keeping with Krashen's SLA model, reading aloud provides an excellent source of these essential ingredients for language acquisition. Over ten years earlier, Carol Chomsky's major study reached the same conclusion. In her research with native speakers of English between the ages of 6 and 10, she found that a strong correlation exists between reading exposure and linguistic development. Her theoretical premise, like Krashen's, is that language is not taught, but learned naturally, as one is developmentally ready for it. Chomsky ends her report with a clear recommendation for educators:

> The best thing we might do for (the child) in terms of encouraging this learning would
> be to make more of it possible, by exposing him to a rich variety of language inputs in
> interesting and stimulating situations" (p. 33).

A story, by its very definition, meets these definitions. It presents language in a meaningful context. If a book is well chosen, it should be interesting to the listeners. When read to, a student can climb beyond his often limited reading level; he is thus assured of more stimulating material. The teacher, through the book selection, can also stretch the learner's proficiency, challenging him to the next level. She can further control this by paraphrasing difficult sections. And, as mentioned in Benefit #2 above, the read-aloud environment is relaxed with few overt pressures. The learner's filter should be open to absorb the rich input.

Reading literature aloud also introduces students to different registers of language. Written language is usually more formal than speech, even when it contains dialogue. How can we expect our students to speak and write more than conversational English if they have never heard it? Literature provides this variety of speech naturally.

In sum, reading aloud is an ideal classroom method for enhancing the second language acquisition process.

7. Reading Aloud Integrates Easily into Any Subject Area of the Curriculum

By using language-based activities to follow-up a read-aloud session, literature can be integrated into any ongoing curriculum area. It is usually tied into the language arts program, but it need not be limited to this area. Literature read aloud, especially non-fiction, can serve as an excellent introduction or enrichment in social studies or science classes. The trend in ESL programs is to use content-based material to teach language. When used in this way, literature read-aloud can be used as the foundation to synthesize both language and content.

Follow-up activities can focus on specific skill development in listening, speaking, reading and writing. They can also integrate these skills with the creative arts, producing a truly interdisciplinary approach. They also are flexible in terms of time, easily limited to a single lesson or expanded into full units. This approach is fully developed through the 27 activities described in Chapter 5 of Part I, "The Curriculum Connection: Follow-Up Language Activities Generated from Literature."

8. Reading Aloud Expands Horizons

On their own, students would probably not pick up certain books. Reading aloud allows you to introduce them to some classics of children's literature, such as *Ferdinand* by Munro Leaf and *Charlotte's Web* by E.B. White. It also allows you to broaden their interests by introducing diverse topics. For example, even non-scientific students can be stimulated by short chapters read-aloud from *Astronomy* by Dinah Moche. Who knows, you may be opening the mind of a future astronaut!

Reading aloud can fill in gaps in students' academic backgrounds. This can be very important to SL students and others in grades K-3 who are not familiar with our culture's basic nursery rhymes and fairy tales that form part of our cultural knowledge. For older SL students, in grades 4-8, an introduction to American history and native American culture through literature will serve them well when they encounter these as content areas.

For mainstream teachers with students of diverse cultural backgrounds, reading aloud is an nonthreatening way to enhance cross-cultural understanding. For example, when a middle school class listens to the humorous but traumatic experiences of nine-year-old Shirley Temple Wong's first year at an American school *In the Year of the Boar and Jackie Robinson* by Bette Bao Lord, they can't help but become more sensitive to their own immigrant classmates.

9. Reading Aloud Stimulates the Imagination

Literature introduces new ideas and images which stimulate the imagination. When we imagine, we dream. When we dream, we become excited. And when we are excited, we feel empowered to create. This creativity enriches our lives and permeates our writing.

The oft-quoted phrase "a mind is a terrible thing to waste" is very true. A child's mind is developed by imagination, among other things. This imagination is stimulated by literature. And so the circle comes round and hopefully cycles on and on.

Children's literature is infused with magic, fantasy and the ridiculous. The hope expressed in "Hug O'War," one of Shel Silverstein's poems in *Where the Sidewalk Ends* stirs the soul while tickling the funny bone. And the image of the plastic Indian who magically comes alive in *Indian in the Cupboard*, written by Lynne Reid Banks, will haunt you long after the book is complete.

While it is true that one's imagination can also be enriched by reading to oneself, it is easier for a young person to be open to the ideas when he is not stumbling over words and concentrating on the reading process. Reading aloud frees the listener.

10. Reading Aloud Opens the World of Literature

Good children's literature possesses the same qualities as good adult literature. It puts us in touch with our own humanity. It expresses what we feel. Good literature is precise, sensitive and rich in meaning. It is education in its broadest sense. Through it, we learn about the world and ultimately about ourselves. Certainly this deserves as much time in the school curriculum as spelling rules!

Reading aloud is like planting slow-growing seeds. As in the story of *The Carrot Seed* by Ruth Krauss, it takes a long time for the roots to attach and new growth to emerge. Someone else may enjoy the ripe fruit, but you will have the satisfaction of having participated in the life of the plant.

Review the verbs used in this chapter to describe the benefits of reading aloud: it provides, bonds, focuses, improves, stimulates, introduces, enhances, integrates, expands and opens. Can something this easy and inexpensive really be so good? YES! Reading aloud will probably be one of the most pleasurable things you share with your students. And it just may be the most valuable too, in the long run. Please, don't miss out on the experience, for your students' sake, or for yours. Enjoy!

CHAPTER THREE

The Library Connection:
Criteria for Selecting Read-Alouds

Thousands of children's books line the shelves of libraries and thousands more are published each year. Many books, while quality literature, even classics, are not appropriate as read-alouds. And many good read-alouds work best with experienced listeners. These guidelines will help you choose appropriate books for your read-aloud program. Although they are useful for all students K-8, they are written specifically for the target population: limited English proficient (LEP) students.

The guidelines here include two sets of criteria: the first for selecting individual books and the second for balancing selections over time or for an overall collection.

CRITERIA FOR INDIVIDUAL BOOKS

These criteria can help you make initial decisions about the appropriateness of a book, usually while browsing in a library or bookstore. For a final decision, it is highly recommended that you read the books yourself. For a picture book this takes no more than five to ten minutes, for novels up to two hours. Keep the criteria in mind as you read, but make that final decision yourself. Not all criteria will apply to each book. You know your class and their needs the best. Follow your instincts! Experience is often the best teacher.

These criteria have been posed in question form because when we are cruising the shelves looking for that perfect book, we are asking questions, either of ourselves or to the librarian. "What is this about? Will it work?" Here are some more specific questions to guide you in your search.

1. Do You Like the Book? Does It Attract You?

Your gut reaction to a book is a good starting point. Think of the book as a product and yourself as a salesperson. If the salesperson genuinely believes in the product, this enthusiasm will help to sell it! After you consider your attraction to the book, consider your students'. Do you think they will like it too?

2. Does the Book Relate in Some Way to What You Are Teaching? Does It Help Meet One of Your Curriculum Objectives? _____

If so, you can quickly complete part of your lesson plan book: briefly state the objective, list the book as material to meet that objective and write in "read aloud to class" as part of your teaching plan. The connection could either be the subject matter, a grammar point, or a cultural or holiday topic. Parents can luckily skip this consideration.

3. Does the Book Address an Age-Appropriate Theme or Topic? Are the Protagonists the Students' Age or Older? _____

This should be reflected in the illustrations as well. Nursery rhymes, for example, are too immature in subject matter, tone and usually illustrations for students above nine years old. This important criterion limits, but does not eliminate, the pool of appropriate picture books for beginning SL students in grades 4 and above. Some picture books, such as the allegorical *The Giving Tree* by Shel Silverstein, appeal to all ages, 5-75. Picture book non-fiction, especially those by the prolific Gail Gibbons, also help fill this gap.

4. Does the Book Have an Easy to Follow Story Line? _____

Elementary age children are basically interested in what happens. The plot should be fairly straightforward, chronological and unambiguous. The narration should be strong, with action predominating. Children's attention wanders during long descriptions and flashbacks tend to cause confusion. Both should be avoided, except for experienced, older listeners.

5. Do the Picture Books Have Clear Illustrations that Help Tell the Story? _____

The illustrations are perhaps the single most important criterion for SL students. They should be detailed and dramatic, ideally able to almost tell the story on their own. Both the teachers and students depend on the pictures to explain new vocabulary or situations. The particular style is not as important as its full visual description of the mood and scene. Be careful to avoid abstract art and artistic stereotypes.

Beginning SL students will be "reading" the pictures, much like pre-schoolers. For this reason, the amount of text per page should be limited, with art predominant and the layout uncluttered. With increased language proficiency, the balance should shift to more text. Even when selecting novels, don't overlook the presence and importance of the illustrations. When they are not explaining the text, they help set the tone.

Because of the fuller illustration, choose single volumes over collections, whenever possible. Children enjoy a sense of completion when they finish listening to a whole book. Many artists take great pride in illustrating individual books of fairy tales, legends, songs and poetry. Those by Paul Galdone, Brinton Turkle and Trina Schart Hyman are aesthetically pleasing as well as descriptively rich.

6. Is the Book Large Enough to Be Seen Comfortably by a Group? _____

The size of the group and the seating arrangement will dictate the size of the book. Most 9 X 12 inch books, which is a large but normal size picture book, can be seen easily by up to 10 students.

This criterion applies mainly to picture books and decreases in importance as text predominates over art. This is another criterion that parents can ignore altogether, when reading cozily at home with one to three children.

Many publishing houses are now printing "Big Books," which are large size editions of regular picture books. These can be seen comfortably by up to 30 students. Many of these come in kits, with additional support material, including regularly sized book editions. While an exciting trend, check out the quality of the individual Big Book. Not all are original literature and the quality of the illustrations vary widely.

7. Does the Book Contain Predictable Patterns? _____

These include rhyming as well as repetition of words, patterns, refrains or entire sentences. These are commonplace in nursery rhymes, songs and poems, but also found in many picture books. Predictable patterns add to the fun of a story. They also help children memorize books, even when they are not trying. For example, many of my students who cannot produce a grammatically correct sentence can nevertheless repeat from memory the name of the most honored first son of the House of Chan, "Tikki tikki tembo, no sa rembo, charri barri ruchi, pit peri pembo."

These predictable patterns help students learn to read. After hearing the pattern read aloud in the context of a story, chanting it orally follows easily. The transfer to the written symbols is more manageable than if students first encounter the words in print. They are already "user friendly." Rhymes are particularly good for reading skill development. The vowel sound remains the same, with only the consonants changing.

8. Does the Book Use Grammatical Structures Slightly Beyond the Level of Your Students? _____

When it does, it provides "comprehensible input," an essential ingredient for the language acquisition process. (See Benefit #6 in Chapter 2, "The Theoretical Connection: The Benefits of Reading Aloud" for a discussion of this concept by Stephen Krashen.)

For beginners, look for fairly simple language structures, with a limited number of tenses and repetition of patterns. For intermediate and advanced level students, language need not be as controlled. When planning grammar lessons, choose books that model specific structures. For example, I have taught regular and irregular past tense using *The Fox*, an engaging singable book by Peter Spier.

9. Does the Book Use (but not overuse) Dialogue? _____

Dialogue is good for reading aloud because it allows the reader to vocally dramatize the different characters. As a follow-up activity, some of the students can read the lines, while others role play the actions. And there you have a simple play!

Dialogue reads quickly, giving a fast pace to a story. It also develops characters through communication rather than through description. This creates authenticity in a story. It also adds informality which makes a story even more accessible.

In order to expose students to a variety of written English, do not lean too heavily on dialogue dominant books. In excess, they overshadow other qualities of literature, such as the cadence of narrative prose. They begin to sound like television scripts.

10. Does the Book Use Only Small Amounts of Nonstandard Language, Literary Metaphors and References to Unfamiliar Experiences? _____

These are a positive challenge for advanced listeners and do expand the richness of literature. For beginner and low intermediate SL students, however, they are a distraction from understanding the basic story and should be reduced, or avoided altogether. (For a further discussion of reading aloud non-standard language, see p. 20 in the next chapter, "The Classroom Connection: Techniques for Reading Aloud.")

CRITERIA FOR BALANCED SELECTIONS OR FOR OVERALL COLLECTIONS

Over time, book selections should represent a variety of topics, cross cultural themes and literary genres. These considerations were taken into account in the selection of the "Read-Aloud Library" in this book. The information is presented here to serve as guidelines for a teacher's, librarian's or parent's own balanced selections.

1. Book Topics

The 19 topics listed below cover most of the basic themes of elementary ESL programs as well as many from the general elementary curriculum, excluding mathematics. They can be found as headings in the Listing of Books by Topics (p. 58).

Family Relationships
Life Passages (Birth, Marriage, Divorce, Death)
House/Home
Friendship
Emotions/Values
School/Learning
Basic Academic Skills (Alphabet, Calendar, Colors, Numbers, Opposites, Shapes, Sizes, Time)
Clothing/Body
Holidays
Food/Nutrition
Community (Places, Shopping, Transportation)
Recreation/Sports
Role Models (Heroes, Careers)
History/Geography (United States and World)
Immigration/Cross-cultural Adjustment
Animals (Birds, Farm, Pets, Prehistoric, Sea, Wild, Zoo)
Seasons/Weather
Science (Growth, Health, Space)
Imagination/Monsters/Magic

2. Cultural Themes

Part of children's education involves understanding their culture and finding their own place in it. Many of the students in the United States today come from a multicultural background. In addition, many children function in one culture at home and in another at school. Depending on their particular situation, they may lack knowledge of certain aspects of their home or school cultures. For newly arrived Hispanic refugees, this usually means an unfamiliarity with the modern American community and how it functions. For young Vietnamese born in the United States, it may mean an unfamiliarity with their own cultural traditions. In addition, the United States has historically been a country of immigrants. For all students in our schools, exposure to this immigrant past enhances cross-cultural understanding in the present.

Children's literature can be a rich source for expanding our students' cultural horizons. Literature selections should include a balance from the following cultural themes. Depending on the needs of your students, some themes will require more attention than others.

1. Childhood background of familiar nursery rhymes, fairy tales, legends and fables.
2. American culture and customs (e.g. family life)
3. Contemporary American community, (e.g. modern hospitals, shopping centers)
4. American history
5. Immigration stories
6. Cross-cultural experiences
7. Diverse cultural traditions

3. Literary Genres

Over time, students should be introduced to a variety of literary genres. Some genres lend themselves better to certain themes or topics and some are more appropriate for certain ages (novels, for example). To provide balance in a full collection or over the course of a school year, however, incorporate as many as possible in your book selections.

Picture Books
    Wordless picture books
    Nursery rhymes
    Fairy tales
    Folk tales
    Singable books
    Fables
    Myths and legends
    Concept books
    General
Easy Readers
    Beginner level
    Intermediate level
Poetry
    Individual/narrative poems
    Collections
Fiction
    Short stories
       individual (under 50 pages), collections
    Short novels (50-100 pages)
    Long novels (over 100 pages)
    Historical fiction
    Modern fantasy
    Contemporary realistic fiction
    Mysteries/Suspense
    Science Fiction
Non-Fiction
    Picture book non-fiction
    General non-fiction
    Biography/autobiography
Anthologies

Selecting appropriate read alouds for a particular audience is not as easy as picking books off a shelf. I hope these criteria help facilitate the process, so as to encourage teachers to use literature more frequently in their classes.

CHAPTER FOUR

The Classroom Connection:
Techniques for Reading Aloud

Once you have convinced yourself (and your principal) of the benefits of reading literature aloud and have selected one or two books, you are ready to perform. Or are you? It is not as easy as it looks to do it well, but neither is it very difficult. Actually, most people find reading aloud a pleasurable experience. Here are some considerations to incorporate into your planning and some classroom-tested techniques. It is hoped that these will guide you and your students towards a successful read-aloud experience.

1. Arrange a Special Place for Reading Aloud

Many classrooms have an all-purpose, open area. This serves as an ideal read-aloud center. Create the needed space by moving as little furniture as possible. Whatever setting you decide upon, use the same one regularly. In this way, the children will come to anticipate "story time" by movement to a certain area.

Seat the children in a semicircle, either in chairs, on mats or on the floor. Place yourself in a comfortable chair in the front. Then arrange the children and yourself so all of them can see the illustrations. This requires the reader's head to be above that of the students. Being at this level also helps your voice to project better.

As an experimental seating arrangement, I once tried sitting on the floor in a circle with my students. I thought it would create a relaxed, informal atmosphere. Many wanted to sit next to me, but those who did couldn't see the pictures well. Some students abused the informality by lying down on the floor. They soon became distracted. A few even fell asleep, plus my back hurt. What a fiasco! That was a short session! The next day, I was back in my rocking chair, they in their little chairs in the old semicircle. So much for the experiment!

2. Set Aside a Regular Time for Reading Aloud

The classroom teacher should select a time during the day that the class would benefit from a relaxing but educational interlude. Different times will work best for different classes and their schedules. It can be just the perfect way to start the day, to unwind after an active recess or to end your time together. It can also be a component of the language arts block.

It is, of course, best to read aloud every day. Students enjoy it and come to eagerly anticipate their "story time." Even when this is not possible, read aloud regularly. Let students know in advance when that time will be. Anticipation builds excitement. When reading a chapter book, it is important to continue reading it on a daily or near daily basis. Otherwise, the momentum of the story is broken.

Many ESL teachers see their students for only 30-45 minute blocks of time and in some cases, only a few days a week. In these situations, it is more difficult to set aside a regular time for reading aloud. Integrating reading aloud into the curriculum increases the likelihood that it will happen. That is also why the following technique is realistic.

3. Plan How You Are Going To Use the Book

Think through the role that a chosen book can play in your lesson planning. Then incorporate those ideas into your unit objectives and weekly plan book. Literature can serve diverse functions in completing the school curriculum. It may be an introduction to a social studies or science unit. It may illustrate a grammatical point or cover a particular vocabulary unit or current holiday. In these cases, follow-up activities (see Chapter 5) enhance its integration into the curriculum. Or it may just be for fun, with no particular relevance to any specific part of the curriculum or any intended follow-up. It provides a good balance to mix a few of these "free" selections with ones that later become associated with school work.

Once you have planned how you will use a certain book, it is important to communicate your intentions to the students. Some school districts now require this. I have found that students always do better if they know why we are doing something. Students as young as six can understand brief explanations. For example,

> "Today I will be sharing with you a wonderful story, *Pancakes for Breakfast*, written by Tomie dePaola. What do you think it may be about? (Accept responses.) Listen to find out. In the next few days we will be talking about foods for breakfast and if you are especially good, we will plan, cook and eat a breakfast meal together, right here in school! Won't that be fun?! Now please sit quietly and enjoy the story."

For older students, an introduction to *In the Year of the Boar and Jackie Robinson* might include a brief description of it as an immigrant story of a 10 year old Chinese girl and a mention that "later this month we will be talking and writing about our own immigrant experiences."

4. Prepare for the Reading Session Itself Ahead of Time

First preview the book silently. Then read it aloud to yourself or ideally to an audience. This allows you to practice your reading and to experiment with pacing, timing and any dramatic expressions you may want to incorporate. This will help you decide the amount of time the book will take as a read-aloud and to estimate the necessary number of sessions needed to complete it. This read-aloud practice also serves as a final confirmation of an earlier decision to use the book. It is much better to change your mind now than in the middle of class. With chapter books, you should have read the whole book before making the initial decision to use it. For nightly preparation, it is advisable to read aloud the portion for the next day, so it is fresh in your mind.

Once you have read the book aloud at home and are sure that you will use it, try to gather visual aids that will enrich its presentation. These also function well as part of a short introduction to the read-aloud session. For example, with *Caps for Sale*, by Esphyr Slobodkina bring in a stuffed toy monkey (or two or three) and a variety of caps. For *A Chair for My Mother* by Vera Williams bring in a big glass jar. Tell the children that one of these appears prominently in the story and let them guess its function. Later on, as a follow-up, encourage the class to collect their own coins for a special class purchase. A popular choice is refreshments for a class party. It is nice to leave these props, along with the book, in an available place in the classroom, so that the students can interact with them during any free time.

5. Anticipate Distractions and Plan for Them

As much as possible, try to eliminate interruptions during a reading session. First, at the beginning of the year, highlight any of your behavioral expectations that are particularly appropriate for read-aloud sessions and communicate these clearly to the students. One standard one is

> "Try not to interrupt when the teacher is talking/reading. But if you have something
> important to share, please raise your hand and wait to be called on."

Be sure to communicate sanctions for inappropriate behavior as well. One that has worked well for me is,

> "If the reader needs to speak to a listener more than once, (except for an emergency),
> the listener needs to leave the story circle for the rest of that session."

It is helpful to explain briefly why these guidelines and sanctions are necessary. This tends to work better with older students. These rules are even more effective if they are developed cooperatively by the class as a whole, with all students and teacher(s) participating. It is usually necessary to review them periodically throughout the year.

Second, consider the physical needs of the children. If they have just finished seatwork, lead them in some short stretches before settling into sitting again. Also allow them time to get a drink of water or go to the bathroom, if needed. Explain that doing these things during the reading time disrupts everyone's concentration. Of course, there are always emergencies! For example, it seems like I am always reading during fire drills!

Third, make sure that all the children are comfortably seated with unobstructed views of the book, so that you won't be interrupted with cries of "I can't see!" If it is impossible for students to all see at one time, assure them that you will move around so that they *will* all be able to see the pictures.

Fourth, alert the students to any anticipated interruptions for that particular reading session. For example, a team of visiting school officials may be in the building or a parent volunteer may be coming into the room to work with an individual student. We all handle distractions better if we know about them ahead of time.

6. Read Slowly and Dramatically

Reading too fast is the single greatest problem. Give yourself enough time so that you don't feel a time pressure. Also be conscious of articulating the words carefully. Listeners depend on this articulation for their comprehension.

To this slow, clear reading, add elements of drama. You don't need a degree in acting, but be aware that reading aloud is a performance. For example, modify your voice for different characters and use nonverbal facial expressions and body movements to enhance the meaning. What your SL students may miss in the words they can pick up from these nonverbal cues. Act out! It's OK, in fact, it's great fun for the reader! And your listeners will love it!

Finally, consider elements to help pace your reading. Correct breathing is important. Pause to take deep breaths regularly. Drinking sips of water from a nearby glass helps with this pacing as well as with your vocal comfort. You will be surprised how dry your throat can get when reading for 10-15 minutes. Pacing is also related to capturing the rhythm of a text. Often this rhythm will change during the story. This is easier to gage in books with predictable patterns, rhymes and melodies.

In the end, remember that it's better to read a smaller amount slowly, clearly and dramatically than to rush through a longer portion.

7. Edit and Paraphrase Judiciously

Authors intentionally write to a wide audience. As teachers of limited English speakers, we often need to modify the language to communicate the message. Try to use as much of the original language as possible, striving to maintain a balance between respecting the prose as written and editing it to the proficiency level of your students. This freedom to orally edit books extends the range of literature appropriate for SL students. It provides yet another advantage of reading aloud.

There are many valid reasons for orally editing a text. First, while some novels capture their audience in the first paragraph, others take a while to warm up. If you think a book is worthwhile, read selectively from the slow introduction, providing your listeners just enough information to develop the story line. Let them know you are doing this, so that they won't be surprised if they read the book themselves.

Second, some children's classics use language patterns and vocabulary that are more complex than the comprehension level of your students. You can preserve the story by orally simplifying the language. Be advised that this does require some extra preparation for a smooth presentation. *The Just So Stories* by Rudyard Kipling, with their flowery samples of Victorian English, do very well with some judicious language and vocabulary simplification. It is also a good example of a classic worth the editing effort.

Third, some fast-moving action books contain an occasional long description which will likely lose your listeners. Don't be timid! Omit it or edit it down. Maybe next year they will be ready for it.

Fourth, some excellent books contain nonstandard language (often referred to as "dialects"). Some examples are *The Boy Who Didn't Believe in Spring* and *John Henry*, both of which contain some black English and *The Witch of Fourth Street*, which includes other ethnic variations of English (e.g. Italian, Irish, Jewish). Authors often use nonstandard language in dialogues to authenticate the characters. While stories with dialect are very entertaining when told by a gifted story teller, they are often difficult to convincingly read aloud by the rest of us. Also, this nonstandard language can be very confusing to students with limited English proficiency. In addition, as teachers, in a formal, school setting, we may be uncomfortable modeling non-standard speech.

It is quite simple to orally transform the occasional written dialect into standard form without sacrificing the overall tone of the story. On the other hand, be warned that some of the book's ethnic flavor is lost in the translation. Therefore, do not hesitate to read the dialogues as is, if you are comfortable with the language and you think that your students will understand it and be able to differentiate it from the standard speech taught in school curriculums.

For each of these editing reasons, it is the teacher or librarian that must make the final decision about how much of the text to orally modify. As long as editing still retains the basic integrity of the literature, I feel it is better to orally edit than to eliminate a book altogether.

8. Limit Your Read-Aloud Sessions to 5-15 Minutes

Listening is hard work that requires concentration and conditioning. Build up gradually from 5 to 15 minute sessions. This is particularly true when the majority of your audience is limited English speakers. For most ESL classes, which are only 30-45 minutes, these short reading sessions allow time for follow-up activities and for frequent re-readings. This time limit applies to both picture books and novels.

Any book can be interrupted at appropriate breaking points. Stopping at that point before you lose your audience requires sensitive monitoring of both the literature and the class, but it is important. It is always better to leave students hanging than to leave them bored.

Once your students have built up their listening skills and your schedule has some extra time, by all means read aloud for longer than 15 minutes. Longer sessions encourage listeners to become more fully absorbed in a story. This is especially beneficial for older students engrossed in full-length novels.

9. Allow Time for Discussion

Literature provides a rich source of "comprehensible input" that often stimulates a meaningful desire to communicate. Allow time after the story for students to share their reactions, even if you are not planning any special follow-up activities that day. Often these brief, unplanned sessions generate the most authentic opportunities for language production.

On the other hand, do not force responses this first time. If a few general questions do not stimulate conversation, move on. Many legitimate reasons exist for lack of response. Some students need to hear a book a few times before understanding it enough to respond, some others may initially feel inhibited by their limited English proficiency. Or sometimes, a book can be so stirring that the best response is a few moments of quiet time for reflection. For those books integrated into the curriculum with structured follow-up activities, there will be ample later opportunities for communication.

Time for discussion is best after the book or chapter has been completed. Sometimes, however, young children's reactions emerge spontaneously in the middle of a story. Guide your students to concentrate on listening to a book or chapter through the first time, so as to not break the flow. Encourage them to hold their thoughts for the discussion time immediately after a story. This takes training, especially for the younger ones.

10. Remember Practice Makes Perfect

For most people, reading aloud is a learned skill. Like many things, it improves over time. Give yourself a lot of opportunities. Remember, the better you become at something, the more you enjoy it. Don't be too tough on yourself and don't be afraid to try. Your listeners will appreciate your efforts!

CHAPTER FIVE

The Curriculum Connection:
Follow-Up Activities Generated from Literature

The benefits (of reading aloud) are greatest when the child is an active participant, engaging in discussions about stories, learning to identify letters and words, and talking about the meaning of words. (*Becoming a Nation of Readers*, 1985: 23)

INTRODUCTION

In earlier chapters, I discussed the benefits of reading aloud to limited English proficient (LEP) students and techniques to do this successfully. This chapter focuses on classroom activities that develop language skills from literature sources. Through these activities, teachers can reinforce any given language objective. In this way, the literature selections become integrated into the rest of the ESL or language arts curriculum.

These activities represent a smorgasbord of ideas, developed during my years of ESL teaching. Some are tried and true favorites that will probably be familiar to many of you. Others I have evolved from the input of school in-services, professional conferences and journal literature. In these cases, I have noted their professional sources. Still others I have developed anew for my own classroom needs (e.g. cooperative murals, collective book reports). All the activities included have been classroom tested.

For purposes of discussion, I have divided these classroom activities as follows:

1. Listening
2. Speaking
3. Reading
4. Writing
5. Creative Arts

In the life of a classroom, divisions into the above skill areas are less distinct and most good activities involve a mixture of skills. Nevertheless, such a division helps teachers focus on areas that need attention. To create a well-balanced unit, teachers, in their planning, should include suggestions from each section. For an overview of the activities, see the list at the end of this introduction.

The description of each activity includes a rationale and a detailed explanation of how to implement it, often with examples. This is supplemented with other tips for class management as well as some personal anecdotes relating how certain activities have worked in my own classroom.

After each description, I recommend some literature that is compatible with it. The full bibliographic and annotated format for these books can be found in "Part II: Read-Aloud Library" and also through the various indexes at the end of the book.

The teacher should carefully select the activity as well as the literature to meet both the grade and the proficiency level of the learners. I delineate these for each activity. However, as most ESL and special education classrooms, and many mainstream ones, serve a range of language proficiency levels and grades, the activities are designed to be expandable regarding language difficulty and age range.

Initially, most of these activities are best demonstrated with the whole class. The teacher stimulates the creative process, fields ideas and blends together the whole. Ultimately, however, the goal is for the students to work independently, either in small cooperative groups or individually, depending on the activity.

My preference is for cooperative, small group work.[1] This works especially well for middle school students (grades 4-8). It encourages communication, simulates the development of ideas and allows the integration of students with varied proficiency levels. The teacher's role then becomes that of facilitator, helping the various groups in turn.

Through these activities the students take ownership, responsibility and hopefully some pride in their work. I have observed over and over again that students feel better about learning when they do it themselves. After all, they are the learners. As teachers, we are there to stimulate them and facilitate their acquisition of their linguistic competence. Through these activities we move them towards more independent learning, in cooperation with their peers or by themselves.

In summary, this chapter has two goals. First, to provide an easy-to-use set of language activities that integrate literature into the curriculum and facilitate language acquisition. Second, to serve as a springboard to stimulate the creation of new activities for language development through literature. Have fun and enjoy the activities with your students!

LANGUAGE ACTIVITIES GENERATED FROM LITERATURE

Listening Activities
    Introduction   **25**
    1. Do it again: Listening Reinforcement
    2. Share it: Peer Reading
    3. Listen for it: Directed Listening
    4. Act it out: Nonverbal Role Playing

Speaking Activities
    Introduction   **28**
    1. Check it out: Oral Comprehension Questions
    2. Join in: Shared Reading
    3. Tell it like it is: Story Retelling
    4. Make it up: Round Robin Story Telling
    5. Experience it: Language Experience

Reading Activities
    Introduction   **33**
    1. Read it yourself: Independent Reading
    2. Chart it: Reading Skill Development
    3. Review it: Collective Book Reports
    4. Unscramble it: Sentence Strips
    5. Put it in order: Sequencing
    6. Cloze it: The Cloze Procedure
    7. Fill it in: Fill in the Blanks

Writing Activities
    Introduction   **38**
    Chart A "The Composing Process
    1. Copy it down: Student Anthologies
    2. Publish it: Story Writing
    3. Be a poet: First Letter Poetry
    4. Finish it yourself: Story Endings
    5. Write it like it is: Dictation
    6. Reconstruct it: Story Reconstruction
    7. Write about yourself: Autobiographies

Creative Arts
    Introduction   **45**
    1. Book it: Bookmaking
    2. Paint it together: Cooperative Murals
    3. Perform it: Class Performances
    4. Play it out: Dramatization

LISTENING ACTIVITIES

Introduction _____

You might ask, "Why do follow-up listening activities when students have just listened to the book?" The answer is that many students, especially kindergartners and beginners, need extra aural experience. Yet this reinforcement needs to be varied to avoid boredom. Also, for beginning students, listening activities can be designed so that oral comprehension is indicated without requiring production. The four activities recommended include listening to a different presentation of the same story, peer reading, directed listening and nonverbal role playing.

1. DO IT AGAIN!   *Listening Reinforcement*

ESL Level: Beginner-Intermediate   **Grades: K-8**

The first reading of a book is most effectively done teacher to students. Teachers experienced in reading aloud read with facial expressions and body language that help explain the text as much as do the illustrations. Also, students seem to understand better with familiar human interaction.

Yet, hearing a story again (and again) is an important part of the learning process, and although it can be a teacher model each time, it need not be. In fact, the variation of presentation modes can be stimulating for the students. So, whenever possible, arrange for tapes, film, filmstrips and even videos of books for second and third presentations.

Many classic stories are available in a variety of media, with more coming out each year. Finding them, however, does require a little more effort than just taking a book off a library shelf. Media sources exist both within the schools and in the community. Most school media centers have their own collection of films and filmstrips of literature, plus they usually have access to a central storehouse for the district, which has an even wider selection. I have always found the school media specialist to be very helpful in locating diverse presentations of the book I was using. Most public libraries have a children's record collection, many of which include children's literature. Don't overlook the local video store as a source, even though you will have to carefully seek out the few authentic literature selections. Preview these carefully before devoting valuable class time to them.

Two new resources are helpful in identifying children's literature in a variety of media. *Parent's Guide to Video and Audio Cassettes for Children* (Cascardi, 1988) is a full length book devoted to this topic. Not all of the entries originate from quality children's literature, but many of them do. *The Association of Library Services for Children's (ALSC) Notable Films/Videos, Filmstrips and Recordings* (1989) offers a five page pamphlet, which describes this highly regarded group's recommendations in a variety of media.[2]

Book Recommendations. Ever popular, *The Velveteen Rabbit* by Margery Williams is available in a filmstrip kit, as a best selling children's album narrated by actress Meryl Streep (1985), and as a video from Windham Hill, also released in 1985.[3] Rudyard Kipling's *The Elephant Child* from his *Just So Stories* collection has been produced as a video, also from Windham Hill (1987) and *Corduroy*, the lovable bear story by Don Freeman, has been done by Children's Circle Home Video (1988).

Don't overlook children's literature on records and cassettes. An "oldie but goodie" is Boris Karloff, doing clear, dramatic readings of the *Just So Stories* (1958) and of *The Three Little Pigs and Other Fairy Tales* (1962). More recently, Weston Woods has produced an excellent series of albums, entitled *Picture Book Parade*. These are available through most school and public library systems or directly from the publisher.[4]

Many good books are now packaged in kits for listening center use. The kits include a cassette tape and multiple copies of the book. The equipment for this method allows numerous students to simultaneously listen to the tape on individual headphones, while following along with their own books. *Bill Martin's Instant Readers*, a very popular early elementary series, comes in this format.

2. SHARE IT!   *Peer Reading*

ESL Level: Beginner-Advanced   **Grades: K-8**

Although peer tutoring is a familiar concept in school, peer reading is newer.[5] It involves, quite simply, an older and more language proficient student reading a book aloud to a younger one. It helps all parties involved: the older students with oral reading practice, question asking and general responsibility, the younger students with another model and more listening opportunities and the teacher with an additional semi-independent, small group activity.

In second language situations, mature 3rd graders and older SL students with at least intermediate proficiency should be considered as reading candidates. A grade span of at least three years should establish enough authority in the readers (e.g. 3rd graders to kindergartners, 5th to 2nd graders). For the readers, this provides additional and much needed practice in oral pronunciation and intonation inflection. 100% accuracy in pronunciation need not be the criterion or goal for SL readers, especially if the teacher will be providing an additional reading, either before or after.

Teachers should be warned that peer reading involves some training of the student readers. At least initially this can be time consuming as well as time saving. They need to prepare student readers with techniques for reading aloud (see Chapter 5) and for management of small groups. In addition, older student readers can be trained to provide aural/oral reinforcement at the completion of the story. This can involve asking simple oral comprehension and discussion questions. (For other suggestions, see activities suggested under Listening and Speaking in this chapter.)

Book Recommendations. As a teacher often has certain books in mind to meet curriculum objectives, student readers can be offered a choice of pre-selected books. Alternatively, they can be assigned a book on a given topic. On occasion, the younger students can choose a book they would like read to them or the older students can be allowed to share one of their favorites.

3. LISTEN FOR IT!   *Directed Listening*

ESL Level: Beginner   **Grades: K-8**

Directed listening serves as a simple, aural comprehension check, in a game-like fashion. The teacher asks the children to listen for specific things and to indicate nonverbally when they occur in the story. This nonverbal comprehension can be indicated by a variety of physical gestures: for example, arm raising, head-nodding or even by changing the body position (sitting to standing or vice versa).

To ascertain that the students are really listening to the words and not just getting their answers from the illustrations, it is often necessary to do directed listening without showing the book. For this reason and also to allow for the pleasure of hearing the entire story uninterrupted, directed listening should be done as a follow-up activity and not during a first-reading. This allows students to gain a sense of the whole before being required to listen for component parts, be they language structures, vocabulary or general comprehension.

Using examples taken from *Caps for Sale* by Esphyr Slobodkina, students' listening can be directed to a number of objectives: for example, language structures—action verbs, "Tell me when the peddlar *sits* down under the tree"; vocabulary, "Stand up when the peddlar takes off his *red* cap, his *checkered* cap, his *own* cap"; or general comprehension, "Shake your fists when the peddlar gets angry with the monkeys for the second time."

By asking questions that require an answer, as opposed to just a gestured response, directed listening can easily be converted into a comprehension activity requiring oral production. For example, again from *Caps for Sale*, "What color is the peddlar's own cap?" Mixing these two levels of comprehension (directed listening and oral comprehension) works well in classes with mixed proficiency levels.

Book Recommendations. Directed listening can be used effectively for beginners with almost any book and any grade. For starters, try *Danny and the Dinosaur* by Syd Hoff for K-3 and *Mufaro's Beautiful Daughters* by John Steptoe for older students.

4. ACT IT OUT!   *Nonverbal Role Playing*

ESL Level: Beginner   **Grades: K-3**

After hearing a complete story one time, students are ready to begin to dramatize it. In this activity, dramatizing the story means acting out roles according to the teacher's oral cues, which are taken literally from the story. In effect, the students are using Total Physical Response (TPR) to indicate comprehension of the story without being required to respond yet in English. Speaking can be incorporated, however.

Take, for example, *The Little Red Hen* by Joseph Jacobs, found in many nursery tale collections or as a separate book. In the story, the hen asks three of her friends, a dog, a cat and a duck, to help her with her farm work of planting grain, threshing and carrying wheat, kneading flour, and eating the bread, the finished product.

The teacher assigns the students one of the characters. She then instructs them to act out that role as she reads that character's lines in the story. Although speaking is not required, even the newest beginner will soon be chanting, "No, not I" to the request for help and "Yes, I will" to the request for eating the freshly baked bread from the oven.

If your group contains more students than roles in a story, the teacher can either have the students perform the role play several times with the others enjoying their role as "audience," or double up on the number of actors for each part.

Book Recommendations. Stories for dramatization should include as many parts as possible. Other criteria for choosing books appropriate for nonverbal role playing include predictable lines, a simple plot and actions which are easy to act out. In addition, as many students of this age love to pretend they are animals, stories with at least some animal characters encourage participation.

I suggest nursery tales like *The Gingerbread Man, The Three Billy Goats Gruff, and Goldilocks and the Three Bears*, all found in Tomie dePaola's *Favorite Nursery Tales*. Longer, more complicated folk and fairy tales should be reserved for dramatization when speaking is encouraged. (See *Play it out!* #4 under Creative Arts)

SPEAKING ACTIVITIES

Introduction

Talking about a story just read aloud is the most natural of all follow-up activities. Often a teacher doesn't even plan any activity or comprehension questions, yet the students are so excited by a book that comments and discussion arise spontaneously. This is the best kind of language practice: that which is meaningful, related to content and not focused on structure.

When this communication doesn't arise on its own or at the level at which the students are capable, the teacher should use activities that elicit a natural flow of communication about the literature. Comprehension questions are only one of the activities suggested here. Others include orally joining in on the teacher's reading, story retelling, round robin sharing and participating in and discussing a real life experience related to the shared literature.

1. CHECK IT OUT!   *Oral Comprehension Questions*

ESL Level: Beginner-Advanced   **Grades: 1-8**

Comprehension questions asked at the completion of the first reading give the students opportunities to share their initial reactions to a story. Questions can either be general (e.g. "What did you think about that story?") or specific (e.g."What parts did you like about it?")

During the second or third readings, teachers can ask a variety of questions geared to ascertain general comprehension. Question types should vary from yes/no, to factual (wh-questions), to inference and opinion. This activity prepares students to respond to content area questions in the mainstream class.

In order to increase language proficiency, the teacher should listen for, and at times gently correct, grammatical as well as content accuracy. He should not overdo the error correction, pointing it out only when he assesses that the students can absorb the correction into their linguistic competence.[6]

The issue of whether students should be encouraged to reply in full sentences is controversial. On the positive side, it allows students to practice full grammatical constructions, which prepare them for written expression. On the negative side, it is not natural speech and it can inhibit a focus on content responses. Be advised to request full sentence responses sparingly, with clear objectives in mind and only with more advanced SL students.

Asking questions at break points during a second or third reading is more successful with ESL students than asking them all at the end. Discussion at intervals provides a closer check, with more opportunities to build comprehension and vocabulary. The purpose is to insure as many opportunities as possible for the students to use English in a situational context, in this case, a book discussion.

For 4th-8th grade intermediate to advanced ESL students, the teacher can also introduce literary analysis through interpretive questions. Interpretation, the search for a story's meaning, is often asked through "why" questions. It is confused with evaluation, which requires readers to relate ideas of a story to their own experiences and values. For example, "What is your opinion of _____?" or "Do you agree with _____?" The interpretive approach is well developed by the Great Book Foundation, which calls this method "shared inquiry."[7] The purpose is to engage students in analyzing the story, with their answers defended by reference to the text. Often there is more than one correct answer and a lively debate ensues.

The following interpretive questions come from *Beauty and the Beast* included in the Junior Great Books Series, Level 3: "Why does the Beast, who is so generous to Beauty, threaten her father for picking a single rose?" and "Why does the Beast turn into a handsome prince only after Beauty realizes she loves him as he is?"[8] These questions, like many of the other Great Books questions, are syntactically quite complex and if used with SL students need to be simplified. For example, the last question could be modified to "Why does the Beast turn into a handsome prince at the end of the story" without sacrificing its basic meaning.

These more analytic questions for advanced ESL students should be saved until the end of a second (or even third) reading. For this "shared inquiry" approach, it is helpful to provide copies of the text and encourage students to either follow along with their copy or to read it independently. During the discussion period, where the focus is heavily on content, the teacher should silently note errors in language structures, but correct them later, after the discussion, if at all.

Book Recommendations. Comprehension questions can be developed about any book, from the simplest to the most intricate. Interpretive questions need a fully developed story with intriguing characters and plot scenarios. *The Ugly Duckling* by Hans Christian Andersen and *Jack and the Beanstalk* by Joseph Jacobs do well for this activity.

2. JOIN IN!   *Shared Reading*

ESL Level: Beginner-Intermediate   **Grades: K-6**

Joining in on a familiar chorus or refrain is a natural response. Most children need little enticement to participate in this activity. It's fun, requires little preparation beyond selecting an appropriate book and the students are speaking good English!

After reading a story to students for the first time, the teacher encourages the children to join him on the repeated pattern. A classic is the refrain in *Millions of Cats* by Wanda Gag, "Hundreds of cats, thousands of cats, millions and billions and trillions of cats." Kids receive great pleasure in the humor of enormous numbers of cats descending on the unsuspecting old woman. They also just enjoy large numbers; they're much more fun than 1, 2, 3. Through this joining in, not only are they painlessly absorbing the concept of sequencing groups of numbers, but they are also learning the vocabulary to accompany it. This easily integrates with or reinforces a math lesson on place value.

When a book includes rhymes, rhythmical chants or melodies, joining in becomes even easier and more fun! For example, although the chorus in *When I First Came to this Land* by Oscar Brand is grammatically rather complex ("But the land was sweet and good, and I did what I could"), students seem to learn it quickly. The melody and rhymes facilitate the memorization, as the students associate the words with the tune and rhymes. When the last words of a line rhyme, the teacher can omit this last word and ask the children to produce it. This, in essence, is an oral "fill in the blank" exercise. The cumulative verses of this book lend themselves well to this. For example,

So, I got myself a cow.
And I called my cow,
No milk _____ (now)

So, I got myself a son.
And I called my son,
My work's _____ (done).

Through initially just filling in the final rhymes, my intermediate third grade students happily memorized this whole book! Although this was not my objective, it was certainly a pleasant learning bonus! Teachers do need to check that this oral production is accompanied by comprehension. (See *Listen for it! #3* under Listening Activities and *Check it out!*, the previous activity in this section.)

This joining-in oral activity lends itself not only to second readings but also to the third, fourth and other additional renditions that you will likely share of special favorites. After a while, joining in ceases to feel like a separate activity but integrates itself into the flow of spoken English, characteristic of a lively ESL classroom.

In a relaxed manner, this activity effectively imprints correct language structures and sentence patterns as well as expanding vocabulary. Many years after leaving the small South Pacific island where I had taught 5th and 6th grade Fijian children in the Peace Corps, I returned to discover that the English they remembered best was in the songs and rhymes I had read and sang to them!

Book Recommendations. Particularly successful for joining-in are books with rhymes, choruses, predictable refrains and melodies. *Just Like Daddy* by Frank Asch, with its short, repeated refrain works well for K-3 beginners, as does *Chicken Soup with Rice* by Maurice Sendak, for more intermediate K-3rd graders. For older students, *The Fox Went Out on a Chilly Night*, a singable book by Peter Spier, with its often repeated chorus, never fails to enchant students. How my intermediate students strive to learn all of its many verses continues to amaze me!

3. TELL IT LIKE IT IS! *Story Retelling*

ESL Level: Advanced Beginner-Intermediate **Grades: K-6**

Story retelling provides marvelous practice in forming ideas into sentence patterns. First, read the book without interruptions or expectations. On the second (or third) presentation, simply show the pictures and ask the students to tell you the story, page by page. During the first attempt, the teacher might need to prompt the students with sentence starters or vocabulary reminders. By the third or fourth "readings," the intermediates, at least, should be able to generate most of the story in cooperation with their classmates.

In this activity the students do not need to create sentences entirely on their own, with just a picture stimuli. They have the written language of the literature to provide them an excellent model. They also have their teacher's pronunciation, intonation and expression model to imitate.

In most cases, capturing the general idea seems adequate, but the teacher may want to emphasize exact word restatement for tense or other grammar practice. Students themselves, however, will strive to reproduce the story exactly. It is very gratifying to see them take such pride in their own retellings!

Book Recommendations. Books with clear, numerous illustrations are essential for this activity. Other important criteria are limited text per page (usually a sentence or two), and relatively short book length.

For K-3rd grade, try *The Very Hungry Caterpillar* by Eric Carle with its appetizing food, predictable past tense, popular refrain ("But he was still hungry") and beautiful surprise ending. Also popular with this age group is *Alexander and the Terrible, Horrible, No Good, Very Bad Day* by Judith Viorst. It is not as depressing as it sounds. In fact, it's quite funny. For older students (4th-8th grades), I would recommend the Native American folktale, *Gift of the Sacred Dog* by Paul Goble, plainly told and exquisitely illustrated.

4. MAKE IT UP! *Round Robin Storytelling*

ESL Level: Beginner-Intermediate **Grades: 1-6**

Hearing one story will often stimulate a child's imagination to other creative possibilities. One way to capitalize on this, while simultaneously developing both listening and communication skills, is by round robin storytelling.

The teacher begins by sharing aloud the germ of an idea, stimulated by a story previously read aloud. For example, using *The Frog Prince* by The Brothers Grimm, begin with the following:

Once upon a time, there lived a beautiful, but unhappy princess named _____.
While she was wandering outside her castle grounds one day, she met a _____

The students, taking turns around a circle, add a sentence or two in the creation of their own collective tale. They need to listen carefully in order to logically continue the story line.

The role of the teacher in this activity varies, depending on how the groups are constituted and his objectives. When the students can work independently and cooperatively, in small groups of 3-5, his role is to oversee the various stories, as they unfold. Alternatively, he may choose to keep a larger group (up to 10) together to allow more intervention and direction. In this case, he can supply alternatives if the children get stuck or develop the story inappropriately.

He can stop a student at a key point to build dramatic tension. He also needs to sense when the story has reached completion and would benefit from closure.

The teacher can use repetition in a number of ways in this activity. At intervals, he can repeat the cumulative offerings or challenge certain students to try to do it. He can also reinforce correct language patterns by repeating the students' original contributions, making any needed revisions orally, but without comment. Discussing grammatical errors would distract from the main objective: self-generated, creative communication.

Beginning SL students can contribute to a mixed ability group, with some help often needed to structure their ideas. This help can be provided by the teacher or by other students. If a teacher has a group of advanced beginners, this activity can be modified for them. In this case, he supplies them a scenario and encourages them to finish the thought. He then builds upon their responses to develop the story himself, continuing to give different students chances to add on. This scales down the activity from round robin storytelling to dialogue storytelling. After practice with this teacher-centered approach, the students progress to more student-student storytelling.

Book Recommendations. Imaginative stories work best as a stimulus for round robin story-telling. *Esteban and the Ghost* by Sibyl Hancock can stimulate the creation of other ghost stories. These are especially popular around Halloween with all elementary-age students.

As a fairy tale recommendation, try a sentence starter based on *The Shoemaker and the Elves* by The Brothers Grimm. I have often wondered about the life of the tiny elves, both before and after they so nimbly sewed the poor shoemaker's shoes. Why did they sew those shoes for him night after night? Where and how did they live? Why did they have no clothes? How did their lives change once the shoemaker and his wife made them fine clothes? Use questions like these above to stimulate the students' imagination. Then begin something like,

Once upon a time there were two elves named _____ and _____. They were very poor but clever. One cold winter day they _____

Just because our students have limited English proficiency does not mean they have limited imaginations. I am constantly impressed with the creative stories they develop collectively and cooperatively.

5. EXPERIENCE IT!   *Language Experience*

ESL Level: Beginner-Intermediate   Grades: K-6

Plan an experience in conjunction with a topic presented in a book. Usually this works best after reading the book, as a real life communication opportunity, using the vocabulary and structures introduced in the literature. For example, cook pancakes after reading *Pancakes for Breakfast* by Tomie dePaola,[9] or visit a playground after reading the non-fictional *Playground* by Gail Gibbons. Sometimes, however, it makes better sense to experience the event first and then read about it. For example, after planting seeds with the class, read *The Carrot Seed* by Ruth Krauss, which shares the patience needed for a seed to sprout.

These experiences often serve as cultural introductions, as in the cases of the pancakes and playground. These experiences also provide teaching situations which introduce the language and context of social expressions needed by students outside the classroom: for example, requests ("Will you please pass the syrup?"), sharing ("It's my turn on the swing now.") and appreciation ("Thank you, Kim, for setting the table.")

All of this—the story, the vocabulary, the structures and the children's own experiences—can be additionally reinforced in a language experience story, written cooperatively, as a culminating activity for the mini-unit. The teacher asks each child to orally share something of the previous experience as she writes the student's contributions on the board or chart paper. This popular teaching strategy personalizes and preserves the experience as well as providing an original composition for possible reading and writing practice. Even if the age, proficiency level or situation does not warrant further expansion into reading and writing, the teacher should, at least, read back the language experience story to the students, pointing out the flow of words as she reads.

As a concluding activity, I would recommend having the teacher read aloud the original book again. In addition to generating a unifying sense of closure and additional reinforcement of vocabulary and structures, it also affirms literature as an important source of life experiences.

Book Recommendations. Any book that lends itself to a feasible school experience or field trip would be appropriate. Non-fiction subjects lend themselves well to the language experience approach if you can find books for ESL students, at suitable proficiency and maturity levels.

Gail Gibbons is a rising star in this arena, although her books are intended primarily for curious and language mature pre-schoolers. Currently very popular and prolific, she has written numerous non-fiction picture books about practical life and community experiences (e.g. *Trucks, The Department Store, Fire!Fire!, and Zoo*). She has also written books on all the major U.S. holidays. These can usually be experienced, at least partially, in school settings. All of Gibbons' books include clear pictures with word labels and simple explanations, appropriate for advanced beginners to low intermediates.

An excellent series at the intermediate ESL proficiency level is *The New True Books*, by Children's Press. It includes over 75 titles on a variety of non-fiction topics, from automobiles to libraries to weather experiments. All are fully illustrated with a mixture of photographs, pictures and diagrams.

READING ACTIVITIES

Introduction

In the elementary grades, stimulating students' interest in reading and learning how to read absorbs considerable class time. Reading aloud is crucial for both these important goals. The reading activities included here develop reading skills from this original oral stimulus. They incorporate reading both as a decoding skill, to be learned separately, and more holistically, as part of the integrative language acquisition process.

The activities suggested are of three types: 1) those that focus on the reading process itself, either in chart stories or in independent reading; 2) those that serve as a culmination of listening and speaking activities, as in strip stories or language experience stories; 3) those that combine with writing skills, often serving as a first step towards free writing, as in cloze tests or collective book reviews.

1. READ IT YOURSELF!   *Independent Reading*

ESL Level: Beginner-Advanced   Grades: K-8

Introduction to pleasure reading is an important educational objective for all students, kindergarten through 12th grade. *A Nation of Readers* (1985), in their review of the research on reading, report a significant correlation between independent reading, both in and out of school, and gains in reading achievement and vocabulary.

The teacher should make available for independent reading all books initially read aloud to the class. The students should be encouraged to "read" them, whether they can read the words or just the pictures. They are either reading the author's words or creating their own. Both are important in the reading process. For bilingual students, this nonverbal processing can occur in either their native language or English.

Often the most difficult parts of reading on one's own are getting started and setting aside the time. By reading the book aloud first, the teacher is stimulating interest that hopefully encourages students to read it themselves, either now or later when they discover it in the library. Providing time and space in the classroom also encourages independent reading habits. Ten minutes can be set aside for silent reading time once or twice a week. This is often identified by the acronyms SSR (Sustained Silent Reading) or DEAR (Drop Everything and Read). In these programs, the whole class participates, including the teacher. Silent reading time can also be given as a reward for special behavior or achievement. In this situation, students are invited into the reading corner and excused from another assignment.

This reading corner need not be fancy or even large. A cozy spot, decorated with a soft rug for sitting, comfortable pillows for leaning against, some cuddly stuffed animals and a few good books, attractively displayed on low shelves, are all that's necessary. If you can't create this kind of space, improvise. The goal is to make it separate and appealing.

For a more structured reading activity, a book can be integrated into the class work as a reading center activity. Aside from reading the book, no additional requirements need be made. However, a variety of age and ability-level assignments can be developed. For example, for kindergarten, "Draw your favorite picture;" for 1st-2nd grades, "Draw and write a sentence about a funny or happy scene;" for 3rd-6th grades, "Describe one character or event;" for 4th-8th grades, "Write a paragraph summarizing the book." The books, but not necessarily the activities, should be changed regularly, about once every week or two.

Book Recommendations. Books selected for read-alouds can be more difficult than those chosen for reading skill development. So, guide the students to easier ones for independent reading, to not cause them frustration. Those with clearly detailed illustrations will help students recollect the story. Remember that this is not like a basal reading program, however, and mastery should not be expected.

Each annotation in *Part II: Read-Aloud Library* indicates, under the "genre" category, those books that are classified as "easy readers". All of these books are listed together in the

Literary Genre Index. Books for independent reading need not be limited to this classification, however, depending on the proficiency level of your students.

There are many good options. *Green Eggs and Ham* and *Hop on Pop*, both by Dr. Seuss, are popular easy-reading choices for the K-3 set, even if they can't yet read. For non-fiction, consider the easy-reading 28 page picture book biography of *Martin Luther King* by Magaret Boone-Jones, suitable for 2nd-6th grade, advanced-beginner ESL students. Sports-minded middle school students seem to devour the short stories in *Strange but True Basketball Stories* by Howard Liss. This series is also available for baseball and American football. These are language appropriate for intermediate ESL readers but may not initially appeal, if the sport described is not indigenous to the student's own culture. As sports do bridge the international and communication gap, introducing SL students to them, through literature, meets an important cross-cultural objective.

We all enjoy an absorbing novel. For 2nd-5th graders, Judy Blume's *The Tales of a Fourth Grade Nothing* and *The One in the Middle is the Green Kangaroo*, are some of the most popular. Monitor some of her others more closely. For older, more advanced readers (4th-7th graders), consider the engaging novels of Katherine Patterson, especially her Newbery Award winner, *The Bridge to Terabithia.*

2. CHART IT!   *Reading Skill Development*

ESL Level: Beginner-Intermediate   **Grades: 2-8**

Chart stories serve as one source of reading instruction. They are, simply, the text of a nursery rhyme, song or poem, copied verbatim onto large chart paper and clearly displayed on a classroom easel or on the chalkboard. This is a useful technique for SL students because by the time they are introduced to the written medium, they will already have heard the story aloud and had opportunities for oral comprehension, vocabulary development and pronunciation practice. The next major step is to transfer this oral competence to written symbols.

There are four basic stages in this whole language approach to reading. First, the teacher begins by reading the text aloud from the chart paper, running her finger under the words as she reads. Second, she then asks the group to read along, again running a finger under the words. She may want to do this a few times chorally before going on to the third step, individual practice. Here the teacher focuses on specific skills, depending on the age and level of the students. For example, "Show me an *s*," "Read me the word *boy*" or "Point out the word that rhymes with *moon*." For comprehension practice she may ask, "Read me the word/sentence that shows where the cow jumped." Fourth, for older or intermediate students, revert back to the whole, giving individual students an opportunity to read the complete story. Most students love to do this. The teacher can involve a second student by letting him serve as pointer, the one who follows the words on the chart.

The teacher can extend this reading practice by having the students copy the selection into their anthologies (see *Copy it down! #2* under Writing Activities). They then have their own copy to practice these reading skills independently.

Book Recommendations. Individual and fairly short rhymes, poems and songs do well here. They can come from a separate book or be part of a collection.

My younger students (K-2) always enjoy the short nursery rhymes in the stiff, cardboard collections of *Saying Rhymes* and *Counting Rhymes*, both published by Brimax. Intended for pre-school native-speakers, they appeal to grade school ESL students because of their brevity, cuteness and cheerful illustrations.

For older students (4th-8th grades), many of the humorous poems by Shel Silverstein in *Where the Sidewalk Ends*, and by William Cole in *Poem Stew* are short enough to write on chart paper. They tickle the funny bone while capturing various aspects of the modern experience. Using a masterful manipulation of language, rhyme and rhythm, they serve as wonderful introductions to the genre of poetry.

3. REVIEW IT!   *Collective Book Reports*

ESL Level: Beginner-Intermediate   **Grades: 4-8**

This adaptation of book reviewing develops oral comprehension skills and then transfers these to the literate medium — reading and writing. As a preparation for the commonly assigned book reports, this activity uses modified language experience techniques. (For a full explanation of language experience stories, please see *Experience it! #5* under Speaking Activities.) The purpose of collective book reports is to introduce literary analysis in a written format without requiring independent writing skills.

The teacher chooses questions to explore, one at a time. For example, "Describe the main character." or "What did you like/dislike about this book?" In reference to Rudyard Kipling's *The Elephant Child*, students might respond to the second question as follows:

I didn't like the python snake. (Beg.)
I liked when the elephant child spanked his mother and father. (Int.)
I liked that the elephant child didn't know what the crocodile eats for dinner. That was funny. (Adv.)

The teacher writes each child's contribution on the chalkboard, creating a collective review. For example, "Mai said that. . . . ." She can either quietly correct grammatical structures while recording the oral responses or write it verbatim and sensitively use error analysis with the class to correct first drafts. I would recommend moving from teacher to class revision as the students' written language proficiency increases or to individualize this according to the ability of the students.

When all contributions have been recorded, the class then has its own original reading text, as with a language experience story. Phonics and reading skill development can then be practiced with this. (For details see *Chart it #2* in this section.) For example, "Read me the sentence that tells what the elephant child did to his parents." or "Point to a word with a silent *e*/long *i*/or rhymes with lake." Choral and individual sentence reading should also be practiced.

This activity can easily flow into writing skills if students are asked to copy a question and a few favorite responses. They should also be encouraged to add a few more additional responses of their own. I would discourage having them copy all the sentences, as the educational value can be achieved with just a few. For a more permanent record, the teacher can transfer the group review to chart paper.

Book Recommendations. For these class book reports, the teacher needs to use longer, more substantial stories, but they still should not be overly complex. For intermediate 3rd-5th grade ESL students, try some of the other *Just So Stories* by Rudyard Kipling. *Stone Fox* by John Gardiner, also appropriate for this age and ESL ability, is a dramatic, action-packed adventure with strong character development. It lends itself to serious discussion of commitment, bravery, and family loyalty. Older intermediate students (5th-8th grades) enjoy individual legends from *Greek Gods and Heroes* by Alice Low.

4. UNSCRAMBLE IT!   *Sentence Strips*

ESL Level: Intermediate   **Grades: 3-8**

In this variation of a scrambled sentence exercise, students develop communication skills by cooperatively reconstituting events of a story. The teacher prepares for the activity by writing events from a story already introduced orally onto individual strips of paper or note cards. She then divides the class into groups of 4-6. Each group should have their own set of cards. Each student has only one piece of information and no one knows the whole. Their first task is to read and memorize their own sentence and then return the card to the teacher. Second, each student, in turn, reads their sentence aloud to the group. Third, they orally discuss among themselves their sentences in order to logically sequence their component strips. Finally, they physically arrange themselves in the correct order and present the whole story aloud, making modifications as needed. (Gibson, 1975)

This relatively simple activity accomplishes many objectives: cognitive sequencing, focused communication, careful listening, oral and reading comprehension, memorization and pronunciation. In addition, peer communication and collaborative learning styles are enhanced. As an added benefit, the teacher can observe the process, as she is not directly involved in the task completion himself.

For optional written follow-up, the teacher can dictate the collective sentences in the correctly sequenced order. However, this might be overkill for this activity. So, unless the class particularly needs written reinforcement at that time, I would recommend leaving well enough alone.

Book Recommendations. Sentence strips can be constructed from almost any story book, basal reading text or content area textbook. This technique provides a good opportunity to reinforce non-fiction material, although selections need not be limited to them.

Biographies are very popular with 3rd-8th graders. Those by Jean Fritz are especially well-written and engaging, as well as informative. They are appropriate for an advanced intermediate ESL level. Start with *And Then What Happened Paul Revere?* or *Where Do You Think You're Going, Christopher Columbus?* Both are major figures in American history and material from these books have proven successful with sentence strips.

Stories with an obvious time sequence provide helpful clues for sentence strips. For example, try *Humphrey, the Lost Whale* by Wendy Tokuda and Richard Hall, which follows such a sequence. This is the true story of a whale inadvertently trapped in a river and his dramatic escape.

5. PUT IT IN ORDER!   *Sequencing*

ESL Level: Intermediate-Advanced   **Grades: 4-8**

This activity, like the previous one, also develops sequencing skills. Here the students orally contribute any events or descriptions about the story that they can remember. The teacher records them all on the chalkboard, chart paper or overhead projector, correcting any oral errors as she writes. The students' task is to then put their collective offerings into the correct story sequence.

This can be done as a cooperative small-group assignment in class, but I prefer each student to struggle with it on their own, as homework. So, I create a worksheet by copying these sentences and drawing a blank line (_____) in front of each sentence. The directions read, "Put these story events in the correct order by placing a 1, 2, 3, etc. in front of the appropriate sentences." As a model, I start them out with number one filled in correctly.

The next day, the students orally justify their orderings, which provides academic communication practice, approximating that used in mainstream classes' content area discussions. On occasion, there can be different opinions about the sequence, especially when descriptions of characters and settings are included along with events. Discussion ensues, with the teacher or a designated student, writing the agreed upon number on the original class copy.

I like this particular sequencing activity because, as in *Language Experience* and *Collective Book Reviews* (see #5 under Speaking Activities and #3 in this section), it takes the students' own ideas and uses them to practice language skills, focusing mainly on speaking and reading. I have also used this student-generated story sequence as the basis for cooperative mural making. (See *Paint it together!* #2 under Creative Arts.)

Book Recommendations. Almost any story can be used for sequencing. The actual sequence generated will vary with the difficulty of the selected book and the proficiency level of the students. Books should have a well developed plot. This allows for a variety of selected events and descriptions to create a unified whole. Consider the dramatic, short biography about a brave, young woman during the American Revolution, *Deborah Samson Goes to War* by Byrna Stevens or any of the *Favorite Fairy Tales Told Around the World* by Jane Yolen.

6. CLOZE IT!   *The Cloze Procedure*

ESL Level: Intermediate-Advanced   **Grades: 4-8**

The cloze procedure is an integrative assessment measure which checks for overall story comprehension. It is also pragmatic, providing specific practice in reading, grammar and spelling skills. As an assessment measure, the cloze test has proven effective, with its scores correlating positively with those of standardized reading comprehension tests. (Cohen, 1980; Oller, 1979) Although the cloze can be used as a test, it need not be limited to that use. It also functions well as a regular classroom or homework activity assessing general comprehension.

To prepare a cloze, select two or three paragraphs verbatim from the text, leaving out every fifth, sixth or seventh word. Retain the first few sentences intact to set the context. Alternatively, the teacher can summarize a longer story, but this requires more work. To complete a written cloze, the students are instructed to fill in the blanks. Either exact word scoring or contextually appropriate word scoring can be used.

Teachers like the cloze procedure because it is a relatively easy measure to construct, administer and score. Students enjoy this activity, too, because it can be done fairly quickly and they can easily check their work against the original. Also, when they have completed both the test and its check, they will have a part, or sometimes all, of a familiar book.

Book Recommendations. As with book selections for strip stories, almost any book with a well-developed plot can be adapted successfully for cloze exercises. The difficulty of the book selection will automatically correlate with the grammatical and comprehension complexity required to complete the cloze.

For low intermediates try any of the six Black American folk tales in Julius Lester's *The Knee High Man and Other Stories*. Or, this technique could be used at chapter intervals, as a comprehension check for longer fiction. For this genre, consider the universally appealing *Charlotte's Web* by E.B. White, as much loved by adults as by children.

7. FILL IT IN!   *Fill in the Blanks*

ESL Level: Intermediate-Advanced   **Grades: 3-8**

The old tried and true technique of fill in the blanks still has validity today. It provides practice in both overall reading comprehension *and* discrete grammar points. The teacher can focus on one structure or tense by controlling what is omitted. A cloze test, by contrast, is more random. (See Activity #6 above.) There, one encounters a mixture of grammatical and vocabulary items.

The singable book *The Fox Went Out On a Chilly Night* by Peter Spier is a good choice for this activity because it is filled with both regular and irregular past tense verbs (e.g. went, prayed, had, reached, ate, were etc.). First the teacher reads the book aloud, encouraging the students to join in and sing it together during the second or third readings. Second, she copies the whole story onto chart paper, from which the class practices reading skills. Third, she covers up all the past tense verbs. The class practices that structure by guessing what is under the paper. Fourth, she transfers the story onto paper for duplication, leaving a blank for all the past tense verbs. At the top she lists the infinitive form of each verb. In the directions, she tells the students to choose the correct verb and to put it in its correct form. This assesses both contextual comprehension and grammatical knowledge of the specific skill taught. This assignment can be done with equal success for homework, individually during class time, or as a group activity.

Book Recommendations. If the teacher plans to include the whole book, fairly short picture books that include sentences with contextual clues work best. Use *Bears in the Night* by Stan and Jan Berenstain for prepositions and *Gilberto and the Wind* by Marie Halls Ets for simple present tense, first and third person singular. Both are appropriate for younger elementary students at the low intermediate proficiency level.

An alternative for older and more advanced students is to select sentences from longer books. In this case, numerous examples of the grammatical structure being studied should be chosen. I would recommend taking advantage of the natural language in *Charlie and the Chocolate Factory* by Roald Dahl, for a mixed verb review. This is an absolutely delightful read-aloud with a strong, underlying message.

WRITING ACTIVITIES

Introduction _____

Writing has been traditionally perceived as the most difficult and advanced language skill. The audio lingual approach to second language teaching encouraged students to attempt it only after the structures had been mastered in listening, speaking and reading. More contemporary ESL methodologies, in an attempt to break this writing phobia, introduce writing throughout the learning cycle, not limiting it to the final skill.

The new process-centered approach to writing encourages this by viewing writing as recursive stages of rehearsing, organizing, drafting, revising and editing. See Chart A "The Composing Process" for a visual summary. This is a developmental process and does not expect grammatical or orthographic perfection in the early stages or from beginning writers. Expression of ideas and creativity is primary. This approach, developed for native speakers and popularized through The Bay Area Writing Project, is appropriate for second language learners as well.

The writing activities recommended here, as follow-ups to read-aloud stories, run the gamut from copying (e.g. dictation) to creating (e.g. poetry and story writing). Some can be used as an immediate follow-up (e.g. story endings), while others require reading as a prerequisite (e.g. story reconstruction).

I strongly believe that writing should accompany all stages of language learning. Accordingly, activities have been included that span the ESL proficiency levels, from beginners (e.g. student anthologies) to advanced (e.g. autobiographies). In addition, be encouraged to try most of these writing activities with all but your basic beginners, even those identified for "intermediate-advanced." You may have to make some modifications and set realistic expectations, but engage the students in the writing process as soon as possible.

1. COPY IT DOWN!   *Student Anthologies*

ESL Level: Beginner   **Grades: 2-8**

In this activity, students copy nursery rhymes, short poems, chants or songs from a chart story or a book into their own notebook. Copying is an important and often overlooked skill for second language learners. It is all too easy for the students if the teacher types and distributes the poem or song. The students miss the important step of studying it visually and correctly transferring that visual representation to their paper. This copying step also psychologically identifies it as their own.

Students are encouraged to take pride in their book, using their best handwriting. They should also be provided opportunities to illustrate their selections. In this way, this activity becomes more than a copying exercise, as the students create their own illustrated anthologies.

In many instances, I prefer the old-fashioned classroom materials of chalkboard and chart paper to overhead projectors and computers because the former emphasizes the human interaction, so significant in language learning. However, if a class has access to a computer or even a typewriter, the students have the "modern" option of typing or printing their "books."

A key in this activity is to allow students to make selections, so that their books truly represent their favorites. For older children (grades 4-8), I suggest the title, "The Anthology of _____ (their full name)." For younger ones, (grades 2-3) use "My Song Book" as a title, since most rhymes and poems are singable as well.

This has always been a very popular activity in my classes, with the books being read and reread throughout the year. They also serve as a review of earlier work, coming in handy for oral practice when there are just a few minutes at the beginning or end of a class. Students regularly ask to take their books home to share with their family. I often hear younger (and also older) siblings chanting the words too!

CHART A

THE COMPOSING PROCESS

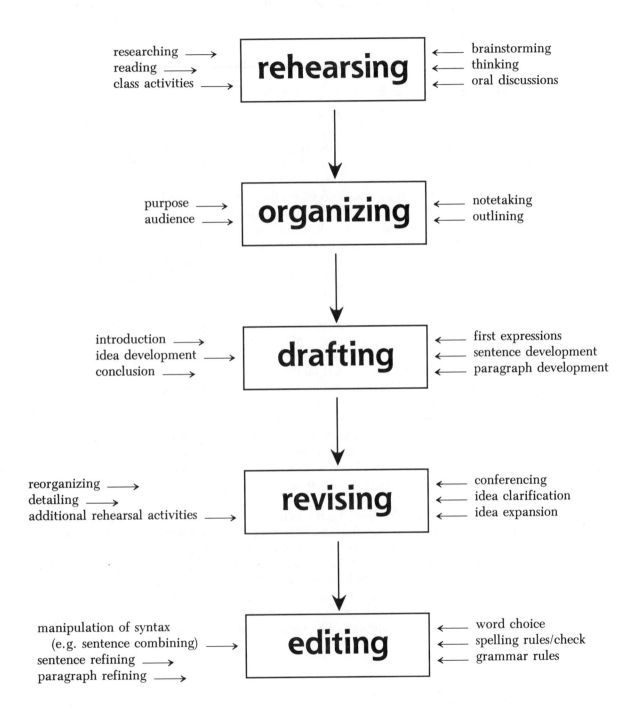

Book Recommendations. For the younger children, Mother Goose rhymes are just perfect for a student anthology. In addition, *Chicken Soup with Rice* by Maurice Sendak lends itself well to this activity, for children up to 4th grade. The book includes short rhyming poems for each month, each with a variation of the same, catchy refrain. Students just love these!

For the older children, the definitive *Random House Book of Poetry* offers quite a varied selection. Jack Prelutsky, who has contributed original poems for each section introduction, is quite appealing to the students.

2. PUBLISH IT!   *Story Writing*

ESL Level: Intermediate   **Grades: K-8**

Story writing takes the students beyond copying to creating their own story. The structures of the story read aloud provide the model for the new book. The young authors should not feel constrained by the framework of the original literature, using it as a springboard, not as a chain. Imagination is the key to this activity. Since this essential human quality knows no age limit, this activity has an open age span.

When story writing is introduced for the first time, it works best as a whole group activity, with the teacher leading the students through the process. For the K-1 students, the teacher will need to continue as facilitator, asking for suggestions and serving as scribe for the children's ideas. Most likely, they will create a class story. For students in grades 2-8, after the initial whole group modelling, this works especially well as a cooperative small group activity, with one student assigned as scribe and each group creating their own story. Alternatively, students may choose to work on their own. The advantage of the group process is the cross-fertilization of ideas.

Through this activity, teachers can introduce the concepts of revising for ideas and editing for language. Either teacher or peer conferencing can be used (Calkins, 1986). The story may go through two or three drafts before the students and teacher consider it finished. Word processing programs, like Bank Street Writer, facilitate this revision process. When complete, the student authors write or type the final version, illustrate it, sign their names and make a cover. The oral sharing of their stories with their classmates is particularly fun!

Teachers who use this technique regularly may be interested in taking this one step further — to publication, by starting an informal class publishing "company." Let the class choose the company's name. Each student assigns each of his books a copyright date, makes a title page and a book jacket. They also write a brief biographical statement and a book summary for the jacket. For this purpose, the final text should be typed, ideally with a computer. Then, with the help of the xerox machine (or the computer), the teacher can make copies.

Whether you make simple final versions for class consumption or expand this into "publishing," the students enjoy it immensely. They feel very empowered by their role as authors, and they are meeting the dual objectives of language learning and creative writing.

Book Recommendations. Proper book selection is particularly important for this activity. The primary keys are repeated patterns and also rhyming. The structures provide the patterns, with the students changing, in the beginning, only the rhyming words, usually nouns. A particularly good choice for younger students (K-3rd grade) is the very funny, *Oh, A Hunting We Will Go* by John Langstaff. The verses repeat the following pattern:

> Oh, a hunting we will go
> A hunting we will go.
> We'll catch *a fox*
> And put him in *a box*
> And then, we'll let him go.

Other verses are more challenging, including one of my favorites,
"We'll catch an armadillo and put him in a pillow." It ends with the reassurance,

We'll just pretend
And in the end
We'll always let them go.

When the students make their own verses, they are practicing the future tense and its important contraction (we'll).

When I First Came to this Land by Oscar Brand, appropriate for older students (grades 4-8), also offers the important rhyming and repeated patterns. By changing the key rhyming words in each verse, the students can transform the setting from an early 20th century, rural immigrant experience to a contemporary urban one, the reality of most immigrants today. For example, consider the refrain and one verse:

When I first came to this land,
I was not a wealthy man,
So, I got myself *a duck*
And I did what I could.
And I called *my duck*,
Out of luck.

That verse would feel more contemporary if, following the rest of the pattern, he got himself a car that wouldn't go far!

Book selections need not be limited to rhyming. For prose, try *Fortunately, Unfortunately* by Beverly Charlip and *Q is for Ducks* by Mary Elting, an alphabet guessing game.

3. BE A POET!   *First Letter Poetry*

ESL Level: Intermediate-Advanced   Grades: 3-8

Poetry uses language, especially vocabulary and modifiers in a concise way to capture feelings and summarize thoughts. SL students can and should be introduced to this written medium as well as to prose. The story writing, described above, involves a lot of rhyming, modelled on structured patterns. Thus it can be considered poetry. Not all poetry needs to rhyme, however.

As a summary activity for a read-aloud, create a non-rhyming poem based on the first letters of a key word from a book. Like a story that is created from a book's repeated patterns, this activity also has a structure: the first letters of the word.

Begin by collectively deciding upon this word, selecting either the title, key or theme from a book. Write it vertically on the board, i.e.

S
A
R
A
H

The selected example names the main character in *Sarah, Plain and Tall* by Patricia Mac-Lachlan. With this guide, the students add a word or series or words beginning with the first letter to create a unified whole. The completed poem should reflect the essence of the book. For example, from the above,

S   strong, serious Sarah
A   are you
R   ready to live with us
A   at our
H   home?

Initially, this is best demonstrated with the whole class. The teacher stimulates the creative process, fields ideas and blends together the whole. Ultimately, however, the goal is for the students to work independently, either in small cooperative groups or individually.

Book Recommendations. An initial letter poem can be drafted from almost any book, nonfiction as well as fiction. The book should be substantive in theme and content in order to stimulate words and expressions. It is helpful to use fairly short titles, at least initially, so that the poem composing process remains manageable.

Try "Casey" from *Casey at the Bat* by Ernest Lawrence Thayer, a famous book length poem about baseball. It was written over 100 years ago, but is still just as stirring today.

C   Classic
A   American
S   Slugger
E   Eager but still
Y   Yearning

4. FINISH IT YOURSELF!   *Story Endings*

ESL Level: Intermediate-Advanced   Grades: 3-8

Writing story endings serves as a controlled introduction to creative writing, as well as a check on the students' comprehension of the story read aloud. To activate it, simply stop before the conclusion of the first reading of a suspenseful book and instruct the students to write their own endings.

Be sure to identify students who are already familiar with the chosen story. Allow them to either write the real ending or to create one they find more satisfying. Emphasize to them the importance of keeping the ending a secret.

Encourage the students to focus initially on the expression of their ideas: to simply put their thoughts in writing. Editing for grammar and spelling more appropriately enters the writing process at a later stage. As this activity is basically a short, one time thought stimulator, it will not provide as many opportunities for editing as the longer writing assignments (see story, poetry and autobiography writing in this section).

Writing story endings can be done either as a class activity or as homework. For best results, students should share their own endings before the teacher reads the "real" one. Anticipation builds if you can schedule this for the next day. Through class discussions, encourage the students to compare their endings with the original. Make them feel that theirs have validity too.

Book Recommendations. For advanced students, a good book for this is *Sarah, Plain and Tall* by Patricia MacLachlan, an engaging, short novel which deservedly won the 1985 Newbery Award for best children's literature. The reader doesn't know until the very end whether Sarah will stay to marry the children's widowed father.

A shorter book, appropriate for more intermediate students, and also with a dramatic ending, is *The Girl Who Loved Wild Horses* by Paul Goble. This imaginative Native American legend, with stunning artwork, won the Caldecott Award as the best picture book of 1979.

5. WRITE IT LIKE IT IS!   *Dictation*

ESL Level: Beginner-Intermediate   Grades: 2-8

Dictation is an important and often overlooked writing task. It requires individual resynthesis of orally generated data into correctly written form, including syntax and spelling. Although the internal linguistic process is quite complex, the actual class task is relatively easy to facilitate.

After listening to, speaking about and possibly reading from a read-aloud book, the teacher dictates a few sentences of the text verbatim. He carefully reads each phrase, a few times, and then rereads the entire sentence at the end. The students are instructed to write down exactly what they hear.

This activity can be used with a range of ages and ESL proficiency levels. Start with short dictations, allowing students to become accustomed to the combined listening-writing focus. One to two sentences will suffice for second graders. Move up gradually to a paragraph for older students. To individualize this activity for the inevitable range of abilities in the same class, allow beginners to stop at one point, intermediates at another and advanced at yet another.

Upon completion, students compare their own dictation with the original. To facilitate this correction process, teachers should make at least one copy of the material to be dictated. Beginners can be at work correcting, ideally at a separate table, while the intermediate and advanced students are still writing the dictation. Adequate time should be provided for all students to correct their work. With this immediate feedback, students learn a lot from their mistakes.

Teachers can modify this whole sentence dictation model by giving students a sheet on which part of the story is written. The teacher reads aloud the written part and gives the students time to complete the blanks from the oral dictation. This variation is not intended as a creative, sentence ending exercise, but rather as a modified dictation and cloze task, combining the benefits of both.

Book Recommendations. As with cloze exercises, any age and proficiency appropriate book can be selected for dictation.

6. RECONSTRUCT IT!   *Story Reconstruction*

ESL Level: Intermediate-Advanced   **Grades: 5-8**

Story reconstruction is more challenging than dictation because it requires remembering and synthesizing the entire story and then expressing this in the written medium. This is a good assignment for SL students because it provides some guidelines, with the goal being independent writing.[10] As such, it can be considered a first step towards unstructured summary writing, a common assignment in high school. Yet this is also different than summary writing because details are requested.

This activity should be done only after familiarity with the story is assured. This usually takes at least two oral readings. To get the reconstruction underway, the teacher can begin this orally, as round robin story retelling (See *Tell it like it is! #3* under Speaking Activities). The book can be referred to at this oral stage. He then gives the students a series of key words or events from the story, either on the chalkboard or as a handout. The task is to retell the story in writing, with as many details as can be remembered. Students should use exact words from the story whenever possible and include the listed words and phrases. During the writing stage, the book should be off limits.

The writing can be followed-up with another reading of the story, if it is short enough, so students can listen for what they remembered (and forgot). The teacher can allow students to revise their reconstruction after this additional reading.

The teacher can help students to include certain grammatical items in their reconstructions. For example, if a few adjectives are listed as part of the start-up phrases, the students are guided to more colorful descriptions. Also, storytelling usually evokes the past tense. If the teacher wants students to practice this tense, it is helpful to include a few examples in the guide words.

The difficulty of this assignment can be controlled by the complexity of information and structure provided in the foundation phases. In fact, if there are at least two distinct levels in the same class, the teacher may want to present two different sets of guide words.

Book Recommendations. Relatively short books or short stories within a collection lend themselves well for story reconstruction. Additionally, books for this activity should have clearly developed story lines and characters with interesting details. Fairy and folk tales meet this criteria well. For a cross-cultural dimension to this genre, try *The Day it Snowed Tortillas* by Joe Hayes, a short anthology of Mexican American tales. In non-fiction, consider the amusing science story about geology, *The Magic School Bus Inside the Earth* by Joanna Cole. This book can be used to check comprehension of subject matter as well as language.

7. WRITE ABOUT YOURSELF!   *Autobiographies*

ESL Level: Intermediate-Advanced   Grades: 5-8

Thinking about one's life and expressing it in writing are lofty goals for 5th to 8th graders. Nevertheless, this is a good age for reminiscence about one's childhood. Recognizing this, many middle/junior high schools include autobiographical writing as part of their language arts program. With support, advanced SL students can participate in this writing activity, either within their regular classroom or through a modified assignment in their ESL class.

Historical fiction, biographies and/or autobiographies read aloud to middle/junior high students serve as a stimulus for such autobiographical writing. If the book selections represent childhood immigration or cross-cultural experiences, they also provide important role models for ESL students. Most books can be completed within a month, if read to the students in chapters (or shorter segments) a few times a week. Once into the book, the students eagerly anticipate the next reading, with it often becoming the highlight of the class period.

During the read-aloud period, the teacher should use various comprehension checks at selected intervals, including cloze, writing their own chapter endings and oral questions. The teacher should engage the students in general discussions as well, highlighting the affective component and emphasizing cross-cultural immigration experiences. Literary analysis of the story leads into stylistic analysis of the writing itself. This information becomes part of the students' writing arsenal and subconsciously is incorporated into their own writing.

From these discussions, consciously guide the class into the writing process. Decide upon and explain the writing assignment—either short and focused around one significant event of childhood or a major autobiographical project. Plan at least three weeks for a full autobiography. It is also possible to individualize the expectations, depending on the students' differing proficiency levels. In either case, consider this a full writing project worthy of all the stages of the composing process: rehearsing, organizing, drafting, revising and editing. Refer to Chart A "The Composing Process" (page 39) for the specific activities involved in the various stages of writing.

Many SL students have led dramatic young lives that provide an important forum for cross-cultural sharing. Students should be encouraged to write for an audience beyond their teacher. When some 6th grade ESL students shared their autobiographies at a parent-student assembly, there was respectful silence. Middle-school American students can begin to understand the journeys and struggles of their immigrant and refugee classmates. Only in this way will they truly begin to work together sensitively, in schools, and later, in life.

Book Recommendations. Most books appropriate as models for autobiographical writing are full length children's literature, usually over 100 pages. For SL students, cross-cultural literature focusing on childhood experiences should be the primary criteria in book selection. Luckily, a few gems exist.

My absolutely highest recommendation is *The Year of the Boar and Jackie Robinson* by Bette Bao Lord. In this humorous but sensitive account, the author recounts her own nine year-old immigrant year from China to Brooklyn, New York. Although in a fictional format, the author claims it is based on her actual experiences. Consider also *The Night Journey* by Kathyrn Lasky, another fictional account, about a young Jewish girl's escape from oppressive Tsarist Russia. It is told three generations later to and through her Americanized granddaughter, the author. A slightly different perspective is provided in *The Land I Lost*, non-fiction by Huynh Nhuong. Although not about the immigrant transition, the author vibrantly captures his childhood adventures of his native land, Vietnam. It offers rich insights into another culture.

CREATIVE ARTS ACTIVITIES

Introduction

Creative arts activities usually synthesize all four language skills while focusing on a different activity altogether. The ones recommended here include drawing, painting, singing and acting. They often function well as the culminating project of a unit. Although language or classroom teachers are not arts specialists, they should use a variety of mediums to help develop the language proficiency of their students. This creates a stimulating language/teaching experience for both the students and the teacher. It also touches upon different gifts of the students, awakening in them other satisfying means of self-expression. Elementary-age children both love and need this exposure to the creative arts.

Ultimately, although teachers are often identified by their subject area, e.g. ESL, math or reading, we are all teachers of the whole child. The creative arts, integrated with language skills, can help nurture this wholeness. This is especially true for ESL students, whose sense of wholeness and self-esteem is usually diminished by limited proficiency in their second language.

In addition, all of the creative arts activities included here foster cooperation and collaboration. This is somewhat true for *Book Making* but especially so for *Cooperative Murals, Performance* and *Dramatization*. In these activities the students need each other to complete the assignments. They provide meaningful opportunities for communication and develop positive feelings and a sense of community within the class. These ingredients equate with the "comprehensible input" and "low affective filter" that Krashen (1985) identifies as key to his developmental theory of second language acquisition.

1. BOOK IT!   *Bookmaking*

ESL Level: Beginner-Intermediate   **Grades: K-2**

Having students recreate a book after reading it aloud is a good, fun follow-up for young children. It provides excellent opportunities for vocabulary practice, oral story retelling, and written expression. Be prepared for this activity to take two to three thirty-minute class periods, especially if writing is involved. Don't worry that students' "books" don't exactly replicate all of the original. As long as they are speaking and writing the vocabulary and telling a story, it's meeting the objectives!

To begin this activity read a selected book aloud, inviting students to join in from the second reading on. Check for oral comprehension. Be sure to have available paper, crayons, markers and ideally, several copies of the book. Then, instruct the students to draw a series of pictures in sequence that tell the story. Encourage them to talk about their pictures and hence the story, even before their entire "book" is complete.

Beneath their drawings, have the students add words or a sentence. For some beginners and kindergartners, the teacher will need to write their orally reported word or sentence on their drawings. For advanced beginners, record their dictation onto the board, instructing them to copy it into their book. For intermediate first and second graders, encourage them to write about the pictures independently. Accepted invented spelling. Upon completion, the students have their own illustrated books, of which they are usually very proud. As with *Student Anthologies* (see #2 under Writing Activities), these "books" can be used for developing reading skills.

Consider cooperative bookmaking as an alternative. In this modification the children work together in groups of 2-5 to make group books. Excitement increases as two to three books are in process at one time. The children can be divided either by proficiency, to accommodate diverse levels of books, by mixed proficiency, to assure a role for all, or by individual choice, to allow students to work on their favorite books. Be sure to plan time at the end for oral group presentations, another opportunity for language expression. The cooperative model has the added advantage of increasing the amount of basic interpersonal communication skills (BICS), a fundamental goal of language acquisition.[11]

Book Recommendations. Books selected for this activity should be short and simple, with numerous clear, colorful illustrations. A key to success here is that the children really enjoy the original. An indication of this is their requesting it over and over again.

I have found that *The Very Hungry Caterpillar* by Eric Carle meets all of these criteria and lends itself beautifully to book-making. Young children take great pleasure in drawing the colorful butterfly at the end. Also try the full version of *Mary Had a Little Lamb* by Sara Hale and *Whose Mouse Are You?* by Robert Kraus.

2. PAINT IT TOGETHER!   *Cooperative Murals*

ESL Level: Beginner-Intermediate   **Grades: 2-6**

In cooperative mural making, a class artistically recreates a story previously read aloud. This is an interdisciplinary blend of the creative arts, literature, communication and language skill development.

Although it requires significant teacher preparation and supervision, I have consistently found this activity a winner. It's fun! Students think it is a special treat to paint in ESL class. They also enjoy contributing their part to a whole class creation and take great pride in the communal finished product.

Like the previous art activity in this section, *Book it!* cooperative murals provide not only a creative outlet for ESL students but also a relaxed setting for the development of basic, interpersonal communicative skill (BICS) development. During this group painting project, students use English to describe their painting, to share materials and to help and get help from others for their artistic endeavors. The students also spontaneously tell the story.

In preparation, the teacher needs to gather art supplies from the school's art center, including large paper, poster paints, brushes, smocks etc. If it can be arranged, it is easier to do the painting in the art room itself.

A number of language activities precede the actual painting. First, as a class, divide the story into plot segments and sequence them correctly (see *Put it in order! #5* under Reading Activities). Second, discuss how each segment can be portrayed artistically. Third, with this discussion as a stimulus, have the students select the various parts. Fourth, instruct the students to sketch out a picture of their portion and to write about it underneath. This component works well as a homework assignment, priming them for the painting the next day.

On the painting day, first give the students adequate time to paint their sketch on individual sheets and to carefully write a corrected version of their description underneath. Second, help the students to logically organize the segments onto large, mural-size paper. Third, write a short description of the project, have one of the students copy it neatly in one corner and have everyone sign their name. Fourth, conclude by rereading the original book. This provides closure and also an increased personal investment in listening carefully to the story. It is often necessary to postpone the final reading of the story until the third day.

Realistically, this project also requires some finishing touches after school or during a free period. For example, some students may need extra time to finish their painting or writing. Also, the pasting or taping together of the individual paintings onto the large paper takes time. Whenever possible, I try to arrange for a few students to help me with this. We all enjoy this time together.

The whole project, with the reading aloud, sequencing, homework assignment and painting takes two to three full class periods. The finished product is quite impressive, especially if laminated, and well worth the effort. One of ours was hung in the school office for months!

Book Recommendations. Myths, legends and fairy tales work well for cooperative mural making. Books with strong illustrators, like Paul Galdone, Trina Schart Hyman and Ezra Jack Keats, mentioned below, provide aesthetically pleasing models, an important criterion when artwork is a main focus. Also look for stories with a variety of characters and settings that will appeal to both girls and boys.

The traditional fairy tale, *Little Red Riding Hood* illustrated by Galdone, with a wolf, hunter, little girl, grandmother, house and woods provides such a mixture for advanced beginners in the 2nd-4th grades. For more intermediate and slightly older 3rd-5th graders who are beginning to experience the competition between sexes, consider "Atalanta," a liberated version of an ancient Greek myth about a foot race. This story is found in *Free to be You and Me*, edited by Marlo Thomas.

For 5th-8th grade advanced beginners, I highly recommend the American legend, *John Henry*, powerfully illustrated by Keats. The boys, especially, find a lot of strong images in this story. For the more intermediate students of this age, try *St. George and the Dragon* illustrated by Hyman. A classic legend set in medieval times, it contains elements of danger and suspense, which translate dramatically into pictures. It also has a beautiful damsel in distress, who is rescued by a handsome young man on a white horse. Many of the girls fight over this picture and I have learned how to spread out variations of this scene among a number of girls.

3. PERFORM IT! *Class Performances*

ESL Level: Beginner-Advanced   Grades: 1-8

Students prepare various short poems, songs and choral readings to present at an international, school, or community function. Most of the selections they perform are first introduced as literature read-alouds.

This activity provides motivation for oral pronunciation and sentence intonation practice. It also assures comprehension and usually memorization of the pieces presented. In addition, the students gain important skills in self-confidence, from performing publicly.

Because of the energy involved in planning, rehearsing and performing, plan to do this once a year, usually in the springtime, after the classes have built up a repertoire of songs, poems and stories. Begin by explaining to the children about the performance opportunity and encouraging them to do it. If you can't convince them, don't push it. Try at a later date for a different event. Once the class has voted to participate, the teacher selects the performance numbers for each class, with the students' input. Do this as a review of their songs, poems and stories, most of which have been preserved on chart paper. This review is always fun! Students like so many selections that it is often difficult to limit them. Try to incorporate some bilingual pieces, which can be performed in English and another language.

The final program usually includes about two to three short numbers per class, with eight to ten the total number. On occasion, brave, individual students will ask to perform short pieces as a duet. Try to incorporate this request. The total time is usually 10-15 minutes. End with a finale in which all the groups participate. One year we finished with the song "We are the World." In preparation, the students made flags of their countries, attached them to long sticks and waved them during this number. It was very moving.

Rehearsal needs to be done regularly so that the children know the material well. It helps to write the words on a sheet for home practice. With each class, rehearse for about three to four weeks total, trying to limit it to 10 minutes three times a week, except for the final week. In this way, this activity does not overwhelm the rest of the curriculum. During rehearsals instruct the children in standing properly, articulating their words clearly and projecting their voices. Whenever possible suggest body motions or actions to express the song. This gives the children something to do with their hands and aids the audience's comprehension. This can be done easily with most nursery rhymes.

To familiarize the students with the whole routine, do at least one dress rehearsal with all the classes together the week of the performances. Try to get permission to use the music room or the stage for this practice. At this time explain carefully any travel or evening plans. This usually involves coordination with families.

At the time of the performance, the children are always nervous. This is normal and part of the learning experience. In your introduction to the audience, explain that these students are new to The United States and are just learning English. The children usually do just fine and the audience applauds warmly, amazed with their poise and English language ability. Their parents are proud beyond belief!

In the end, I find this activity is well worth the effort. These special events create lasting memories. The students learn poems and songs they remember long after their ESL years are over. Even more important than that, they learn to overcome nervousness with poise and character. They learn that they can do more than they thought they were capable of. They feel good about themselves and their abilities. These feelings significantly affect a child's attitude towards learning. As an added benefit, this activity helps to integrate multicultural *parents* into the school community, as they come to watch their children perform.

Book Recommendations. Nursery rhymes, short poems and singable books make excellent performance choices. *Tomie dePaola's Mother Goose* offers many choices for the younger children. A shortened form of *When I First Came to this Land* by Oscar Brand is popular with the older ones. A two-group choral reading of *Just Like Daddy* by Frank Asch, with its liberated, surprise ending, is also fun to perform.

4. PLAY IT OUT!   *Dramatization*

ESL Level: Intermediate-Advanced   **Grades: 3-8**

Students, with their teacher's help, can enjoyably create and perform a play from one of their favorite books. This activity integrates all four language skills, builds self-confidence through performance and develops a collaborative learning style, as students contribute according to their different abilities and skills.

Dramatization develops along a continuum of modest, classroom-based activities. It can be stopped at any step and need not involve a complicated, staged production. Performing for others, however, can certainly be one final goal.

As you read through this continuum of activities, think of *Cinderella* by Charles Perrault. As the first step of the continuum, students nonverbally act out parts according to lines read from the book. (See *Act it out! #4* under Listening Activities). Either the teacher or possibly another student can do the reading.

Second, the teacher or students read the narration, priming students for the speaking lines (i.e. direct speech). If there are more students than roles, the teacher can divide the class into two play groups, assigning a leader to each.

Third, for more familiarity with the story, provide copies of the text for class or homework reading. The specific assignment (in addition to reading it) is to underline the dialogues (i.e. the direct speech) in the story.

Fourth, have students work in small groups to write a play from the story, culling out the dialogues they have already underlined. This will need some initial modelling and direction from the teacher. Make sure the students understand and include the role of the narrator. The teacher circulates to help with this challenging writing project. This step could be eliminated by providing the students with a pre-written play of the story, but the students would lose the valuable experience of synthesizing and writing it themselves.

Fifth, students assign the roles among themselves and read their play to the other groups. Give groups time to practice their parts. The class always enjoys these readings tremendously. Each play will be a little different, which should be noted as acceptable to the students.

If interest is still alive, proceed to step six. Still working in small, cooperative groups, students memorize their parts, design simple costumes, props and sets, in preparation for final production. This performance can either be done in class, for other classes, or at a school wide assembly. It is realistic that only some students will want to continue to this performance level. The teacher can combine them into one group and give them some independent class time to work together, while starting the rest of the class on another activity.

Book Recommendations. Folk or fairy tales lend themselves well to dramatization. Also look for books with numerous characters, dialogues and clear action. *Snow White and the Seven Dwarfs* by Walt Disney (not in the RAL) and *The Bremen Town Musicians* by Ilse Plume meet these criteria.

For SL students, an interesting alternative to *Cinderella* by Charles Perrault, suggested above, is *Yeh Shen* by Ai-Long Louie. This is a beautifully illustrated, modern picture-book edition of the original Chinese tale. Its author claims that the Chinese story predates the European one by over 1000 years.[12]

Notes

1. For more information on cooperative learning, see its succinct description in a two page pamphlet by Jacob and Mattson (1987) or the full teacher resource book by Kagan (1985), one of the noted leaders in the field. Full citations are given in the Reference section.

2. *The Association of Library Services for Children's (ALSC) Notable Films/Videos/Filmstrips and Recordings* (1989) is available from ALSC, ALA, 50 East Huron St, Chicago, IL 60061. For a single copy, send 50¢ and a self-addressed, stamped #10 envelope, with payment.

3. Windham Hill Records, P.O. Box 9338, Stanford, CA 94309

4. Weston Woods publishes material in a variety of media, in addition to records—filmstrips, tape cassettes, motion pictures and hardcover books. For a complete catalogue write them at Weston Woods Studios, Weston, CT 06883.

5. Dr. Shirley Brice Heath has done research on peer reading in California. She had 5th and 6th grade Hispanic girls successfully reading to kindergartners and first graders for 20 minutes two times a week. As this research activity becomes adopted into the ongoing school program, the school plans to use both 5th and 6th grade boys *and* girls. Dr. Heath presented an overview of the program and the results of her research to the WATESOL Spring Conference, 1987.

   Paired reading is a related trend. That is generally defined as an adult being matched with a child to provide the youngster oral reading practice. For a report on this approach, see Topping (1986, 1985, 1984), *National Paired Reading Conference Proceedings.*

6. Error correction after the initial expression of ideas is compatible with Krashen's monitor hypotheses. This argues that grammar and error revision should not interfere with the development of thoughts nor should it be substituted for comprehensible input. The Monitor focuses on the conscious study of rules. According to Krashen's theory, this should occur later in the speaking process because it affects linguistic performance (the output), and not the acquisition of linguistic competence (the input). For further explanation, see Krashen (1985), pp. 1–4.

7. The Great Books approach is sponsored by the Great Books Foundation out of Chicago, Illinois. They provide a set of readers for Grades 2–12 and also for adults. Each set is complemented by a Leader's Guide, which has interpretive questions prepared for each story. The foundation regularly runs training sessions throughout the United States in their "shared inquiry" approach to literary analysis. This training is a prerequisite for using their materials. For more intormation, contact them at 40 East Huron Street, Chicago, IL 60611.

8. *Great Book's Leader Aid, Level 3.* 1984. Chicago, IL: Great Books Foundation, p. 30.

9. A full unit plan for integrating *Pancakes for Breakfast* into the ESL curriculum was developed by Grace Fritz, an ESOL teacher in Montgomery County Public Schools, Maryland. A summary of it appears in the Washington Area of Teachers of English to Speakers of Other Languages (WATESOL) Newsletter (Dec. 1987). Mrs. Fritz also spoke on this topic to the Elementary What Works Workshop at the WATESOL Conference (March, 1987).

10. This activity was demonstrated with a secondary-college level reading text by Professor Jean Mc-Conochie, during her seminar on "Literature and ESL" at Teacher's College, Columbia University in New York City (July, 1986).

11. This term, basic interpersonal communication skills (BICS) was first introduced by Cummins (1981) to explain the first level of language proficiency. The second and higher level of language proficiency expected in schools he identifies as cognitive academic language proficiency (CALP). Research has indicated that the first can usually be acquired within two years, the second requires four to eight, depending on the age on arrival (AOA) of the students (Collier, 1987). Bibliographic citation is provided in the Reference section.

12. The Cinderella story first appeared during the T'ang Dynasty (618–907 A.D.) written by Tuan Ch'eng-Shih. It received wide distribution throughout China, when it was included as part of an encyclopedic work that went through many editions during the centuries. As the oldest European version of Cinderella comes from an Italian tale of 1634, Cinderella seems to have traveled from the Orient to the Occident.

    This information comes from Ai-Ling Louie, in her preface to *Yeh-Shen, A Cinderella Story from China.* (1982). Full bibliographic information and annotation appear in *Part II: Read-Aloud Library.*

PART TWO

Read-Aloud Library

CHAPTER ONE

Introduction

From the thousands of books that line the library shelves, the "Read-Aloud Library" recommends over 260. These books are specifically chosen to address the language learning needs of limited English proficient students in pre-kindergarten through eighth grade. Of course, more than 260 appropriate books exist. My decision here is to fully annotate a limited number, providing comprehensive information about each. Based on my classroom experience, this is more helpful than simply a long list of titles and authors.

The literature chosen balances fiction and non-fiction, contemporary and classics, novels and picture books. While fiction is the traditional choice when selecting a read-aloud, non-fiction, especially social studies and science books, also offer advantages. It is an excellent way to introduce content-based material and to stimulate interest in these fascinating subjects. And if your students do not yet have the proficiency to read the books independently, you are opening their ears and eyes to the world beyond!

Individual books usually provide a better read-aloud experience than anthologies. There are more illustrations and less text per page. Nevertheless, it is important to also include a few anthologies in this collection. They can serve as a teacher resource and also be used directly as a read-aloud. This usually works better with more intermediate and advanced students.

All the books recommended are quality literature, written for native speakers, with appeal to an audience beyond second language (SL) speakers. The key criteria for selection here is that the book succeeds as a read-aloud. Look in Chapter 3 of Part I for guidelines to select read-alouds specifically for SL listeners.

In addition, I have utilized two more general criteria for this "Read-Aloud Library." First, upon the advice and request of numerous librarians and booksellers, only those books currently in print are included. While many out-of-print books still exist on library shelves, it is often difficult to find used copies and impossible to locate new ones for purchase. A few exceptions do make this list, and they are so identified. Second, I checked that all the books were available in the public libraries where I live. Since they were, I assume they are also available in most other metropolitan areas.

ORGANIZATION OF THE READ-ALOUD LIBRARY

Most collections of annotations are written by librarians. Reflecting their training, they usually organize their selections either alphabetically or by literary genre. This collection was compiled by a teacher; hence, it is organized by teaching topics. Since teachers usually choose books to coordinate with textbook topics or curriculum units, this topical organization is intended to facilitate the teacher's selection process. This, in turn, enhances the likelihood that the literature will become more fully integrated into the curriculum.

To develop a comprehensive but manageable list of topics I thoroughly reviewed all levels of two major elementary ESL series and *The ESL Miscellany* (1981), which includes detailed lists of notional, functional and situational topics. The RAL topics also incorporate the standard themes of most ESL and elementary school curricula. The full list appears on page 15 in Chapter 3 of the "Read-Aloud Guidelines."

Within each topic, the books are organized from easy to advanced and from kindergarten to junior high age. An attempt has been made to include a range of proficiency levels and age ranges for each topic.

The books in the Read-Aloud Library are intended to serve as instructional material. Therefore, the annotations are written to provide enough information so the teacher can make sound educational decisions about their usage. Accordingly, the annotation format covers more than the standard bibliographic data and short prose description. It is hoped that this additional information enhances the usefulness of the literature in a classroom setting.

1. Standard Bibliographic Information

This includes the full title, author/s, illustrator/s, name of publisher and date/s of publication. The title, author's and illustrator's names are quite clear. The publishers, however, begin to overlap because in recent years some publishing companies have been acquired by others. Many of the original companies still retain some of their identity as imprints (or divisions) of the larger firms. I feel it is important to know both the original publishing house because of their reputation and the current one, for ordering purposes. Therefore, I list them both, with the current publisher first and the original in parenthesees: for example, Macmillan (Thomas Y. Crowell).

In the "Listing of Books by Topics," I cite the earliest publication date—the original copyright. This sets the book in its correct time period. However, in the annotation itself, I also give the latest publication date. This information is helpful for ordering purposes. In addition, if a book has been published separately with a cassette or a teacher's guide, I list that in the annotation as well.

2. Page Numbers

The number of pages usually correlates with the level of difficulty. It also allows an estimate of the time needed to read a book aloud. This information can be especially helpful in evaluating the appropriateness of juvenile fiction, which varies in length from 50 to 250 pages. Most selections included, except for anthologies, do not exceed 200 pages.

3. ESL Proficiency Level

To my knowledge, no other comprehensive attempt exists to categorize children's literature by ESL proficiency level. It is helpful for both ESL and regular classroom teachers to keep this criterion in mind when making literature selections. After some experimentation, I decided to limit the ESL proficiency levels to three: beginner, intermediate and advanced. When a book seems to span two proficiency levels, both are listed. My decision on how to categorize a book was based on a combination of syntax, vocabulary, book length and complexity of subject matter.

While most ESL programs divide students according to these basic categories, in reality, students' language acquisition progresses along a continuum that doesn't always fit into these neat divisions. Therefore, these proficiency levels are intended as helpful guidelines, not as a straightjacket. For example, a beginner can absorb at least partial comprehension of an intermediate level book, and an advanced learner, can still find challenge with an intermediate level one.

4. Grade Level

Literature decisions for SL students must consider the grade level appropriateness of a book, as well as its ESL proficiency level. For example, beginner ESL middle school students should find the easy reader, *Are You my Mother?* too juvenile. This criterion is discussed more fully on page 13 in Part I (Chapter 3). The following categories are used: Pre-K-1, K-3, 2-5, 4-8, 6-8. When a book seems to span more than one grade grouping, both are listed. In considering the appropriate grade categories, I consulted the publisher's recommendation, when available, yet I have also made independent decisions. I often assigned lower grade ranges than other annotators because the multicultural population usually has had less exposure to literature. As with ESL proficiency levels, classification of literature by grade (or age) requires flexible interpretation.

Keep in mind that some SL students are still placed in lower grades because of their limited English proficiency. In these cases, consider the student's age rather than grade when making independent book recommendations.

5. Literary Genre

In order to introduce the students to a variety of literary styles, it is important to balance book selections, over time, according to genre. By attending to this category, this collection attempts to achieve that balance for grade levels K-8. This criterion is developed more fully on page 16 in Chapter 3 (Part I), where a full listing of the literary genres appears. These include those generally used in children's literature, with a few independent flourishes added: in particular, the term "singable books" and the division of novels into short (less than 100 pages) or long (100-200 pages). See the "Literary Genre Index" for a listing of the RAL by genres.

6. Ethnic Group

All children are enriched by participation in a multiethnic society. LEP students contribute to this ethnic diversity and are gladly counted in the statistics by the administration. Yet the standard instructional materials do not always contribute to their positive self-image. Literature shared with a class provides an opportunity to affirm diverse cultural traditions of our multicultural society. These include different kinds of stories, both fiction and non-fiction. Some highlight a particular ethnic heritage: for example, *The Land I Lost* about the author's childhood adventures in Vietnam. Others focus on life stories, found in biographies of those from ethnic backgrounds: for example, *Jackie Robinson*, about the famous, black American baseball player. Yet others concentrate on the immigration experience coming to America: for example, *Lupita Mañana*, about a teenage brother and sister's dangerous escape from Central America.

In keeping with these values, this collection includes literature that presents diverse ethnic groups in a positive, nonstereotypic manner. If a book includes characters of a major ethnic group, that information is listed under this category. For the Asian and Hispanic groups, ethnic subcategories are included as well: for example, Asian-Korean, Hispanic-Puerto Rican. It is hoped that inclusion of this information will encourage cross-cultural awareness in all students. To identify books according to ethnicity, use the "Multicultural Index."

7. Vocabulary

To facilitate the selection and planning process, it is helpful for teachers to know what vocabulary topics are included in a book. This category addresses that need. For each book, it highlights the key vocabulary. These are selected from over 65 standard topics. Often it specifies subsets of the basic topics. For example, in *The Knee High Man and Other Tales* the vocabulary listing includes "animals—dog, cat, bear, rabbit, owl, horse, bull, snake." Use this information to help write lesson plans and objectives. To decide which vocabulary to emphasize in follow-up activities, refer to the text.

8. Grammatical Structures

Awareness of the major grammatical structures of a text is important information for teachers of SL students. With this knowledge, teachers can decide upon the suitability of a text as well as its usefulness to teach or reinforce grammar items currently being studied. This category identifies this information for each text. In order to do so in a systematic format, a grammar classification system was developed. It includes numerous grammatical categories, such as the parts of speech (verbs, nouns, prepositions, adjectives, adverbs, conjunctions, articles and pronouns) as well as non-affirmative sentences (e.g. imperatives, tag questions) and object formations. Altogether, it identifies over 55 grammatical structures. Because every book contains numerous syntactic features, only the predominant ones can be mentioned. As with the vocabulary above, often the exact items of a category are specified: for example, in *Sarah, Plain and Tall* "modal auxiliary verbs—can, must." Other times, separate but related grammatical features are listed together: for example, in *The Fox Went Out on A Chilly Night* "prepositional phrases—of place, manner and instrument." It is hoped that this detailed grammatical information will encourage teachers to use literature to help teach discrete linguistic features.

9. Repeated Patterns

Children's literature is rich with repeated patterns. They provide a rhythm to the text as well as many mnemonic devices for language learning. These predictable patterns, like syntactic structures, also generate valuable teaching material for second language students. In order to communicate this information about each book to the teachers, the grammar classification system was expanded to include patterns. The general categories are word patterns (e.g. short vowel sounds, rhyming), sentence patterns (e.g. complex sentences, passive voice), story patterns (e.g. repeated refrain, cumulative repetitions), communication patterns (e.g. dialogues, question/answer sequence) and varieties of English (e.g. academic language, nonstandard language). The full list includes 25 different patterns, each a subset of a general category. For each given text, it is possible to mention only those which predominate.

For more information about this taxonomy, write to me via the publisher, Addison-Wesley.

10. Prose Description

All annotated bibliographies include a narrative about each entry, following the standard bibliographic information. Usually these concentrate on an objective plot summary and are limited to a short paragraph. The annotations in the "Read-Aloud Library" expand beyond this basic information to provide a distinct flavor of a book, taking note of its setting as well as its characters. Special attention is paid to the book's illustrations and also how it enhances cross-cultural understanding. In addition, its usefulness as a teaching tool is highlighted. Each annotation concludes with some statements about the unique contribution of the particular book. An attempt is made to find something positive and distinctive to say about each recommendation. For example, special literary awards, such as the Caldecott and Newbery, are noted. Also, books selected for the excellent television show, *Reading Rainbow,* are mentioned.

My goal is to make these annotations read well. I hope it is like the pleasure many derive from reading well-written recipes in an interesting cookbook, even if one doesn't actually prepare each dish described. I enjoy reading and writing about children's books, especially good ones. I hope to convey this enthusiasm in the annotations.

11. Related Books

Success with one book on a given topic or by a particular author often stimulates the desire to follow up with a related one. This is a positive sign, which affirms literature as both a pleasurable and learning medium. Expansion to a related book also encourages a class to compare and contrast treatment of a given subject or by authors. To facilitate these opportunities, related books are listed — by title, author and date of publication. This category appears following the annotation, as "Related Books."

When these related books are written by the same author, this is noted in a separate entry, "Related Book/s by Same Author." When the relationship is by author only, this is indicated by "Book/s by Same Author." To communicate that a related book is annotated separately in the "Read-Aloud Library," the symbol "RAL" follows the title. Because of space limitations, this category is included for many but not all of the books.

HOW TO USE THE READ-ALOUD LIBRARY

In order to facilitate systematic access to the "Read-Aloud Library," five types of indexes have been designed. The most straightforward, "Listing of Books by Topics," is located at the end of this chapter on pages 58–64. Use this comprehensive subject index when you are looking generally for books. By quickly perusing it, you can identify the recommended books for each topic and where to find them.

Four other groupings of the "Read-Aloud Library" appear in the Index section. They identify the books according to their multicultural group, their literary genre, alphabetically by book title and by their author and illustrator. For each book in each index, page number locations in the RAL are given. These indexes are useful when you know more specifically what book or what kind of book you are seeking.

It is hoped that these series of indexes streamline your selection process. Of course, you needn't be this organized. You can also more casually browse through the annotations until an old favorite or intriguing new book catches your eye.

The final step in "How to Use the Read-Aloud Library" is to locate the books in your local library or bookstore. Begin your search with at least a partial list, with some bibliographic information noted about each book. To refresh your memory, you may find it helpful to take along this book or another collection of annotations.

Allow at least a week between the library trip and when you plan to use the book. You may not find everything you want on the shelf during your first visit. Seek out the children's librarians; they are usually very knowledgeable and helpful. They can reserve books for you at other libraries or have them sent over to your local branch. They can also suggest alternative titles for a given topic. At times, you may need to settle on a second choice. This occasional difficulty in finding books is especially acute for holiday and seasonal books the week/s before the event. Plan ahead!

In conclusion, I hope this introduction guides you through the abundance of information and wonderful literature presented in the following pages. Treat each book as the gem it is and enjoy the experience of just reading about them!

LISTING OF BOOKS BY TOPIC

Family Relationships   65
  Whose Mouse Are You? 1970. Kraus
  The Patchwork Quilt. 1985. Flourney
  The Napping House. 1984. Wood
  I Go with My Family to Grandma's. 1986. Levinson
  Little Red Riding Hood. 1983. Hyman
  Sisters. 1984. McPhail
  Tikki Tikki Tembo. 1968. Mosel
  Yeh-Shen. 1982. Louie
  Mufaro's Beautiful Daughters. 1987. Steptoe
  Rapunzel. 1982. Rogasky
  The Spring of Butterflies and Other Folktales of China's Minority Peoples.
    1985. Liyi
  The Brocaded Slipper and Other Vietnamese Tales. 1982. Vuong
  Tales of a Fourth Grade Nothing. 1972. Blume
  The Summer of the Swans. 1970. Byars

Life Passages (Birth, Marriage, Divorce, Death)   72
  The Tenth Good Thing About Barney. 1971. Viorst
  The Tooth Fairy. 1983. Gregor
  The Giving Tree. 1964. Silverstein
  Knots on a Counting Rope. 1987. Martin/Archambault
  Charlotte's Web. 1952. White
  A Taste of Blackberries. 1973. Smith
  Ramona Forever. 1984. Cleary
  Sarah, Plain and Tall. 1985. MacLachlan

House/Home   76
  Hop on Pop. 1963. Seuss
  In a People House. 1972. Le Sieg
  A Dark, Dark Tale. 1981. Brown
  This is the House that Jack Built. 1987. Underhill
  Bored-Nothing to Do! 1978. Spier
  Amelia Bedelia. 1963. Parish
  The Stories Julian Tells. 1981. Cameron

Friendship   80
  Where is my Friend? 1976. Maestro
  Friends. 1982. Heine
  Happy Birthday to Me. 1981. Rockwell
  Jamaica's Find. 1986. Havill
  What Do You Say, Dear? 1958. Joslin
  A Letter to Amy. 1968. Keats
  Best Friends. 1986. Hopkins
  My Best Friend Duc Tran: Meeting a Vietnamese-American Family. 1987.
    MacMillan/Freeman
  The Courage of Sarah Noble. 1954. Dalgliesh
  Bridge to Terabithia. 1977. Patterson
  Indian in the Cupboard. 1980. Banks

Emotions/Values   85
  Leo the Late Bloomer. 1971. Kraus

Alexander and the Terrible, Horrible, No Good, Very Bad Day. 1972. Viorst
Nobody's Perfect, Not Even My Mother. 1981. Simon
Sam. 1967. Scott
A Hole in the Dike. 1975. Green
Frederick's Fables. 1985. Lionni
It Could Always Be Worse. 1976. Zemach
Aesop's Fables. 1985. Hague
Fables. 1980. Lobel
Free to Be You and Me. 1974. Thomas
Stone Fox. 1980. Gardiner

School/Learning 90
The School. 1975. Burningham
Timothy Goes to School. 1981. Wells
Mary Had a Little Lamb. 1984. dePaola
My Friend Leslie. The Story of a Handicapped Child. 1983. Rosenberg
Miss Nelson is Missing. 1977. Allard
Crow Boy. 1955. Yashima
Angel Child, Dragon Child. 1983. Surat
I Speak English for My Mom. 1989. Stanek
The Master Chess Player. 1976. Chek
The One in the Middle is the Green Kangaroo. 1967. Blume

Basic Academic Skills
    Alphabet 95
Alphabet Block Book. 1979. McKie
A, B, See. 1982. Hoban
Q is for Ducks. 1980. Elting/Folsom
On Market Street. 1981. Lobel
I Unpacked my Grandmother's Trunk. 1983. Hoguet

    Counting/Numbers 98
Bears on Wheels. 1969. Berenstain
One Bear All Alone. 1985. Bucknall
Counting Rhymes. 1980. Brimax
Roll Over: A Counting Song. 1981. Peek
One Two Three: An Animal Counting Book. 1976. Brown
Count and See. 1972. Hoban
The Toothpaste Millionaire. 1972. Merrill

    Days/Weeks/Months/Calendar 101
Chicken Soup with Rice. 1962. Sendak
One Monday Morning. 1967. Shulevitz
A Year of Beasts. 1986. Wolff

    Telling Time/Clocks 103
Around the Clock with Harriet. 1984. Maestro
Bear Child's Book of Hours. 1987. Rockwell

    Colors/Shapes/Sizes 104
Do You Know Colors? 1979. Miller/Howard
Brown Bear, Brown Bear, What Do You See? 1967. Martin
Beside the Bay. 1987. Samton
Shapes. 1986. Kightley

One fish, two fish, red fish, blue fish. 1960. Seuss
Deep in the Forest. 1976. Turkle
Hailstones and Halibut Bones. 1961. O'Neill

Opposites/Modifiers   107
Is it Rough? Is it Smooth? Is it Shiny? 1984. Hoban
Quick as a Cricket. 1982. Wood
Fast-Slow, High-Low. 1972. Spier
Fortunately. 1964. Charlip
Think about Smelling. 1986. Pluckrose

Clothing/Body   110
Old Hat, New Hat. 1970. Berenstain
Hand, Hand, Finger, Thumb. 1969. Perkins
Caps for Sale. 1940. Slobodkina
You'll Soon Grow into Them. 1983. Hutchins
Little Bear. 1957. Minarik
The Elves and the Shoemaker. 1984. Galdone
How and Why: A Kid's Book about the Body. 1988. O'Neill

Holidays

Martin Luther King Day   113
Martin Luther King, Jr. 1968. Boone-Jones

Valentine's Day   114
Bee My Valentine! 1978. Cohen

Chinese New Year   114
Gung Hay Fat Choy. 1982. Behrens

Passover   115
I Love Passover. 1985. Hirsh

Mother's Day   115
Are You My Mother? 1960. Eastman
The Mother's Day Mice. 1986. Bunting
Journey to the Bright Kingdom. 1979. Winthrop

Father's Day   117
Just Like Daddy. 1981. Asch
Poems for Father. 1989. Livingston

July Fourth (U.S.Independence Day)   118
The Star-Spangled Banner. 1973. Spier

Halloween   118
It's Halloween. 1977. Prelutsky
Esteban and the Ghost. 1983. Hancock

Thanksgiving   119
Thanksgiving Day. 1983. Gibbons
Over the River and Through the Woods. 1974. Child

Christmas   120
Peter Spier's Christmas! 1983. Spier
The Night Before Christmas. 1985. Moore/Marshall

Food/Nutrition 121

The Supermarket. 1979. Rockwell
Let's Eat. 1975. Fujikawa
Green Eggs and Ham. 1960. Seuss
The Little Red Hen. 1973. Galdone
The Gingerbread Boy. 1975 Galdone
Think about Tasting. 1986. Pluckrose
Pancakes for Breakfast. 1978. dePaola
The Grey Lady and the Strawberry Snatcher. 1980. Bang
Stone Soup. 1986. McGovern
Cloudy with a Chance of Meatballs. 1978. Barrett
Hansel and Gretel. 1980. Grimm
Poem Stew. 1981. Cole
The Paper Crane. 1985. Bang
How My Parents Learned to Eat. 1984. Friedman
The Milk Makers. 1985. Gibbons
Nutrition. 1985. LeMaster

Community

Places 129

Odd One Out. 1975. Peppe
Bears in the Night. 1971. Berenstain
Playgrounds. 1985. Gibbons
The Fire Station Book. 1981. Bundt
The Little House. 1942. Burton
Fill it Up! All About Service Stations. 1985. Gibbons
The Red Balloon. 1956. Lamorisse
Encyclopedia Brown, Boy Detective. 1963. Sobol

Shopping 133

Corduroy. 1968. Freeman
Ox-Cart Man. 1979. Hall
A Chair for my Mother. 1982, *Something Special for Me.* 1983, *Music, Music for Everyone.* 1984, (a trilogy). Williams
Department Store. 1984. Gibbons

Transportation/Safety 135

School Bus. 1984. Crews
Traffic: A Book of Opposites. 1981. Maestro
I Read Symbols. 1983. Hoban
We're Taking an Airplane Trip. 1982. Moche

Recreation/Sports 137

Curious George Rides a Bike. 1952. Rey
Play Ball, Amelia Bedelia. 1972. Parish
Yagua Days. 1976. Cruz
Three Days on a River in a Red Canoe. 1981. Williams
Strange but True Basketball Stories. 1972. Liss
Casey at the Bat. 1987. Thayer/Bendis

Role Models

Heroes 140

Amelia Earhart, Adventure in the Sky. 1983. Sabin
John Henry, An American Legend. 1965. Keats
Saint George and the Dragon. 1984. Hodges

Greek Gods and Heroes. 1985. Low
Robin Hood, His Life and Legends. 1979. Miles
Sports Star, Fernando Valenzuela. 1982. Burchard
The Story of Jackie Robinson, Bravest Man in Baseball. 1988. Davidson
The Pride of Puerto Rico, The Life of Roberto Clemente. 1988. Walker

Careers   144
Amelia Bedelia's Family Album. 1988. Parish
I Can Be a Carpenter. 1986. Lillegard
I Can Be a Doctor. 1985. Hankin
Weather Forecasting. 1987. Gibbons

History/Geography
United States   146
When I First Came to this Land. 1965. Brand
The Erie Canal. 1970. Spier
Deborah Sampson Goes to War. 1984. Stevens
Wagon Wheels. 1978. Brenner
And Then What Happened, Paul Revere? 1973. Fritz
Shh! We're Writing the Constitution. 1987. Fritz

World   149
Where the Forest Meets the Sea. 1987. Baker
Maps and Globes. 1985. Knowlton
Take a Trip to Nigeria. 1983. Lye
A Family in China. 1986. Jacobsen/Kristensen
India (My Country Series). 1986. Moon
The Land I Lost: Adventures of a Boy in Vietnam. 1982. Nhuong
Where Do You Think You're Going, Christopher Columbus? 1980. Fritz

Immigration/Cross-cultural Adjustment   152
Molly's Pilgrim. 1983. Cohen
How Many Days to America? 1988. Bunting
The Long Way to a New Land. 1981. Sandlin
The Witch of Fourth Street and Other Stories. 1972. Levoy
In the Year of the Boar and Jackie Robinson. 1984. Lord
A Jar of Dreams. 1981. Uchida
A Boat to Nowhere. 1980. Wartski
A Long Way from Home. 1980. Wartski
Lupita Mañana. 1981. Beatty
The Night Journey. 1981. Lasky

Animals
Birds   157
Owls in the Family. 1961. Mowat
The Ugly Duckling. 1979. Andersen/Cauley

Farm   158
The Farmer in the Dell. 1978. Zuromskis
Baby Farm Animals. 1984. Windsor
Rosie's Walk. 1968. Hutchins
Old MacDonald Had a Farm. 1984. Pearson
Henny Penny. 1968. Galdone
The Fox Went Out on a Chilly Night. 1961. Spier
Our Animal Friends at Maple Hill Farm. 1974. Provensen

Pets 162
Where is it? 1974. Hoban
Where's Spot? 1980. Hill
A Bag Full of Pups. 1981. Gackenbach
Millions of Cats. 1928. Gag

Prehistoric 164
Dinosaur Time. 1974. Parish
Danny and the Dinosaur. 1958. Hoff
Tyrannosaurus Was a Beast. 1988. Prelutsky
Strange Creatures that Really Lived. 1987. Selsam
The Monsters Who Died. A Mystery About Dinosaurs. 1983. Cobb

Sea 166
Humphrey: the Lost Whale. 1986. Tokuda/Hall

Wild 167
A Crocodile's Tale. 1972. Aruego
Gift of the Sacred Dog. 1980. Goble
The Girl Who Loved Wild Horses. 1978. Goble
The Elephant's Child. 1983. Kipling/Cauley

Zoo 169
Dear Zoo. 1982. Campbell
A Children's Zoo. 1985. Hoban
Zoo. 1987. Gibbons
Koko's Kitten. 1985. Patterson

Miscellaneous 171
A Rhinoceros Wakes Me Up in the Morning. 1984. Goodspeed
Oh, A Hunting We Will Go. 1974. Langstaff
The Story of Ferdinand. 1936. Leaf
The Knee-High Man. 1972. Lester

Seasons/Weather 173
Summer Is . . . 1983. Zolotow
The Seasons of Arnold's Apple Tree. 1984. Gibbons
The Snowy Day. 1962. Keats
The Boy Who Didn't Believe in Spring. 1973. Clifton
Gilberto and the Wind. 1963. Ets
Toad is the Uncle of Heaven. 1985. Lee
The Seaside. 1986. Ruis/Parramon
A Day on the River. 1985. Michl
Stopping By Woods on a Snowy Evening. 1978. Frost
Flash, Crash, Rumble and Roll. 1985. Branley
Sunshine Makes the Seasons. 1974. Branley
Weather Experiments. 1982. Webster

Science
Growth 179
The Carrot Seed. 1945. Krauss
The Very Hungry Caterpillar. 1970. Carle
The Lady and the Spider. 1986. McNulty
A Chick Hatches. 1976. Cole

Health/Hospitals   181
My Doctor. 1973. Rockwell
Emergency Room. 1985. Rockwell
Curious George Goes to the Hospital. 1966. Rey
Your Heart and Blood. 1984. LeMaster

Space/Solar System   183
The Planets in our Solar System. 1987. Branley
I Can Be an Astronaut. 1984. Behrens
Space Colonies. 1985. Fradin
Astronomy Today. 1982. Moche

Miscellaneous   185
The Magic School Bus Inside the Earth. 1987. Cole
Top Secret. 1984. Gardiner

Imagination/Monsters/Magic   186
Rain Makes Applesauce. 1964. Scheer
The Three Billy Goats Gruff. 1973. Galdone
Abiyoyo. 1986. Seeger
The Perfect Crane. 1981. Laurin
Beauty and the Beast. 1978. Mayer
The Velveteen Rabbit, or How Toys Become Real. 1983. Williams
Charlie and the Chocolate Factory. 1964. Dahl
The Wizard of Oz. 1982. Baum
Where the Sidewalk Ends. 1974. Silverstein
The Little Prince. 1943. De Saint-Exupery

Anthologies   191
Tomie dePaola's Mother Goose. 1985. dePaola
If You're Happy and You Know It. 1987. Weiss
The Fairy Tale Treasury. 1972. Haviland
Side by Side. Poems to Read Together. 1988. Hopkins
The Random House Book of Poetry. 1983. Prelutsky
The Day it Snowed Tortillas. 1982. Hayes
Favorite Folktales From Around the World. 1986. Yolen
More Classics to Read Aloud to Your Children. 1986. Russell

CHAPTER TWO

Read-Aloud Library Annotations

FAMILY RELATIONSHIPS

WHOSE MOUSE ARE YOU?

by Robert Kraus
New York: Macmillan, 1970

illustrated by Jose Aruego
28 pages

Grades: Pre-K-1, K-3   **ESL Level:** intermediate
Genre: picture book

Vocabulary: family, animals—mouse, cat
Grammar: *wh* questions, prepositional phrases of place, expressions of future time—*will*,
    possessive nouns
Patterns: question and answer sequence, repeated sentence patterns

A lovable, little mouse seeks his family. You feel for him, as he misses his family and then cheer for him as he bravely rescues them. Through his family, he finds his security and identity. The single question or response per page makes this a good read-aloud for young listeners. The repeated patterns and format help the children learn the complex syntax. As an oral follow-up, the class can create their own story, with a different animal in different situations. This also flows naturally into bookmaking, where students, either individually or in cooperative groups, create their own illustrated books based on this story and its patterns.

Related Book by Same Author: *Another Mouse to Feed* (1987)

Book by Same Author: *Leo the Late Bloomer* (1971) in the RAL.

THE PATCHWORK QUILT

by Valerie Flourney   illustrated by Jerry Pinkney
New York: E.P. Dutton (Dial Books), 1985   30 pages

Grades: K-3, 2-5   **ESL Level:** intermediate
Genre: picture book
Ethnic Identity: Black American

Vocabulary: family—grandmother, household, seasons
Grammar: past tense, action verbs, adverbs, adverbial clauses
Patterns: dialogue

Grandmother weaves her family together through her patient sewing of a patchwork quilt. The patches include clothing pieces from all their lives. Originally, it is the granddaughter who bonds with grandma through this unifying project, but ultimately mother and the rest of the family get involved as well. Quilts are symbolic of older generations throughout our society; this one happens to be part of a black family, now comfortably established in the middle class.

The warm illustrations fill the book, but they can't explain every action. With about half a page of text per page there is too much story for that. Thus, this is best for the intermediate level. A *Reading Rainbow* selection.

Quilting groups can be found in nearly every area. It would be very enriching to contact a quilter and invite her to the class to explain this American tradition. The students could interview her with prepared questions and then compare this custom with those in their own cultures.

Related Book: *The Night Journey* (Lasky, 1981), about the strong bond between grandmother and her granddaughter (for older, advanced students), also in the RAL.

Book By the Same Author: *The Best Time of the Day* (1979)

THE NAPPING HOUSE

by Audrey Wood   illustrated by Don Wood
New York : Harcourt Brace Jovanovich, 1984   32 pages

Grades: K-3   **ESL Level:** beginner, intermediate
Genre: picture book

Vocabulary: home, family, pets, weather
Grammar: prepositional phrases of place, adjectives, third person agreement, existential
     sentences—*there is*
Patterns: cumulative repetitions

One dreary, rainy afternoon there is "a napping house where everyone is sleeping," at least to begin with. All the inhabitants of the home luxuriously pile on top of granny, one by one, until a fly humorously wakes them all, again, one by one. It all ends happily in the bright sunshine under a beautiful rainbow. The illustrations are sensational. They help create the joy and magic of this original story. With its cumulative verses and sentence patterns, it is somewhat reminiscent of the song, "There was an old woman who swallowed a fly."

This book is an absolute delight, honored with numerous awards! You feel so good after reading it that both you and your students will want to read it again!

Related Book: *The Farmer in the Dell* (Zuromskis, 1978) in the RAL.

Book By the Same Author: *Quick as a Cricket* (1982) in the RAL.

I GO WITH MY FAMILY TO GRANDMA'S

by Riki Levinson
New York: E.P Dutton, 1986

illustrated by Diane Goode
29 pages

Grades: K-3   **ESL Level:** beginner, intermediate
Genre: picture book, historical fiction

Vocabulary: extended family, places in the community—urban, transportation, colors
Grammar: simple present tense, prepositional phrases of place and of instrument, adjectives
Patterns: repeated sentence patterns and format

The pictures tell the story of a large extended family and their pleasures of coming together at grandma's. It is told in the first person, from the grandchildren's perspective. The early 20th century setting in New York City adds an enriching historical and urban dimension. The text is limited, with easy syntax and numerous repeated patterns. All of this, plus the full illustrations, recommend it as a read-aloud. Especially amusing are the last two illustrations, which capture both the hectic preparation for the family photograph and the serene final product. No words are necessary, but it is likely to stimulate much conversation! This joyful book affirms the value of extended families everywhere.

Related Book: *Over the River and Through the Woods* (Child, 1974) in the RAL.

Book By the Same Author: *Watch the Stars Come Out* (1985)

LITTLE RED RIDING HOOD

by Trina Schart Hyman
New York: Holiday House, 1983

32 pages

Grades: K-3, 2-5   **ESL Level: intermediate, advanced**
Genre: picture book—fairy tale
Ethnic Identity: European

Vocabulary: family—grandmother; household, food, body, places in the community—country; natural environment—forest
Grammar: past tense, exclamatory sentences
Patterns: complex sentences, dialogue

This exquisite edition of this classic fairy tale was justly awarded a Caldecott Honor. The language of the text closely mirrors the original translation, providing it with a familiar ring. The syntax is quite difficult for SL students, with two to three paragraphs of text per page. The familiarity of the story, combined with the detailed illustrations make this challenging but access-ible to intermediate ESL students. Ultimately, it is the magnificent illustrations which set this edition apart and justify its presentation in a read-aloud session. The earthen hues of the palette create a gentle tone and the distinctive borders add to the homey mood. Watch the facial expressions; they are captivating. This is a beautiful work of art to be enjoyed by all ages.

Related Books: *Little Red Riding Hood* (Marshall, 1987) offers a more whimsical edition; *The Three Little Pigs* (Brenner, 1972) presents another hungry wolf.

Related Book By Same Illustrator: *Rapunzel* (1982) in the RAL.

SISTERS

by David McPhail
New York: Harcourt Brace Jovanovich, 1984   27 pages

Grades: K-3   **ESL Level:** beginner
Genre: picture book

Vocabulary: daily activities, opposites
Grammar: infinitives, past tense, auxiliary verb—*to be*
Patterns: repeated format

Sisters don't always get along, some have even been known to fight furiously. This little book relates how two young sisters survive their differences and grow through their shared interests and mutual love. It seems a rather adult perspective on sibling relationships, yet it does affirm the positive. It also provides a model for less than ideal sisters, or siblings in general.

The book is small, limiting its viewing audience to groups of six. The text is minimal, no more than a sentence per page, making it appropriate for beginners. The black and white line drawings help this audience by illustrating each of the actions in the text. It is a sweet book.

Related Book: *The Pain and the Great One* (Blume, 1974) presents a more cynical approach to siblings, also in picture book format.

Book By the Same Author: *Farm Morning* (1985)

TIKKI TIKKI TEMBO

by Arlene Mosel   illustrated by Blair Lent
New York: Holt, Rinehart and Winston, 1968, 1989   45 pages

Grades: K-3   **ESL Level:** intermediate, advanced
Genre: picture book—folktale
Ethnic Identity: Asian-Chinese

Vocabulary: ordinal numbers, names, natural environments, places in the community—rural
Grammar: present perfect tense, conjunctions
Patterns: repeated phrases and sentence patterns, compound sentences

This popular, "pourquoi" story humorously relates how the Chinese came to give all their children short names. The delightful illustrations by the award-winning artist sets the folktale in rural China, providing a flavor for both the characters and the environment. Children delight in the numerous repetitions of the oldest son's long name. It is interesting how they seem to learn that sooner than basic grammatical rules! The book is laced with other predictable patterns as well. Nevertheless, its long sentences and unusual length for a traditional picture book suggest it for more advanced K-3 students and/or for those with good listening skills. It's also a great source for teaching the present perfect tense! Enjoy it with the kids!

Related Book: *The Emperor and the Kite* (Yolen, 1967) is another classic and beautifully illustrated Chinese folktale.

YEH-SHEN

by Ai-Ling Louie
New York: Putnam Publishing Group (Philomel Books), 1982

illustrated by Ed Young
31 pages

Grades: 2-5, 4-8   **ESL Level:** intermediate, advanced
Genre: picture book—folk tale
Ethnic Identity: Asian-Chinese

Vocabulary: family, clothing
Grammar: adverbial clauses, adverbs
Patterns: complex sentences

Yeh-Shen is the Chinese Cinderella story. In fact, it can claim to be the original Cinderella, based on the author's research, which indicates that the Chinese version predates the European one by over 1000 years. Questions of originality aside, this is a beautifully told story, enhanced by the authentic illustrations of Ed Young.

However, it does have limitations as a read-aloud for SL students. The shimmering illustrations, drawn across Chinese panels, do not clearly explain the text, which is set within the panels. Without the visual aids, the syntactically challenging text becomes even more difficult to understand. In addition, there is a lot of text per page. These problems can be offset by using this version in conjunction with a more clearly illustrated Cinderella, such as the one by Galdone. This also presents an interesting cross-cultural sharing.

Related Book: *Cinderella* (Galdone, 1978)

MUFARO'S BEAUTIFUL DAUGHTERS

by John Steptoe
New York: Lothrop, Lee & Shepard, 1987

31 pages

Grades: 2-5, 4-8   **ESL Level:** intermediate
Genre: picture book—folk tale
Ethnic Identity: African

Vocabulary: family, feelings—jealousy; places in the community—rural
Grammar: adverbial clauses, conditionals
Patterns: dialogue

This African folktale tells of two beautiful sisters. One, however, is jealous of the other's loving nature. As in the related European tales, Grimm's "The Little Hut in the Forest" and "Beauty and the Beast," the kind sister loves an ugly creature, in this tale a snake. He later magically transforms to a handsome prince, whom she happily marries. With older students, it is challenging to compare these tales cross-culturally. Steptoe offers a visually magnificent book, steeped in the warmth and pride of African culture. The fine details of dress, landscape and artifacts authenticate the Zimbabwe region of southern Africa. It is a treat for the eyes and well deserving of its Caldecott Honor award and its inclusion in the PBS *Reading Rainbow* program.

For those times when you can't read-aloud yourself, consider the read-along book and cassette version from Weston Woods.

Related Book: *Beauty and the Beast* (Mayer, 1978) in the RAL.

RAPUNZEL

by Barbara Rogasky   illustrated by Trina Schart Hyman
New York: Holiday House, 1982   31 pages

Grades: 4-8   **ESL Level:** intermediate, advanced
Genre: picture book—fairy tale
Ethnic Identity: European

Vocabulary: family, household, feelings, natural environment—forest
Grammar: past tense, conditional sentences, verbs of emotion, adverbial clauses
Patterns: repeated sentence (two-line chant)

Here is the classic fairy tale of Rapunzel, the lovely girl who is raised by a witch and locked up in a lonely forest tower before being rescued by a handsome prince. Rogasky has faithfully retold Grimm's tale, developing it into a very full and satisfying picture book for an upper elementary audience. Every other page contains a full half column of text unobtrusively interwoven with Hyman's dramatic illustrations. The warm earth colors, interspersed with splashes of red and set within delicate borders create a visually strong effect. It is the maturity of the illustrations as well as the detailed text which suggest its appropriateness for older children. Rapunzel matures into a beautiful adolescent and young mother. Of course, she and her prince live happily ever after!

Related Book: *Rumpelstiltskin* (Zelinsky, 1986 or Galdone, 1985)

Related Book By Same Illustrator: *Little Red Riding Hood* (Hyman, 1983) in the RAL.

THE SPRING OF BUTTERFLIES AND OTHER FOLKTALES OF CHINA'S MINORITY PEOPLES

by He Liyi   illustrated by Pan Aiqing and Li Zhoa
New York: Lothrop, Lee & Shepard, 1985   144 pages

Grades: 2-5, 4-8   **ESL Level:** intermediate
Genre: folk tales, short stories
Ethnic Identity: Asian-Chinese

Vocabulary: family, royalty, magical creatures, animals
Grammar: adverbial clauses, past tense
Patterns: complex sentences, dialogue

These 14 folktales come from the minority people of China, who have their own distinct customs and language. Translated by a member of one such group, the tales exude the values of minority people worldwide. They speak proudly of honesty being rewarded, of goodness triumphing over evil, of true love enduring even into death and of poverty overcoming wealth, all with a little help from magical creatures. The stories are rich with the individual cultures, yet with their universal themes, they do not seem foreign. Most are family or love stories. Their length, varying from 3 to 10 pages, makes them convenient for read-aloud sessions of under 15 minutes.

The exquisite illustrations, done by two young Chinese artists, reflect the stories' origins. Each story receives one full-page, color painting. In addition, the entire book, from the moving biographical notes about the author to the stylized design of the chapter headings, is high quality. It reflects a lot of care.

Related Book: *Treasure Mountain, Folktales from Southern China* (Sadler, 1982)—six tales, each about 10 pages long.

THE BROCADED SLIPPER AND OTHER VIETNAMESE FOLKTALES

by Lynette Dyer Vuong
New York: Lippincott, 1982

illustrated by Vo-Dinh Mai
111 pages

Grades: 2-5, 4-8   **ESL Level:** intermediate, advanced
Genre: folk tales, short stories
Ethnic Identity: Asian-Indochinese

Vocabulary: family, life passages
Grammar: past tense
Patterns: dialogue

This collection of five Vietnamese folktales brings to life the people and atmosphere of the olden days. Listeners will be able to identify universal folk themes and scenarios in these stories. Included are Vietnamese versions of Cinderella, Thumbelina, Rip Van Winkle and the Frog Prince.

The stories are long, between 15 and 25 pages each, yet the plots and syntax are straightforward and clear. Because of the length and scattered illustrations, they require good listening skills. Ideally, each should be completed in one sitting. The print is large enough to encourage students to read these independently as well. The author's introduction, story notes and Vietnamese pronunciation guide provide helpful resource material. Well-done.

Related Books: *Toad is the Uncle of Heaven* (Lee, 1985) in the RAL. Also, *Turtle Power* (National Asian Center for Bilingual Education, 1983), a single Vietnamese folktale written in both Vietnamese and English language with picture book format.

Books By the Same Illustrator: *The Land I Lost: Adventures of a Boy in Vietnam* (1982) and *Angel Child, Dragon Child* (1983), both in the RAL.

TALES OF A FOURTH GRADE NOTHING

by Judy Blume
New York: E.P. Dutton, 1972

illustrated by Roy Doty
120 pages

Grades: 2-5   **ESL Level:** intermediate
Genre: fiction—long novel, contemporary realistic fiction

Vocabulary: family, household, places in the community—urban; feelings
Grammar: exclamatory sentences, action verbs
Patterns: dialogue

In this modern classic, ten year old Peter Hatcher tells about his family, concentrating on his greatest problem—his two-year old brother, Fudge. The incidents are clever and the language uncomplicated. The book reads quickly and is hilarious. Judy Blume is a gifted writer. Any school-age child with a younger sibling will easily identify with the feelings, if not the actual episodes. In addition, the urban environment will be familiar to many ESL students.

Each of the ten chapters covers a separate experience, providing convenient stopping points for read-aloud purposes. The chapters also can be used individually for dramatic readings or developed into short plays. This has all the ingredients for a great read-aloud! A sure hit!

Books By the Same Author: Judy Blume has written many popular novels for preteens and teens. They cover various family and personal topics, some in a controversial manner. One benign one, included in the RAL, is *The One in the Middle is the Green Kangaroo* (1967).

THE SUMMER OF THE SWANS

by Betsy Byars   illustrated by Ted CoConis
New York: Penguin (Viking Press), 1970, 1981   142 pages

Grades: 6-8   **ESL Level:** advanced
Genre: fiction—long novel, contemporary realistic fiction

Vocabulary: family, household, friends, places in the community, natural environments—
    mountains, forests, ponds
Grammar: adverbial clauses, action verbs, past tense
Patterns: compound sentences, informal language, dialogues

Sara has a hard time being fourteen. She feels ambivalent and embarrassed about "every-thing," especially herself and her family. Her big orange sneakers, for example, both intrigue and disgust her. It doesn't help to have an older, pretty sister and a younger retarded brother, Charlie.

This is a novel about Sara's coming of age, of her discovering that she can be herself and still fit in. It is also a story of an untraditional family and their anguish when Charlie wanders off and becomes hopelessly lost. Altogether, it is strong, vivid and very gripping. Because of the diverse strands and complex language, it should be reserved for older and more advanced SL students. It definitely deserves the Newbery Medal it was awarded. Highly recommended!

Books By the Same Author: Byars is a popular author, focusing on 4th-8th grade interests in the genre of realistic fiction (intermediate-advanced ESL level required). Her books include *The 18th Emergency* (1973), about a class bully and *Cracker Jackson* (1985), about spousal abuse.

Life Passages

THE TENTH GOOD THING ABOUT BARNEY

by Judith Viorst   illustrated by Erik Blegvad
New York: Macmillan (Antheneum), 1971, 1988   25 pages

Grades: K-3   **ESL Level:** intermediate
Genre: picture book—concept book

Vocabulary: death, emotions, gardening
Grammar: past tense, auxiliary verb—*to be*, adjectives
Patterns: repeated word and sentence patterns

This is a sensitive little book about the death of a young boy's cat. As a family, they observe the customs—mourning, burial, and adjustment. To help focus on Barney's life, Mother encourages her son to think of ten good things about Barney and to share these at the burial in the backyard. He can think of only nine . . . until the end, when his father helps him understand Barney's role as part of nature's cycle.

This is a very useful book to share with primary age children who have lost an animal and even a person dear to them. The topic is somber but the book isn't. The process of affirming one's own loved ones by naming their special qualities, modeled so well in the book, provides an excellent follow-up activity. It gives children a positive way to remember.

Book By the Same Author: *Alexander and the Terrible, Horrible, No Good, Very Bad Day* (1972) in the RAL.

THE TOOTH FAIRY

by Elinor Gregor   illustrated by Winfield Coleman
Hayward, CA: Janus Books (Alemany Press), 1983   32 pages

Grades: K-3   **ESL Level:** beginner, intermediate
Genre: picture book—concept book
Ethnic Identity: multiethnic

Vocabulary: teeth, friends
Grammar: adverbs, adverbial clauses
Patterns: dialogue, repeated format

This large-size book captures the excitement a young girl feels when she loses her first tooth. It also captures her confusion as to which custom to follow—her familiar English one about a tooth fairy, or the Korean, Indian or African ones of her friends. In the story, each child briefly explains their tradition concerning the loss of first teeth. Leah admires them all, but still, she must choose one to follow. Let the children guess how she solves the problem or how they would solve it. Then read the ending to find Leah's solution. This simple book with large black and white line drawings builds cross-cultural understanding. There *is* more than one right way!

As a follow-up mini-research assignment, have the students investigate how other cultures observe this life passage. This usually involves interviews and oral history, two basic learning tools.

Related Books: *Loose Tooth* (Kroll, 1984) and *Tooth Fairy* (Wood, 1989)

THE GIVING TREE

by Shel Silverstein
New York: Harper & Row, 1964, 1988   52 pages

Grades: 4-8   **ESL Level:** beginner
Genre: picture book

Vocabulary: trees, life passages
Grammar: conditionals, conjunctions, past tense, imperatives
Patterns: repeated refrain and format, simple sentences

This is a simple but poignant allegory about the give and take of friendship during the different stages of one's life. It easily leads to interesting discussions on values and numerous writing topics on these themes.

It is an excellent choice for adolescent beginner ESL students because sophisticated topics are covered in easy syntax and packaged in a picture book format. Silverstein's cartoon-like, black and white line drawings depict the different life stages with a mature sense of humor. For all ages, 9 to 99.

Books By the Same Author: *Where the Sidewalk Ends* (1974) in the RAL and *A Light in the Attic* (1981), both collections of Silverstein's poetry.

KNOTS ON A COUNTING ROPE

by Bill Martin, Jr. and John Archambault   illustrated by Ted Rand
New York: Henry Holt, 1966, 1987   32 pages

Grades: K-3, 2-5   **ESL Level:** intermediate
Genre: picture book
Ethnic Identity: Native American

Vocabulary: family, senses, animals—horse; handicap—blindness;
Grammar: future tense, reported speech
Patterns: simple and compound sentences, repeated word patterns

On a dark, starry night, a Native American grandfather and grandson sit together by a campfire, warmed by its glow. The boy asks, "Tell me the story again, grandfather. Tell me who I am." The book relives the boy's life passages, especially his traumatic birth. As each part is told, another knot is firmly tied on the counting rope. Both the storytelling and knot tying strengthen the boy's self-confidence, as he learns to face his greatest challenge—his blindness. The tender and richly authentic Native American illustrations further enhance a very poignant text. A *Reading Rainbow* selection.

This is a wonderful story for reading aloud because of the ongoing dialogue between the two characters. When a single person is reading it, use two different voices to differentiate the characters. This also offers a challenge for two advanced students to present orally.

Related Book: *The Girl Who Loved Wild Horses* (Goble, 1978) in the RAL.

Book by Same Authors: *Barn Dance!* (1986), another *Reading Rainbow* selection.

CHARLOTTE'S WEB

by E.B. White   illustrated by Garth Williams
New York: Harper & Row, 1952   184 pages

Grades: 2-5   **ESL Level:** intermediate, advanced
Genre: fiction—long novel, modern fantasy

Vocabulary: farm, animals—farm; life passages-birth, death
Grammar: past tense, action verbs
Patterns: dialogue

This is one of America's best-loved children's books. It tells of Fern, a young farm girl who so loves the runt of the pig litter that her father saves him and gives him to her as her pet. When Wilbur grows, he is moved to their uncle's farm, where he lives in the barn with other animals. The most special is Charlotte, a beautiful, large spider. She offers Wilbur friendship and ultimately gives him the greatest gift of all, her life, to save his. This story is many wonderful things—at times funny, at others sad, and always absorbing. Interwoven through the animal and human characters are the major life passages—birth, friendship and death.

This is a classic read-aloud. Children are ready for it long before they can read at this level. Although it is a full length children's novel, it is not difficult to understand. The chapters are relatively short (about 10 pages each) and the numerous dialogues move the action quickly. Childhood is not quite complete with hearing this at least once. Adults treasure it too.

Books By the Same Author: *Stuart Little* (1945), *Trumpet of the Swans* (1970)

A TASTE OF BLACKBERRIES

by Doris Buchanan Smith   illustrated by Charles Robinson
New York: Harper & Row (Thomas Y. Crowell), 1973, 1988   58 pages

Grades: 2-5   **ESL Level:** intermediate
Genre: fiction—short novel, contemporary realistic fiction

Vocabulary: friendship, emotions
Grammar: questions—*yes/no* and *wh-*, subject pronouns
Patterns: informal language, dialogue

Jamie did outrageous things. He was sometimes exasperating and embarrassing, but he was always fun. And he was the best friend and next door neighbor of the narrator . . . until he died accidentally, from an allergic reaction to a bee sting. This short novel addresses the very difficult topic of death of a friend with sensitivity and directness. It is written specifically for elementary age students.

If there is a death of a child in your class or in the school, reading this aloud is an excellent way to help the children begin to deal with it. The unnamed narrator is very courageous. The author skillfully allows him to experience the recognized stages of mourning: denial, anger, guilt and acceptance.

This is not an easy book to read, but an important one, for the appropriate situation. Although the book has chapters, it is best read all in one long sitting of about 45 minutes—1 hour. Allow time afterward for discussion.

Related Books: *The Tenth Good Thing About Barney* (Viorst, 1971) for K-3, and *Bridge to Terabithia* (Patterson, 1978) for 4-8, both in the RAL.

RAMONA FOREVER

by Beverly Cleary   illustrated by Alan Tiegreen
New York: William Morrow, 1984   182 pages

Grades: 2-5   **ESL Level:** intermediate
Genre: fiction—long novel, contemporary realistic fiction

Vocabulary: family, sibling rivalry, wedding, household
Grammar: past tense, contractions
Patterns: dialogue

Spunky "blunderful" Ramona! This very grown-up third grader certainly doesn't take life lying down! This is a lively book, filled with funny moments, anticipation and a satisfying ending. Ramona shows us that it isn't always easy growing up. She's a very ordinary, but very wonderful modern-day heroine!

This Ramona novel makes a good read-aloud because it covers topics most students can identify with: being a latchkey kid, fighting with your pre-teen sibling, burying a beloved pet, anxiously awaiting a new baby and planning your favorite aunt's wedding (plus being in it!). As well as good stories to hear, these also provide material for follow-up activities.

Ten television episodes of *Ramona*, some taken from this book, make a good companion to the novel. They are 30 minutes each and available through Churchill Films.

Related Books: *You'll Soon Grow into Them* (Hutchins, 1983) for K-3, and *The One in the Middle is the Green Kangaroo* (Blume, 1967) for 2-5, both in the RAL.

Related Books by the Same Author: There are six other Ramona and Beezus books. Two of them, *Ramona and her Father* (1977) and *Ramona Quimby, Age 8* (1981) have been named Newbery Honor Books.

Books By the Same Author: Beverly Cleary is both prolific and popular. She has written 28 novels for the elementary-age audience, many of which have received awards (including *Dear Mr. Henshaw*, 1984 Newbery Medal). Not all, however, are good read-alouds.

SARAH, PLAIN AND TALL

by Patricia MacLachlan
New York: Harper & Row, 1985   58 pages

Grades: 2-5, 4-8   **ESL Level:** intermediate
Genre: fiction—short novel, historical fiction

Vocabulary: farm, animals, household, family
Grammar: expressions of future time—*will*; modal auxiliary verbs—*can*, *must*; possessive
      adjectives
Patterns: short sentences, simple sentence patterns, dialogues, informal language

Their mother has died giving birth to Caleb, some years ago. As we enter the novel, Caleb and his older sister Anna are yearning for a new mother and Papa for a new wife. Their simple pioneer life on the American Plains has become joyless; no one sings anymore. So, father writes away for a "mail order bride." Thus arrives Sarah, who comes from far away Maine and who describes herself as "plain and tall." Their efforts to build a new family are tentative and touching. This is a fast paced family story with the dramatic tension of whether she will really stay remaining strong until the last page. By not assigning chronological ages to the children, Papa or Sarah, the reader's images remain open-ended, thus extending the age-range of the audience. This is good quality children's literature, well-deserving of the 1985 Newbery award. It deeply reassures the audience of our American dream, not only in the pioneer days of old, but even more poignantly, in our often broken homes of today. A new classic!

Related Books: *Little House on the Prairie Books* (Wilder, 1973), a nine volume set, originally written in the 1930s.

HOUSE/HOME

HOP ON POP

by Dr. Seuss
New York: Random House, 1963, 1987 edition includes a cassette   64 pages

Grades: Pre K-1, K-3   **ESL Level:** beginner
Genre: easy reader, picture book

Vocabulary: household
Patterns: rhyming, initial consonants

Dr. Seuss cleverly uses rhymes and zany illustrations to give beginning readers a book to enjoy. On each page, the rhyming words are in capital letters with bold print, so the students focus on them first. There is also a short, additional sentence underneath. The colorful drawings illustrate the words. Each vignette is independent, with no real attempt to string together a unified story. This makes it almost too long to hold the children's (and certainly an adult's) attention for a single read-aloud session. It is best partially read-aloud to give the children the rhyming model. Then, set them up for oral reading practice in small groups. Or have them listen to the cassette and follow along with their books. Multiple copies are useful for these activities.

Related Books By Same Author: *One fish, two fish, red fish, blue fish* (1960) and *Green Eggs and Ham* (1960), both easy reading, rhyming books and both in the RAL.

Books by the Same Author: *The Butter Battle Book* (1984) is a longer, rhyming picture book about the modern weaponry build-up, for 4th-8th graders. It works well as part of a social studies unit.

IN A PEOPLE HOUSE

by Theo LeSieg   illustrated by Roy McKie
New York: Random House, 1972   26 pages

Grades: Pre K-1, K-3   **ESL Level:** beginner, intermediate
Genre: picture book—concept book; easy reader

Vocabulary: household, food
Grammar: nouns
Patterns: rhyming words and rhyming sentences

A little mouse gaily welcomes a visiting bird into a *People House,* where he lives, and shows him around. On their house tour, he identifies 65 common objects, including furniture, cooking utensils, food and clothing. Each item is independently illustrated and labeled. This is not as dull as it may sound because of the humorous illustrations and the clever rhymes and because the movement through the house functions as a loose plot.

Although it is identified as a beginning reader, much of this vocabulary is actually quite difficult to read. It works very well, when read aloud, as a vocabulary builder or as a review for a house/home unit. Be advised that this is not currently in print, but is still available in many libraries.

A DARK, DARK TALE

by Ruth Brown
New York: E.P. Dutton (Dial Books), 1981   27 pages

Grades: Pre K-1, K-3   **ESL Level:** beginner
Genre: picture book, mystery

Vocabulary: household, natural environment—woods
Grammar: prepositional phrases of place, existential sentence—*there was*
Patterns: repeated sentence pattern

Suspense is masterfully built in this spooky story, as the audience is mysteriously led through the rooms of a *Dark, Dark House* until it encounters . . . ! The richly textured illustrations further enhance the foreboding mood. But not to worry, the book pretends to be scarier than it really is, and children are generally amused rather than frightened by the ending. For read-aloud purposes, the story does generate dramatic reading. It also is easily comprehensible, repeating one basic sentence pattern, varied with different prepositional phrases. The lavishly detailed pictures provide helpful visual clues. This book is especially popular around Halloween time.

Related Book: *In a Dark, Dark Room and Other Scary Stories.* (Schwartz, 1984). This is an easy-reading version, but it is much shorter, with less dramatic illustrations. All around, it is less satisfying.

THIS IS THE HOUSE THAT JACK BUILT

by Liz Underhill
New York: Henry Holt, 1987   32 pages

Grades: K-3, 2-5   **ESL Level:** intermediate
Genre: picture book—nursery rhyme

Vocabulary: household, animals
Grammar: relative clauses, definite articles, nouns-singular, direct objects
Patterns: rhyming, rhythmical chants, cumulative repetitions

Students love the repeated patterns of this popular nursery rhyme, which dates from the mid 18th century. This stunning modern edition not only illustrates each line in exquisite detail, but also sets each scene in the different rooms of Jack's house. Its front and back covers lay out the architectural plans of Master Builder Jack. In this way the rhyme appeals to older students, as they try to fit the characters and scenes into the different rooms.

This nursery rhyme contains repetitions of numerous grammatical structures appropriate for intermediate SL students. This makes it a useful teaching tool as well as a visual and oral delight. The poem challenges its listeners to learn its lines and it provides internal devices, such as rhyming and cumulative repetitions, to help them do it. Encourage your students to try! It's enjoyment for children of all ages!

BORED-NOTHING TO DO!

by Peter Spier
New York: Doubleday, 1978, 1987   46 pages

Grades: K-3, 4-8   **ESL Level:** beginner
Genre: picture book, modern fantasy

Vocabulary: household, transportation—airplanes, engines
Grammar: nouns, simple present tense, third person agreement
Patterns: repeated format, dialogue, short sentences

Two teenage brothers secretly build an airplane with materials pirated from their family's everyday household objects. Much to their surprise, it actually flies! And so do they, as the pilots! Upon discovery, their parents don't know whether to be proud or angry. In fact, they are both! All this activity arises because they were bored, with nothing to do. This story, stimulating by itself, can additionally serve as a provocative introduction for talking or writing about what can arise from boredom.

The detailed and expressive illustrations largely tell the story. Each picture is enhanced by the minimal text which accompanies it—a word, phrase or short sentence. It is one of those needles in the haystack—an age-appropriate story for pre-teens with minimal language skills. Thanks, Peter Spier!

Books By the Same Author: Peter Spier is one of the most talented and prolific modern illustrators. Many of his topics and pictures are very useful for classroom use. The following are annotated in this RAL: *Fast-Slow, High-Low* (1972), *The Star-Spangled Banner* (1973), *Peter Spier's Christmas* (1983), *The Erie Canal* (1970) and *The Fox Went Out on a Chilly Night* (1961). Also, *Noah's Ark* (1978 Caldecott Award Winner).

AMELIA BEDELIA

by Peggy Parish   illustrated by Fritz Siebel
New York: Harper & Row, 1963, 1983   26 pages

Grades: 2-5   **ESL Level:** intermediate
Genre: picture book

Vocabulary: household, furniture, food
Grammar: action verbs-transitive; direct objects, imperative and exclamatory sentences
Patterns: idiomatic expressions, repeated format

One of the most difficult aspects of learning a second language is understanding its idiomatic expressions. At the expense of Amelia Bedelia, America's most popular maid, listeners are humorously introduced to common idioms concerning household chores and food preparation. For example, when Amelia Bedelia is asked to "change the towels" she cuts them into a new shape and when directed to "dust the furniture" she puts dust on it. Through her escapades, students begin to distinguish literal from figurative meanings. All ends happily enough with Mrs. Rogers explaining it all and with Mr. Rogers savoring her lemon pie.

Because domestic work is a common employment of many ESL students' parents and because Amelia, like them, is limited English proficient, some students may be sensitive to even this lighthearted depiction of her predicament. The issue is defused by Siebel's cartoon like drawings, which create a more old-fashioned setting.

Related Books By Same Author: There are more than ten *Amelia Bedelia* sequels. Two of them, *Play Ball, Amelia Bedelia* (1972) and *Amelia Bedelia's Family Album* (1988) are also included in this RAL.

THE STORIES JULIAN TELLS

by Ann Cameron   illustrated by Ann Strugnell
New York: Pantheon, 1981; Knopf, 1987   71 pages

Grades: 2-5   **ESL Level:** intermediate
Genre: short stories, easy reader
Ethnic Identity: Black American

Vocabulary: cooking, gardening, family, household
Grammar: questions—*wh* and *yes/no*, exclamatory sentences
Patterns: dialogue

Childhood is a time of mischief and imagination. The author captures this joyful essence through the story telling gifts of the narrator, Julian, a school-age black American. His gullible younger brother, Huey and his stern, but loving father compliment the lively cast of characters. Mother is there but not a major force.

The six separate stories read easily and each can be completed within a 10 minute read-aloud session. Each centers around a familiar household activity, for example cooking and gardening, but carry an unconventional twist, which makes for delightful listening.

All of the stories can be followed up with hands-on classroom experiences. Two of them shine in this area: one about cooking and eating pudding and another about making wishes on a homemade kite. Language experience stories provide further enrichment. As a different kind of follow-up, make the book available as an easy reader for intermediates.

Related Books: *The Knee-High Man* (Lester, 1972) and *The Tales of a Fourth Grade Nothing* (Blume, 1972), both in the RAL.

Related Books By Same Author: *More Stories Julian Tells* (1986) and *Julian's Glorious Summer* (1987).

Friendship

WHERE IS MY FRIEND?

by Betsy and Giulio Maestro
New York: Crown, 1976, 1987   31 pages

Grades: Pre K-1, K-3   **ESL Level:** beginner
Genre: picture book—concept book

Vocabulary: places in the community
Grammar: prepositions, prepositional phrases of place, past tense
Patterns: repeated format

Lovable Harriet the elephant searches for her friend all over town. This simple story line gives the authors the vehicle to introduce prepositions and prepositional phrases. It also helps them develop the concepts of space, direction and position. Intended as a mixture of story and concept, the book succeeds in meeting these goals. There is even a little suspense, as you don't know the identity of Harriet's friend until the final page.

The bright, uncluttered pictures appeal to young children. They can be seen easily by a large group. They also clearly describe the single sentence on each two-page scene. All in all, it is a good teaching tool and amusing book for young beginners.

Books By the Same Author: The Maestros have specialized in picture books that intend to teach. They call them "word concept books." Students don't realize they're learning. This is the best way! Two that are included in the RAL are *Around the Clock with Harriet* (1984) and *Traffic: A Book of Opposites* (1981).

FRIENDS

by Helme Heine
New York: Macmillan (Aladdin), 1982   30 pages

Grades: K-3   **ESL Level:** intermediate
Genre: picture book

Vocabulary: animals, places in the community—rural; values
Grammar: action verbs, past tense, prepositional phrases of place, adverbs of manner
Patterns: repeated refrain

"Good friends always stick together." This is the positive message of this modest picture book. This theme is repeated, with variations, according to the characters' different situations. And what delightful characters they are! There is Charlie Rooster, Johnny Mouse and fat Percy (the pig). The illustrations warmly capture the animals' friendship and their rather pleasant life together. The book does not present any serious conflicts to be resolved. Rather it bounces along in pleasant vignettes which affirm cooperation and fellowship. These precious qualities certainly deserve all the reinforcement they can get. This book does this with joy and simplicity, in only one to three sentences per page.

Related Books By Same Author: *The Three Little Friends Series* (1982): *The Alarm Clock, The Racing Cart* and *The Visitor*.

HAPPY BIRTHDAY TO ME

by Anne and Harlow Rockwell
New York: Macmillan, 1981

23 pages

Grades: Pre K-1, K-3   **ESL Level:** beginner
Genre: picture book—concept book
Ethnic Identity: multiethnic

Vocabulary: birthday, household
Grammar: simple present tense, action verbs, subject and possessive pronouns-first person
Patterns: short, simple sentences

In this simple book, a young child celebrates his birthday with all the traditional activities, from blowing up balloons, to playing Pin the Tail on the donkey, to opening presents. The party culminates, of course, with eating cake and ice cream. All the way through, everyone seems to have a great time! Each scene is illustrated with ample detail. The book's small size limits its classroom use to groups of about six.

Teachers can use this book to develop vocabulary, to practice simple sentence patterns and to encourage children to share about their own birthday celebrations. As a final project, plan a class birthday party. This really builds a sense of community and the kids will remember it for years!

Related Books By the Same Authors: The authors have written eight other *My World Books* for young people, Pre-K -3. They are similar in size, format and content level.

Books by the Same Authors: This team has also written many other primary concept books. Ones included in the RAL are *Bear Child's Book of Hours* (1987), *The Supermarket* (1979), *My Doctor* (1973) and *Emergency Room* (1985).

JAMAICA'S FIND

by Juanita Havill
Boston: Houghton Mifflin, 1986

illustrated by Anne Sibley O'Brien
30 pages

Grades: K-3   **ESL Level:** intermediate
Genre: picture book
Ethnic Identity: Black American, multiethnic

Vocabulary: playground, feelings, household, family
Grammar: prepositional phrases of place, adverbial clauses, questions
Patterns: dialogues

Pretty little Jamaica has a child-size problem. She finds an adorable little stuffed animal in the park and wants to keep it for her own. Her family is sensitive and supportive, but it is Jamaica herself who figures out her own solution. Discussion of this book can lead into problem solving and other creative conflict activities.

In addition, the illustrations contribute positive role models, both of black Americans and of interracial friendship. The last picture of two happy friends-one black and one white-is particularly moving. This one small book does a lot!

Related Book: *Playgrounds* (Gibbons, 1985) in the RAL.

WHAT DO YOU SAY, DEAR?

by Sesyle Joslin   illustrated by Maurice Sendak
New York: Harper & Row, 1958, 1986   48 pages

Grades: K-3   **ESL Level:** beginner, intermediate
Genre: picture book—concept book

Vocabulary: greetings, manners
Grammar: *wh*-questions, present tense-simple present and present continuous
Patterns: dialogues, repeated sentence, question and answer sequence

What do you say when you bump into a crocodile on a crowded city street or when the Queen feeds you so much spaghetti that you don't fit into your chair anymore? From these and nine other delightfully absurd situations, conventional greetings and etiquette are suggested. Each scenario is presented on one page, ending with the repeated refrain, "What do you say dear?" The one line answer is given on the following page. This design encourages the students to guess the proper responses. Role playing can also be incorporated. The text describing the situations is somewhat complicated, and may need to be rephrased for beginner ESL students. The cartoon-like illustrations of Caldecott Medal winner Maurice Sendak lend additional humor to the already funny text. It is thoroughly enjoyable! Plus the children do learn manners!

Related Book By Same Author: *What Do You Do, Dear?* (1961)

A LETTER TO AMY

by Ezra Jack Keats
New York: Harper & Row, 1968, 1984   28 pages

Grades: K-3   **ESL Level:** intermediate
Genre: picture book
Ethnic Identity: Black American

Vocabulary: friendship, birthday, weather—rain, places in the community—urban
Grammar: past tense, adverbs of manner
Patterns: complex sentence patterns, dialogue

School-age children often become embarrassed about friendships with the opposite sex. So it is with Peter, who secretly sends a letter to invite Amy to his birthday party. During the read-aloud session, encourage the children to guess if she will come. A follow-up discussion helps young children to explore their feelings about friendships with girls and boys.

The illustrations dramatize the text by expressing Peter's confused feelings and by capturing the ominous weather and the birthday party ending. The text and the illustrations combined also introduce much basic vocabulary.

Related Books By Same Author: *Peter's Chair* (1967), *The Snowy Day* (1962), and *Whistle for Willie* (1964). Peter and his dog Willie are the main characters in these books as well, all set in the same urban environment. Only *The Snowy Day* is included in the RAL.

Book by the Same Author: *John Henry, An American Legend* (1965) in the RAL.

BEST FRIENDS

compiled by Lee Bennett Hopkins   illustrated by James Watt
New York: Harper & Row, 1986   48 pages

Grades: K-3, 2-5   **ESL Level:** intermediate
Genre: poetry

Vocabulary: friendship, emotions
Patterns: rhyming, repeated word patterns

"Lying atop each other-on a sled-one boy to the other said: Even if I live to one-hundred-and-ten, you will always be my fren." This tender, short poem, "Atop," by Prince Redcloud, is one of eighteen on friendship selected for this collection. Others include gems by Jack Prelutsky, Judith Viorst and Langston Hughes. Each is short, from four to twelve lines, and independently illustrated. Collectively, they cover the range of experiences involved in friendship—the laughing, the playing and the fun as well as the less positive memories. The poems also touch upon the emotions of friendship, including poignant poems about anger and sadness. A few deal with moving away and missing friends, but the overall mood is upbeat. The themes are universal and the vocabulary and illustrations contemporary. These easy poems on a familiar topic serve as a nice introduction to the genre of poetry.

MY BEST FRIEND DUC TRAN
MEETING A VIETNAMESE-AMERICAN FAMILY

by Diane MacMillan and Dorothy Freeman   illustrated by Mary Jane Begin
New York: Julian Messner/Simon & Schuster, 1987   42 pages

Grades: 2-5   **ESL Level:** intermediate
Genre: short stories
Ethnic Identity: Asian-Indochinese

Vocabulary: extended family, community, customs, food, friendship
Grammar: questions—yes/no and wh-, past tense
Patterns: dialogue

For young people, honoring one's culture of origin yet adjusting to America's is a delicate balance. This book addresses that by sensitively explaining how the Vietnamese live in the United States. The authors use the friendship of two 4th grade boys-one American and one Vietnamese to introduce the Vietnamese-American culture and customs. Based on extensive research by the authors, it is an interesting blend of factual information in a fictional setting. It is also an unusual length—too long for a picture book yet not complete enough for a full novel. But what this book lacks in dramatic conflict, it makes up in cross-cultural understanding. The varied and complex language structures limit its use to intermediate and advanced ESL students. It is ideal for sharing in classrooms with both Vietnamese and American students.

Related Books in the Same Series: *My Best Friend Mee-Yung Kim: Meeting a Korean-American Family* (1989), *My Best Friend, Martha Rodriguez: Meeting a Mexican-American Family* (1986) and *My Best Friend Elena Pappas: Meeting a Greek-American Family* (1986).

THE COURAGE OF SARAH NOBLE

by Alice Dalgliesh   illustrated by Leonard Weisgard
New York: Macmillan (Aladdin Books), 1954, 1987   54 pages

Grades: 2-5   **ESL Level:** intermediate
Genre: fiction—short novel, historical fiction
Ethnic Identity: Native American

Vocabulary: natural environments, household
Grammar: auxiliary verb—*to be*, past tense
Patterns: dialogue, repeated sentence

This classic pioneer story of faith, courage and friendship has a timeless appeal. Not an action-packed thriller, this is a modest novel about a very admirable young person. Based on true events, in 1707 eight year-old Sarah Noble accompanied her father into the colonial wilderness of Connecticut to build their new family home. Wild animals and Indians were just two of her very real fears, especially when her father leaves to bring the rest of the family. Yet her mother's advice, "Keep up your courage, Sarah Noble" and her own inner faith carry Sarah through some remarkable adventures.

This straightforward story offers a gentle introduction to the fascinating world of historical fiction. Its brief chapters and overall short length recommend it as a read-aloud. Its medium-size print and generous white space on each page suggest it as a follow-up independent reader. The small but ample pictures create a warm, soft mood, which enhance the attractiveness of this short novel. A Newbery Honor Book.

Related Books: *The Sign of the Beaver* (Spear, 1983) is a pioneer story of this same era for older students. *Wagon Wheels* (Brenner, 1978) is a pioneer story of a later era for this same age, in the RAL. See also *Stone Fox* (Gardiner, 1980), on courage, in the RAL.

BRIDGE TO TERABITHIA

by Katherine Paterson   illustrated by Donna Diamond
New York: Harper & Row (Thomas Y. Crowell), 1977, 1987   128 pages

Grades: 4-8   **ESL Level:** intermediate, advanced
Genre: fiction—long novel, contemporary realistic fiction

Vocabulary: friendship, feelings, death, school, family, places in the community—rural
Grammar: past tense
Patterns: dialogues

Students new to American culture will easily identify with the two main characters in this novel. Although both are Anglo Americans in a country setting, one is an urban transplant and the other a rural misfit. Together these 5th graders, a girl and a boy, form a special friendship and create their own magical kingdom, Terabithia. Their experiences at school and with their peers are vibrant and their emotions are strong and real. Every aspect of this moving novel, especially its traumatic ending, recommends it as an outstanding read-aloud. Juvenile literature doesn't get much better than this! A Newbery medalist.

Book By the Same Author: Katherine Patterson has written many excellent pre-adolescent novels, including *The Great Gilly Hopkins* (1978).

INDIAN IN THE CUPBOARD

by Lynne Reid Banks   illustrated by Brock Cole
New York: Doubleday, 1980   181 pages

Grades: 4-8   **ESL Level:** intermediate, advanced
Genre: fiction—long novel, modern fantasy
Ethnic Identity: European—British, Native American

Vocabulary: family, friendship, household
Grammar: questions, exclamatory sentences
Patterns: dialogues, nonstandard language—some British English, some Native American
English

The story starts, innocently enough, when a British boy named Omri receives a plastic Indian, a cupboard and a little key for his 9th birthday. The adventure soon begins when the Indian comes to life in the cupboard and Omri befriends him. Little Bear, the two inch Iroquois chief of another era, culture and country, is a fully developed character. The Indian man and British boy share a very endearing relationship, with Omri forced to make life decisions about Little Bear's very existence.

Because Omri acts so maturely, his chronological age of nine does not diminish the novel's attraction for older students. In addition, Omri has two older brothers, adding the realistic element of sibling rivalry.

What makes this story so satisfying is the author's ingenious blend of the genres within children's fiction—fantasy, adventure and humor and realism. It is also an excellent read-aloud. The story moves quickly, engaging the audience with numerous realistic encounters. The masterful use of dialogue also quickens the pace and builds suspense. OUTSTANDING!

Related Book By Same Author: *The Return of the Indian* (1986). This sequel is still exciting, but not as special as the original.

Emotions/Values

LEO THE LATE BLOOMER

by Robert Kraus   illustrated by Jose Aruego
New York: Harper & Row (Thomas Y. Crowell), 1970, 1987   28 pages

Grades: K-3, 4-8   **ESL Level:** beginner
Genre: picture book—fable

Vocabulary: family, emotions
Grammar: auxiliary verb—*to be(was)*, modal auxiliary verb—*could,* negation, pronouns—*he*
Patterns: short sentences, repeated word and sentence patterns

Poor Leo. He couldn't do anything right. "What's wrong?" his impatient father wanted to know. "Nothing," sighed his mother. "Leo is just a late bloomer." Unwatched, Leo does bloom, as do most of us, given the time and a nurturing environment.

This simple story, written with just a sentence or two per page and graced with colorful illustrations of a lion family, was intended for younger children. But treated as an allegory, it appeals to all ages. It can be especially comforting for students frustrated with the early stages of second language acquisition.

Related Book by Same Author: *Whose Mouse Are You?* (1970) in the RAL.

ALEXANDER AND THE TERRIBLE, HORRIBLE, NO GOOD, VERY BAD DAY

by Judith Viorst   illustrated by Ray Cruz
New York: Macmillan (Atheneum), 1972, 1987   29 pages

Grades: K-3, 2-5   **ESL Level:** intermediate
Genre: picture book—concept book

Vocabulary: feelings, household, places in the community—town
Grammar: conjunctions, adjectives
Patterns: repeated word pattern

This is just the book to choose for a "terrible, horrible, no good, very bad day." By hearing about Alexander's misadventures, our own don't seem so terrible. Nor do we feel so alone. The author's premise is that everyone has bad days, but they can be improved if you talk about them. Even older children enjoy this story because of its message, which is delivered with humor. After the read-aloud session, create your own class version of this story. This can be done through round-robin story telling and/or as a cooperative writing project. Both the book and the follow-up activities are fun and very therapeutic!

Book By the Same Author: *The Tenth Good Thing About Barney* (1971) in the RAL.

NOBODY'S PERFECT, NOT EVEN MY MOTHER

by Nora Simon   illustrated by Dora Leder
Niles, IL: Albert Whitman, 1981   30 pages

Grades: K-3, 2-5   **ESL Level:** beginner, intermediate
Genre: picture book—concept book
Ethnic Identity: multiethnic

Vocabulary: emotions, family, household
Grammar: simple present tense, third person agreement, pronouns—first and third persons
Patterns: repeated sentence patterns, repeated format

This concept book affirms everyone's efforts and deals openly with feelings, frustrations and failures. It also carries the important message that "even though everybody's good at some things, nobody's perfect!" The brief text and warm illustrations capture numerous family, work and school situations with a page or two devoted to each vignette. There is even one scene about learning English as a second language.

It is somewhat confusing when the authors use the first person to describe unrelated situations with different characters. Despite this, the book succeeds in directly addressing a basic human struggle and in suggesting sensitive ways to encourage each other. It's very upbeat and affirming. It also lends itself well to a class discussion of feelings.

SAM

by Ann Herbert Scott   illustrated by Symeon Shimin
New York: McGraw-Hill, 1967   33 pages

Grades: Pre K-1, K-3   **ESL Level:** intermediate, advanced
Genre: picture book
Ethnic Identity: Black American

Vocabulary: emotions, family, household
Grammar: imperative, negative and exclamatory sentences
Patterns: repeated refrain

Young Sam wants to be part of the activities of his older siblings and his parents. But they are all busy and don't want to be disturbed. In frustration, Sam cries and cries. Only then, do they all realize how neglected he feels. Mother rallies them together, comforts Sam and finds him something special to do, just for someone his size, and right by her side. The rest of the family looks on approvingly. Ah, all's well that ends well.

Russian born Symeon Shimin's fine-lined black and white drawings are warmed with orange-gold coloration. They sensitively portray the black family and capture their emotions. The illustrations are powerful and add depth to an already touching story.

A HOLE IN THE DIKE

by Norma Green   illustrated by Eric Carle
New York: Harper & Row (Thomas Y. Crowell), 1974   32 pages

Grades: K-3, 2-5   **ESL Level:** intermediate
Genre: picture book, short story
Ethnic Identity: European—Dutch

Vocabulary: natural environments
Grammar: past tense, conjunctions
Patterns: simple and compound sentences

This colorful picture book retells the exciting story of a little Dutch boy who bravely saves his country, Holland, by holding his finger in the dike. The story resonates with values of courage and patriotism. It was first created by Mary Mapes Dodge, an American woman who had never been to Holland. She told it to her children, making it up as she went along. It was first published over 100 years ago, as part of her book, *Hans Brinker* or *The Silver Skates*. The story line remains clear, with the language and vocabulary offering challenges for SL students.

Eric Carle's illustrations authenticate the Dutch rural environment. They are also bright, large and full of attractive details. These qualities contribute to make this an excellent read-aloud choice.

Books by Same Illustrator: *Brown Bear, Brown Bear, What Do You See* (1983) and *The Very Hungry Caterpillar* (1970), both in the RAL.

FREDERICK'S FABLES

by Leo Lionni
New York: Pantheon Books, 1985   132 pages

Grades: K-3, 4-8   **ESL Level:** intermediate
Genre: fables, anthology

Vocabulary: animals, natural environments

This volume gathers together 13 of Lionni's popular animal fables. Having all these stories together enhances them, as does the introduction by Bruno Bettleheim, a noted child psychologist. Lionni has also taken care to maintain some of the important features of single volumes. The page size is as large as the originals, the texts are unabridged and the illustrations, which fill each page, have been carefully selected from the originals. Even though the stories are less than ten pages each, they do not seem cramped.

Lionni's fables affirm the individual and their unique gifts. Although no single moral appears at the end, as in Aesop's fables, the messages are clear. They celebrate strength of character. Smoothly integrated with their brilliantly colored illustrations, they also celebrate the beauty of our world and the power of the imagination. These are ageless stories to be read, reread and treasured.

Related Books By Same Author: Most of these stories can also be found as individual picture books.

IT COULD ALWAYS BE WORSE

by Margot Zemach
New York: Farrar, Straus and Giroux, 1976   27 pages

Grades: 2-5, 4-8   **ESL Level:** intermediate
Genre: picture book—fable
Ethnic Identity: European—Jewish

Vocabulary: farm animals, family
Grammar: imperative and exclamatory sentences, *yes/no* questions
Patterns: dialogue, repeated sentences

"Once upon a time in a small village a poor, unfortunate man lived with his mother, his wife, and his six children in a little one-room hut." All was not sweetness and light (surprise surprise!). The accommodations were crowded, the children noisy and everyone argued. Could it possibly get any worse? With the rabbi's "help," it does get much much worse, until . . . again following the rabbi's advice, all the additional animal "guests" leave. In comparison, the original family, by themselves again, are peaceful and happy. Such is the clear moral of this Yiddish tale: appreciate what you have for *It Could Always Be Worse.*

The drawings which fill each page are both humorous and lovely. Students who come from poor, crowded, rural conditions anywhere in the world can identify with this story and its dilemma. Fables work best for seven year olds and above. The moral seems lost on younger children.

Related Books: *"Could Be Worse"* (Stevenson, 1977) and *Too Much Noise* (McGovern, 1967) are two different versions of the same story in different settings.

AESOP'S FABLES

selected and illustrated by Michael Hague
New York: Holt, Rinehart and Winston, 1985   27 pages

Grades: 2-5, 4-8   **ESL Level:** intermediate, advanced
Genre: fables, anthology

Vocabulary: animals, values, places in the community
Grammar: adjectives, adverbs of manner, prepositional phrases of place
Patterns: repeated format

Aesop's fables with their short, punchy tales and their sentence-ending morals have been both entertaining and educating children for generations. They continue to play an important role today. There are many collections of Aesop's fables. In keeping with the targeted audience of language minority students and a read-aloud perspective, I have selected this particular edition. Hague has included only 13 of Aesop's most popular fables rather than attempting a comprehensive anthology. This allows each fable to be honored with its own page (or two) and its own illustration. These handsome illustrations done in earth colors are large and fully descriptive. In addition, Hague has abbreviated many of the fables, making them easier to comprehend than the fully detailed versions. This thin book gives students a sense of accomplishment. Here is quality, not quantity.

Related Books: *The Aesop for Children* (Winters, 1919, 1947) is the classic version with 126 fables and *When Small is Tall* (Reit, Hooks and Boegehold, 1985) is an expanded picture book version of three fables from Aesop.

Book By the Same Illustrator: *The Wizard of Oz* (1982) in the RAL.

FABLES

by Arnold Lobel
New York: Harper & Row, 1980   41 pages

Grades: 2-5, 4-8   **ESL Level:** intermediate
Genre: fables

Vocabulary: animals, values, places in the community—country
Grammar: future tense—*will*, exclamatory sentences
Patterns: repeated format, dialogue

Here are 20 different fables, freshly created in modern times and offering ageless morals. The individual stories read easily, filled with action and dialogue. The morals at the end cause one to chuckle. Each fable is neatly contained on a single page with a large illustration facing it. Together they provide a separate unit, with easy viewing for a read-aloud audience.

Lobel has illustrated his own stories. The colors are soft and the whole artistic effect is very satisfying. However, one cannot depend on the single illustrations to explain the accompanying text. This is, therefore, best for an intermediate and above proficiency level. Honored with the Caldecott Medal.

Related Book By Same Author: *Prince Bertram the Bad* (1963), a picture book with a strong moral.

Related Book: *Aesop's Fables* (Hague, 1985) in the RAL.

Books By the Same Author: Lobel is a celebrated artist-author. Among his many books are *Frog and Toad are Friends* (1970), a Caldecott Honor Book, *Frog and Toad Together* (1972), a Newbery Honor Book, and *On Market Street* (1981), done with his wife Anita, in the RAL.

FREE TO BE . . . YOU AND ME

edited by Marlo Thomas, Gloria Steinem and Letty Cottin Pogrebin
New York: McGraw-Hill, 1974, 1987   144 pages
Grades: K-3, 2-5   **ESL Level:** intermediate
Genre: anthology
Ethnic Identity: multiethnic

Vocabulary: friends, family, school, emotions

This upbeat collection of stories, songs and poems (25 altogether) affirms that all children, regardless of sex or ethnic origin, can be what they want to be. This liberating message is captured in the catchy title song, which appears with words and musical notation as the first selection. The entire book appeals to all children, but carries an especially powerful message of hope to immigrant and refugee children here in the United States. The pieces are punchy and most are humorous. They put children in touch with feelings and provide alternatives to stereotypes. One of my favorites is "Atalanta" a liberated version of a traditional fairy tale. The selections vary in length from half a page to six pages. The book's large size and colorful, varied illustrations suggest it as a classroom read-aloud.

An excellent record and tape have been made from this book. It greatly enhances the collection, as it provides another medium of aural reinforcement. Plus, it's great fun!

Related Book By Same Editors: *Free To Be . . . A Family. A Book About All Kinds of Belonging* (1987). This is also very good, but because this sequel came out 13 years later, it is hard to switch attachments from an old favorite to a new star.

STONE FOX

by John Reynolds Gardiner   illustrated by Marcia Sewall
New York: Harper & Row (Thomas Y. Crowell), 1980   81 pages

Grades: 2-5   **ESL Level:** intermediate
Genre: legend, short novel
Ethnic Identity: Native American

Vocabulary: farming, family—grandfather; places in the community, emotions
Grammar: exclamatory sentences, questions
Patterns: dialogues

This short novel, based on a Rocky Mountain legend, offers many positive features. First, it is a gripping adventure story about a dog sled race. Second, it is a touching family story about a ten year old boy who is determined to help his ailing grandfather save his potato farm. Third, it is extremely well written for the elementary grades—fast paced, action packed and spiced with dialogue. Fourth, it packs a powerful ending. Fifth, it is one of those "page turners" that is difficult to put down. In addition to all this, it contains a strong Native American character, who turns out to be one of the story's heroes. It's an absolute winner!

Book By the Same Author: *Top Secret* (1984) in the RAL.

SCHOOL/LEARNING

THE SCHOOL

by John Burningham
New York: Harper & Row (Thomas Y. Crowell), 1975   19 pages

Grades: Pre-K-1   **ESL Level:** beginner
Genre: picture book—concept book

Vocabulary: school
Grammar: action verbs—transitive; plural nouns—countable
Patterns: repeated word patterns and format

This small book succinctly describes, both in words and pictures, the basic activities of kindergarten and first grade. Its 27 words are spread across nine pages. Facing each page of brief text is a colorful illustration explaining the activity. It is a perfect book for introducing young beginner ESL students to basic school vocabulary. Following the read-aloud session, allow the students to make their own book about school. This gives them further opportunity to talk about this vocabulary and to write it, if they are ready. A very useful little book.

Related Book: *Timothy Goes to School* (Wells, 1981) in the RAL.

Books By the Same Author: Other "Little Books" include *The Baby, The Rabbit* and *The Snow,* all written in 1975.

TIMOTHY GOES TO SCHOOL

by Rosemary Wells
New York: E.P. Dutton (Dial Books), 1981   28 pages

Grades: Pre K-1, K-3   **ESL Level:** intermediate
Genre: picture book—concept book

Vocabulary: greetings, school, clothing, emotions
Grammar: past tense, negation
Patterns: repeated sentence patterns, dialogue

It is hard for Timothy to be a newcomer on the first day of school, especially when the teacher pairs him with "perfect" Claude. Clothing is very important, even at this early age, as is social acceptance by peers. Timothy's mom provides reassuring home support, but ultimately it is Timothy himself who finds his own place and makes his own first friend.

The cute animal characters remove this a step from reality, yet the experiences and feelings are very real. Hearing about someone else's struggle with a school adjustment helps young people deal with it themselves. They can discuss how they felt when they were new. They can also develop affirming ways to welcome other new students, including those with limited English proficiency.

Related Books: *My First Days of School* (Hamilton-Merritt, 1982), *What's Good for a Five-Year Old?* (Cole, 1969), *Will I Have a Friend?* (Cohen/Hoban, 1967)

MARY HAD A LITTLE LAMB

by Sara Josepha Hale   illustrated by Tomie dePaola
New York: Holiday House, 1984   30 pages

Grades: K-3   **ESL Level:** intermediate
Genre: picture book—nursery rhyme

Vocabulary: school, places in the community—rural, small village; animals
Grammar: past tense, relative clauses, pronouns-possessive and object
Patterns: rhyming, repeated word patterns

When individual nursery rhymes or poems are expanded into fully illustrated picture books, they usually make excellent read-alouds. That is the case here. Plus, artist dePaola's research uncovered all six verses of the poem, which he includes. The last 12 lines unfamiliar to most of us, affirm the value of love and kindness to animals. As a whole, it is a very gentle poem, much richer than its more common, first 12 lines. The singsong melody (included at the front) and the repeated word patterns encourage students to more easily learn the words, and the clear illustrations help explain them.

Using a neo-primitive style, dePaola's large drawings authenticate the poem's origin in 19th century rural America. They also provide a rare opportunity for modern children to "visit" a one-room school house and meet the school marm. Well-done!

Books By the Same Illustrator: *Pancakes for Breakfast* (1978) and *Mother Goose* (1985), both in the RAL. Also, *Favorite Nursery Tales* (1986) and *Strega Nona* (1976), Caldecott Honor Book.

MY FRIEND LESLIE
THE STORY OF A HANDICAPPED CHILD

by Maxine B. Rosenberg   photographs by George Ancona
New York: Lothrop, Lee & Shepard, 1983   45 pages

Grades: Pre K-1, K-3   **ESL Level:** intermediate
Genre: non-fiction picture book
Ethnic Identity: Asian American, multiethnic

Vocabulary: school, friendship
Grammar: simple present tense, third person agreement
Patterns: complex sentences

This is the story of Leslie, a physically handicapped, five year old, as lovingly told by her classmate, Karin. Karin describes her friend and her multiple handicaps in an objective, straightforward manner. She explains some of the difficulties Leslie has in school and that the other children have with her. Most of the anecdotes affirm Leslie's presence in a mainstream kindergarten classroom as a positive experience for all concerned. This serves as a good introduction for children who will interact with the handicapped, especially those their own age.

The candid black and white photographs express the warm friendship between the two girls. They also clearly capture many primary school activities. This provides an excellent opportunity to practice school-related vocabulary.

MISS NELSON IS MISSING

by Harry Allard   illustrated by James Marshall
Boston: Houghton Mifflin, 1977, 1987 edition includes a cassette   32 pages

Grades: K-3   **ESL Level:** intermediate
Genre: picture book

Vocabulary: school
Grammar: exclamatory sentences, *wh*-questions
Patterns: dialogue

Students learn valuable lessons in classroom behavior through the disappearing act of their sweet teacher, Miss Nelson and her terrible substitute, Miss Viola Swamp. James Marshall's illustrations accentuate the humor of the situation. The message, however, will not be lost. The drama and mystery of the students' predicament allows for dramatic reading in what is usually a spell-binding, read-aloud session. No one will dare to squirm!

The author and artist have combined for two popular sequels. Both are good. Of the two, I prefer *Miss Nelson Has a Field Day* because it introduces a new problem, a football team that won't listen and can't win. It's the mean, ugly Coach Swamp to the rescue!

Related Books By Same Author: *Miss Nelson is Back* (1982) and *Miss Nelson Has a Field Day* (1985)

Book by the Same Illustrator: *The Night Before Christmas* (1985) in the RAL.

CROW BOY

by Taro Yashima
New York: Penguin (Viking Books), 1955, 1976   37 pages

Grades: K-3, 2-5   **ESL Level:** intermediate
Genre: picture book
Ethnic Identity: Asian-Japanese

Vocabulary: school, natural environments—mountains
Grammar: adverbial clauses, adjectives
Patterns: complex sentences

This touching story of a rural Japanese school boy tells of a child who marches to a different drummer. It tells of his fears, his accommodation and finally his success. And it tells of the special teacher who nurtures his gifts and encourages Chibi to share them with the school. Chibi's story carries a timeless message. The illustrations help to transport us to this quiet mountainside village, a far different culture than the predominantly urban Japan.

Although the story is simple and the text limited to one to three sentences per page, the language structures and patterns are quite complex. This limits its use to intermediate level ESL students. This serious book quietly affirms the special qualities of us all. A picture book classic!

Book By the Same Author: *Momo's Kitten* (1961)

ANGEL CHILD, DRAGON CHILD

by Michele Maria Surat   illustrated by Vo-Dinh Mai
Milwaukee, WI: Raintree, 1983   36 pages

Grades: K-3, 2-5   **ESL Level:** intermediate
Genre: picture book, contemporary realistic fiction
Ethnic Identity: Asian-Indochinese

Vocabulary: school, seasons, prejudice, emotions
Grammar: adjectives, action verbs
Patterns: dialogue

Going to a new school in America brings out both the angel and the dragon in Ut, a Vietnamese girl. She is also sad, because she misses her mother, who is still back in Vietnam. One boy, in particular, teases her about her Vietnamese clothing, that he calls "pajamas." Ultimately, they fight and as punishment, the principal locks them into a room to resolve their problem. Out of this emerges greater understanding and friendship. Her former nemesis encourages the school to help bring Ut's mother to America. Through a Vietnamese fair, they raise the money.

The Vietnamese artist's soft water color paintings evoke both the Vietnamese and the American cultures. Even though they don't explain every line, they do capture the major scenes and the underlying emotions.

Related Books: *My Best Friend, Duc Tran* (Macmillan/Freeman, 1987), a non-fiction picture book for intermediates in grades 2-5 and *A Long Way from Home* (Wartski, 1980), a novel for 4th-8th grade intermediates, both in the RAL.

Books By the Same Illustrator: *The Brocaded Slipper and Other Vietnamese Tales* (Voung, 1982) and *The Land I Lost: Adventures of a Boy in Vietnam* (Nhuong, 1986), both in the RAL.

I SPEAK ENGLISH FOR MY MOM

by Muriel Stanek   illustrated by Judith Friedman
Niles, IL: Albert Whitman, 1989   29 pages

Grades: 2-5   **ESL Level:** intermediate
Genre: picture book—concept book; contemporary realistic fiction
Ethnic Identity: Hispanic-Mexican

Vocabulary: places in the community—urban
Grammar: simple present tense
Patterns: dialogue

This book focuses on one of the critical issues for Hispanic parents—that their children know more English than they do. School-aged Lupe helps her mother with English, as they interact in the Anglo community. Lupe has mixed feelings about her role as translator for Mom, especially when her Mom decides to learn English herself. The author effectively uses Lupe herself to tell the story as a first person narrative.

The dramatic conflict is rather weak, yet the book succeeds in creating a strong mother-daughter bond. It also provides a positive role model for working class Mexican immigrants.

Related Book: *A Chair for My Mother* (Williams, 1982) in the RAL.

THE MASTER CHESS PLAYER

retold by Chia Hearn Chek   illustrated by Kwan Shan Mei
Singapore: Federal Publications, 1976, 1981 (available in the United States through
Janus Books)   31 pages

Grades: K-3, 2-5   **ESL Level:** intermediate
Genre: picture book—folk tale
Ethnic Identity: Asian

Vocabulary: musical instruments—flute; games—chess; family, friendship
Grammar: adverbial clauses, adverbs of manner
Patterns: dialogue, complex sentences

Tohan and Benppo are ten-year old friends from Mongolia. Tohan's father, a poor weaver, wants his son to succeed in life, so he sends him to town to learn different skills: first, how to read and write, then how to play a musical instrument and finally, how to play chess. Tohan obeys his father, becoming proficient in each skill area, although at the time he cannot see their purpose. As the story unfolds, Tohan uses his education to save both his own life and that of his friend.

The story is engaging, but the text is longer than most picture books. The style is rather flat and, in addition, filled with complex constructions. For all these reasons, it requires good listening skills.

Related Books By Same Author: This is part of a series, *Folktales from the Orient*. In all, there are fifteen titles, each a separate picture book, with the same author and illustrator. The tales cover many of the lesser known Oriental cultures, including Borneo, Maori and Pakistani.

THE ONE IN THE MIDDLE IS THE GREEN KANGAROO

by Judy Blume   illustrated by Amy Aitken
Scarsdale, NY: Bradbury Press, 1967, 1981   39 pages

Grades: 2-5   **ESL Level: intermediate**
Genre: fiction—short novel, contemporary realistic fiction

Vocabulary: school, family
Grammar: past tense, subject pronouns
Patterns: dialogue, informal language, short sentences

This one is for the middle child, who struggles to be special. Here, he wildly achieves that by landing a special part in the school play. Kids love to read Judy Blume's novels. This, her first one, is no exception. Be advised that it is "safe," not covering any sensitive issues, except for sibling rivalry. Because of its simple language structures and short sentences, it works well as an easy reading "novelette" for intermediate students. Because it's funny and fast paced, it also succeeds as a read-aloud for the whole class. A natural blending of school and home.

Related Books By Same Author: *Tales of a Fourth Grade Nothing* (1972) in the RAL, and *Freckle Juice* (1978).

 **Basic Academic Skills**

ALPHABET

ALPHABET BLOCK BOOK

by Roy McKie
New York: Random House, 1979   22 pages

Grades: Pre-K-1, K-3   **ESL Level:** beginner
Genre: picture book—concept book

Vocabulary: animals
Grammar: auxiliary verb—*to be*, present tense
Patterns: repeated sentence pattern

Intended for a pre-school audience, this small, unassuming alphabet book captures the attention of early elementary students as well. I find it one of the most successful first teaching books for the alphabet. Perhaps it is the capital letter in bold print, followed by the same repeated sentence pattern for all letters, beginning with "A is for alligator." Perhaps it is the single picture for each letter. Perhaps it is the cute illustrations. Perhaps it is the cardboard paper and spiral binding that allows students to repeatedly use the book without destroying it. Perhaps it is the last two pages that put it all together as the full alphabet, with each picture in reduced size next to its boldfaced capital letter. Probably, it is the combination of all these.

A, B, SEE

by Tana Hoban
New York: Greenwillow Books, 1982   32 pages

Grades: K-3, 4-8   **ESL Level:** beginner
Genre: wordless picture book, concept book

Vocabulary: everyday objects, household, animals, food, tools
Grammar: nouns
Patterns: repeated format

Tana Hoban tackles yet another learning concept in a highly sophisticated presentation. She introduces the alphabet through stunning black and white photographs of familiar objects. Each letter is highlighted on its own page with an attractive collage of two to seven objects. This wordless design requires either the teacher or students to generate the names of the vocabulary. They can easily expand them into sentences, using a repeated, simple pattern (e.g. P is for pretzel). This format also provides good material for the students' own picture dictionaries.

This book, like many others of Hoban's, is extremely useful for working with older, beginning SL students. It can be appreciated by learners ages 5 to 65!

Books By the Same Author: Tana Hoban has mastered the fine art of concept books, which are very useful for beginning SL students. Because she uses photographs, her books also appeal to a wide age span. Others included in this RAL are *Count and See* (1972), *Is it Rough? Is it Smooth? Is it Shiny?* (1984), *I Read Symbols* (1983), *I Read Signs* (1983), *Where is it?* (1974) and *A Children's Zoo* (1985).

Q IS FOR DUCK

by Mary Elting and Michael Folsom   illustrated by Jack Kent
Boston: Houghton Mifflin, 1980   60 pages

Grades: K-3   **ESL Level:** beginner, intermediate
Genre: picture book—concept book

Vocabulary: animals
Grammar: simple present tense, third person agreement, auxiliary verb—*to be*, action verbs, indefinite article—singular
Patterns: repeated word, sentence pattern and format

This is a clever twist to the traditional alphabet book. Here, the letter is identified by the predicate, usually the action of the subject. For example, the book is entitled *Q is for Duck* "because a duck quacks" and earlier in the alphabet, "J is for Kangaroo because a kangaroo jumps".

This imaginative presentation offers many advantages for the SL student. First, it encourages guessing, and hence unconscious language use. Second, students readily learn the two grammatical patterns because of their abundant repetitions. Third, the book allows students to expand their vocabulary of action verbs. This is helpful because nouns are usually learned more easily. Fourth, the drawings clearly explain both the action as well as the noun. As a bonus, they are also whimsical. And fifth, this riddle format stimulates the students to create their own riddles and present them to the class. This is a fun book with a lot of language learning potential!

ON MARKET STREET

by Arnold Lobel
New York: Greenwillow Books, 1981

illustrated by Anita Lobel
36 pages

Grades: K-3, 2-5   **ESL Level:** beginner, intermediate
Genre: picture book—concept book

Vocabulary: shopping
Grammar: nouns—count and mass, plurals
Patterns: rhymes, repeated format

In this most unusual alphabet book the Lobels invite you to shop along Market Street. The treasures you will find there are represented by the letters of the alphabet. The book is given more substance than most alphabet books by the two poems which introduce it and provide its surprise ending. A page is devoted to each letter, with its capital letter and word of the object accompanying the illustration. It is the drawings which truly set this book apart. They are exquisitely crafted and finely detailed.

This serves as an excellent model for the development of the students' own alphabet books. Because of the shopping theme and the sophisticated artwork, its appeal expands to older elementary age students and on to adults. Attractive and very creative!

Books By the Same Author: See *Fables* (1980) in the RAL.

I UNPACKED MY GRANDMOTHER'S TRUNK

by Susan Ramsay Hoguet
New York: E.P. Dutton, 1983

28 pages

Grades: K-3, 2-5   **ESL Level:** beginner
Genre: picture book—concept book

Vocabulary: animals, household
Grammar: count nouns—singular, indefinite articles-singular, conjunctions—*and*
Patterns: repeated words, cumulative repetitions

This is a beautiful picture book, an alphabet review, an introduction to initial sounds and a memory game, all wrapped in one. The old childhood game (and this modern book) start with "I unpacked my grandmother's trunk and out of it I took a . . . " An object that begins with the sound of its first letter is removed from the trunk, repeated and then added to cumulatively throughout the alphabet. The goal is to repeat all the previous words, as you add one more.

The book can be enjoyed as is, as a read-aloud. Most classes will hopefully be stimulated enough by it to create their own round-robin version. A page of game directions is included to facilitate this. Have fun!

Book By the Same Author: *Solomon Grundy* (1986)

COUNTING/NUMBERS

BEARS ON WHEELS

by Stan and Jan Berenstain
New York: Random House, 1969   32 pages

Grades: Pre K-1, K-3   **ESL Level:** beginner
Genre: easy reader, picture book—concept book

Vocabulary: numbers—1-21, transportation—bicycles
Grammar: countable nouns—singular and plural
Patterns: repeated word patterns

Some very funny bears have a great time on all sorts of wheels. The authors have a wonderful imagination and the artistic ability to capture humor. In addition, all this humor has a purpose, actually a double purpose—to teach counting and beginning reading. The book is delightfully simple, concentrating on the numbers one through five and on predictable word phrases, (no sentences). Be advised that no numerals are included here, only words. The repetition of the limited vocabulary assures its success as a beginning reader. Students gain additional confidence and motivation by hearing it first as a read-aloud.

Related Book: *One Bear All Alone* (Bucknall, 1985), another bear counting book, in the RAL.

Books By the Same Author: The Berenstains have written other humorous easy reading, concept books. Two included in the RAL are *Old Hat, New Hat* (1970) about clothing and *Bears in the Night* (1971) with prepositional phrases.

ONE BEAR ALL ALONE: A COUNTING BOOK

by Caroline Bucknall
New York: E. P. Dutton (Dial Press), 1985   22 pages

Grades: Pre K-1, K-3   **ESL Level:** beginner, intermediate
Genre: picture book—concept book

Vocabulary: numbers—1–10, animals, places in the community
Grammar: countable nouns-singular and plural, prepositional phrases of location
Patterns: rhyming

At the beginning of the day, there is "One bear all alone, sitting by the telephone." He is rather glum, waiting for some action and some friends. His bear friends materialize in progressive increments of one, and together they discover fun activities to do—from the train to the zoo. Each two-page spread is differently designed, but with enough repeated elements to provide continuity. Each has the numeral and a two-line rhyme on the left page and a full page color picture on the right, with the bears drawn large enough to be easily counted. The bears are cute, the rhymes are clever and the mood is cheerful. Be aware that the vocabulary includes British English, the country of the author/artist.

Related Book: *1 Hunter* (Hutchins, 1982)

COUNTING RHYMES

England: Brimax Books, 1980   12 pages

Grades: Pre-K-1, K-3   **ESL Level:** beginner
Genre: picture book—nursery rhymes

Vocabulary: numbers—1–10, games, body
Grammar: imperatives, action verbs
Patterns: rhyming, repeated word and sentence patterns

This small book contains eight counting rhymes of four to eight lines, each with clear and cheerful illustrations. Its greatest attribute is that children can listen to all eight in a short (5-10 minute) sitting and feel a sense of accomplishment. In addition, the rhymes work well for oral practice with numbers and rhyming, for reading skill development and for the much-loved student anthologies (copying, reading and illustrating). The heavy cardboard pages, laminated for easy cleaning, allow for years of heavy usage. These and the companion volumes (see below) are my students' most popular nursery rhyme books. Economically priced, they are also a good investment, both for school and home use.

Related Books By Same Author: *Saying Rhymes. Playing Rhymes. Singing Rhymes.* (1980). All three books follow the same general pattern.

ROLL OVER: A COUNTING SONG

illustrated by Merle Peek
Boston: Houghton Mifflin (Clarion Books), 1981   25 pages

Grades: Pre-K-1, K-3   **ESL Level:** beginner
Genre: picture book—singable book

Vocabulary: animals, numbers—1–10
Grammar: past tense
Patterns: repeated sentences, repeated refrain

Ten animals and one cute child snug cozily in bed, but alas, it is too crowded. So, one by one, they all roll over and fall out. All this merriment is sung with the same refrain and same simple one-line verse. It's all very simple, but very satisfying to young listeners. At the end, the child is left alone. As he drifts off to sleep, his animal friends magically reappear as part of the wall paper.

This singable book (with the music provided at the end) provides good practice for number identification and counting (1-10) and serves as a natural introduction to the past tense. Its predictable patterns and repetitions also easily elicit class participation.

Related Book: *Ten Bears in My Bed* (Mack, 1974). This book uses the same bedtime song but varies the ways the animals (all bears) exit. One gallops, one flies, another rumbles etc. In the process it also introduces modes of transportation (e.g. trucks, motorcycles). It is more active but lacks the repetitions and comfort of *Roll Over*. I recommend this one for the same age range but more intermediate ESL proficiency level.

ONE, TWO, THREE: AN ANIMAL COUNTING BOOK

by Marc Brown
Boston: Little Brown, 1976   30 pages

Grades: K-3, 2-5   **ESL Level:** beginner
Genre: picture book—concept book

Vocabulary: numbers—1-20, animals
Grammar: countable nouns—singular and plural
Patterns: repeated format

It is hard to find a counting book that includes all the numbers from one to twenty. This is a good one. A page or two is devoted to each number. The numeral, its word equivalent and the singular name of the animal are the only printed text. The rest of the page is filled with imaginative animal groupings of the same number. It is very simple, very attractive and very useful.

The black and white line drawings are understated and dignified with their rust color borders. The bright red numerals and bold black print attracts the eye. Because of this somewhat sophisticated design, the book can be used with a wide age range of beginners to teach numbers and counting.

COUNT AND SEE

by Tana Hoban
New York: Macmillan, 1972   40 pages

Grades: K-3, 4-8   **ESL Level:** beginner
Genre: picture book—concept book
Ethnic Identity: multiethnic

Vocabulary: numbers—1-100
Grammar: countable nouns—plurals
Patterns: repeated word patterns

This counting book effectively uses well-composed black and white photographs to illustrate counting objects. The objects are interestingly selected from varied urban scenes, from garbage cans, to school buses to interracial friends sitting on a curbside.

Each two-page spread of numbers 1–15 includes one page for the number as numeral, as word and as a dot set, and the other for the full page photograph. These three representations of the number allow for the teaching of different stages of numerical skill development. Although there are no sentences in the text, they can easily be generated from the illustrations. The inclusion of key numbers from 20-100 expands the book's usefulness. This is a sophisticated and comprehensive counting book that can expand beyond the early years to 8th graders.

Books By the Same Author: See *A, B, See* (1982) in the RAL.

THE TOOTHPASTE MILLIONAIRE

by Jean Merrill   illustrated by Jan Palmer
Boston: Houghton Mifflin, 1972   90 pages

Grades: 4-8   **ESL Level:** beginner, intermediate
Genre: short novel
Ethnic Identity: Black American, multiethnic

Vocabulary: mathematics, business
Grammar: conditionals, questions
Patterns: dialogue, informal language

This book grabs you from the first sentence: "This is the story of my friend Rufus Mayflower and how he got to be a millionaire." Intrigued, one reads on, to discover that Rufus is only 12 years old and in the sixth grade. He makes his fortune, honestly, within one year by producing and selling toothpaste!

Reading the book aloud provides a wonderful opportunity to integrate mathematical and business problem solving with aural language skills. Encourage the students to figure out the problems along with Rufus. It is an excellent choice for middle school SL students because while the math is quite challenging, the language is not. The informal text, heavily laced with short dialogues and declarative sentences, will allow most students beyond the basic beginner level to participate.

Another positive aspect of the book is the multiethnic blend of strong characters. Rufus, the business man, is a black boy; his best friend, the narrator, is a white girl; and the maker of their commercials is an Asian American.

Book By the Same Author: *The Pushcart War* (1964) is a very readable, longer novel (223 pages), also for 4th-8th graders, that explains, through a story, how wars begin.

DAYS/WEEKS/MONTHS/CALENDAR

CHICKEN SOUP WITH RICE

by Maurice Sendak
New York: Harper & Row, 1962; Scholastic, 1986 (includes a cassette)   31 pages

Grades: K-3   **ESL Level:** intermediate
Genre: poetry, picture book

Vocabulary: months, food, seasonal activities
Grammar: future tense, adjectives, contractions
Patterns: rhyming, repeated word patterns

This famous children's author and artist captures the essence of each month in twelve short poems. They are linked together with a comical refrain about eating *Chicken Soup with Rice*. This is Sendak at his rhyming best.

When teaching the months, introduce the book as a whole and then review the individual poems at the beginning of the appropriate month. Although best suited to the intermediate level, the poems are enjoyed by all students. This makes them useful for multilevel classes. Students like to copy them into their own "anthologies." Without being told, they also often memorize them! This can easily be extended into an oral class presentation, with each student mastering a month or two!

Related Books By Same Author: There are three other small books in *The Nutshell Library. Pierre, One Was Johnny* and *Alligators All Around.* All were written in 1962 and are available together on record and tape (Caedmon, 1982) under the title *Where the Wild Things Are* (narrated by Tammy Grimes).

Book By the Same Author: *Where the Wild Things Are* (1963) is an early childhood classic.

ONE MONDAY MORNING

by Uri Shulevitz
New York: Macmillan (Charles Scribner), 1967, 1986   40 pages

Grades: K-3   **ESL Level:** beginner, intermediate
Genre: picture book, modern fantasy

Vocabulary: days of the week, royalty, places in the community—urban
Grammar: future tense, definite article
Patterns: cumulative repetitions, repeated refrain and sentence pattern

Stuck in a city apartment on a dreary rainy day, a clever little boy devises his own entertainment. From a simple deck of playing cards, he creates an imaginary string of royal visitors, which increase with the days of the week. Not to be taken for granted, he arranges to be out, when they come to call, until they arrive on the seventh day, with an irresistible addition! The artistic juxtaposition of a colorful royal entourage with a gray New York street strikes another victory for the world of make-believe! As a follow-up, encourage your students to create their own imaginary escapes from mundane reality.

The predictable patterns, refrains and cumulative repetitions make this an easy book for students to join along with in a read-aloud session. An ALA Notable Book, now in its second edition.

Related Books: *Bored-Nothing to Do* (Spier, 1978) on imagination, for older elementary students, in the RAL. Also, *One Bright Monday Morning* (Baum, 1962) and *Busy Monday Morning* (Dormanska, 1985), other books about days of the week.

A YEAR OF BEASTS

by Ashley Wolff
New York: E.P Dutton, 1986   32 pages

Grades: K-3   **ESL Level:** beginner
Genre: picture book—concept book

Vocabulary: months, animals, family, natural environments
Grammar: plural nouns
Patterns: repeated word pattern

This book beautifully depicts the passage of nature, month-by-month, throughout the year. It also visually traces the activities of two young children and their parents. The brief text, written only in phrases, simply names the animals drawn in the illustration and the month: for example, "White-tailed deer in January," "Skunks and cows in June." The animals are integrated into each richly detailed, two-page scene. This is an excellent source for sentence generating, vocabulary building and story retelling.

Related Book: *January Brings the Snow* (Coleridge, 1987)

Related Book by Same Author: *A Year of Birds* (1984), better suited to intermediate level students.

TELLING TIME/CLOCKS

AROUND THE CLOCK WITH HARRIET
A BOOK ABOUT TELLING TIME

by Betsy and Giulio Maestro
New York: Crown, 1984

31 pages

Grades: K-3   **ESL Level:** beginner, intermediate
Genre: picture book—concept book

Vocabulary: time, clocks, household
Grammar: action verbs, auxiliary verb—*to be*, action verbs
Patterns: repeated format

Harriet, a lovable elephant, cheerfully bounds through a busy, summer day. The authors/ artists coincide her activities with the hours of the day from 8:00 AM to 8:00 PM. For each hour there is a different activity and a black and white clock face, with the time written numerically as well (e.g. 9:00 AM). This book provides a clear introduction or review for both telling time and action verbs. Its big colorful pictures vibrantly fill each page. It is visually alive, intended to both delight and teach young listeners.

Related Book: *All of Grandmother's Clocks* (Ziegler, 1977)

Books By Same Author: See *Where is My Friend* (1976) in the RAL.

BEAR CHILD'S BOOK OF HOURS

by Anne Rockwell
New York: Harper & Row (Thomas Y. Crowell), 1987

30 pages

Grades: K-3   **ESL Level:** beginner
Genre: picture book—concept book

Vocabulary: time, clocks, numbers—1-12; children's activities, household
Grammar: present continuous tense, direct objects
Patterns: repeated sentence pattern and format

At each hour of the day, a cute Little Bear is doing something different, (e.g. getting dressed, playing in the park, listening to a story). The cheerful illustrations capture each of these daily activities, while on each facing page a large, clearly drawn clock tells the time. Under each picture is a single sentence. This pattern repeats from 7 AM until Little Bear's bedtime at 8 PM. To show the passage over time during the night, Rockwell includes nine small clocks on the last page, one each from 9 PM to 8 AM. As this page includes no words, it serves as a good oral review for telling time. Even though this book seems rather flat, it serves well as a simple presentation of telling time in a story book format.

Related Book: *Clocks and More Clocks* (Hutchins, 1970) is a rather nonsensical story that includes time to the minute.

Books By the Same Author: See *Happy Birthday to Me* in the RAL.

COLORS/SHAPES/SIZES

DO YOU KNOW COLORS?

by J.P. Miller and Katherine Howard
New York: Random House, 1979   28 pages

Grades: Pre K-1, K-3   **ESL Level:** beginner
Genre: picture book—concept book

Vocabulary: colors, animals, flowers
Grammar: nouns, questions, simple present tense, auxiliary verb—*to be*
Patterns: short, simple sentences, repeated format

This very clear, practical book both introduces colors and expands animal and nature vocabulary. Fourteen colors receive their own one to two pages. Each scene is painted in the particular color, with the color name as the title, a short three line text as introduction and most of the page filled with labeled objects of that color. Although an attempt is made to create unified scenes, the book does not pretend to develop thematic stories on each page. With this information, however, beginning students will be able to produce sentences that include objects and color words. A useful, classroom book for teaching colors.

BROWN BEAR, BROWN BEAR, WHAT DO YOU SEE?

by Bill Martin, Jr.   illustrated by Eric Carle
New York: Holt, Rinehart and Winston, 1967, 1983   24 pages

Grades: Pre-K-1, K-3   **ESL Level:** beginner
Genre: picture book
Ethnic Identity: multiethnic

Vocabulary: colors, animals
Grammar: *wh*-questions—*what*, present tense, indefinite articles—*a*
Patterns: rhyming, repeated sentences, question and answer sequence

This is one of Bill Martin's best: a clever rhyming book that skillfully teaches both animals and colors. Eric Carle's large, collage illustrations joyfully add bright, primary color to each of the 11 two-page spreads.

It is a great find for ESL beginners because the single sentence pattern repeats throughout, with only the animal and color names changing. The question and answer format also encourages guessing games. In addition, on the last two pages, the whole story, including the words, repeats in reduced form. This provides the basis for good summary activities. Young children never seem to tire of hearing these sing-song verses. A definite read-aloud favorite!

Books By the Same Author: *Bill Martin's Instant Readers, Sets I and II* (1970s)

Books by the Same Illustrator: See *A Hole in the Dike* (Green, 1975) in the RAL.

BESIDE THE BAY

by Sheila White Samton
New York: Putnam Publishing Group (Philomel Books), 1987   26 pages

Grades: K-3, 2-5   **ESL Level:** beginner, intermediate
Genre: narrative poem, picture book—concept book

Vocabulary: colors, natural environments—seashore; animals, birds, fish
Grammar: adjectives, nouns, simple present tense, third person agreement
Patterns: rhyming, cumulative (visual) repetitions

In this very clever and original book the author/illustrator introduces colors, one by one, to describe life *Beside the Bay*. When a color is first named, a color line is drawn under the word for easy identification. The picture on the facing page includes the newly added color words. Rather than a dry labeling of colors and objects, the concept is ingeniously interwoven into a simple narrative poem that grows from page to page until the end, when it cycles back to the original scene of the blue water and gray sky.

The color words and objects, clearly drawn in the illustrations, plus the rhyming story make this a very useful read-aloud for SL students in the beginning to intermediate range. It is also a lovely literary welcome to the bay, seashore and mountains.

SHAPES

by Rosalinda Kightley
Boston: Little Brown, 1986   31 pages

Grades: Pre K-1, K-3   **ESL Level:** beginner
Genre: picture book—concept book

Vocabulary: shapes, objects
Grammar: nouns, questions—*how many*
Patterns: repeated sentence pattern

This very clever and well-designed concept book introduces ten basic shapes, including circle, diamond, right angle and zigzag. Each shape receives a page by itself, with its name in black letters. On each facing page is a scene with numerous examples of that shape. The students are asked to find as many of that shape as they can. Each shape is color coded and is repeated in miniature under the later drawings. This encourages review and identification of numerous shapes in each of the pictures. The illustrations are bright, cheerful and clear. On the last two pages, each shape and its picture are reproduced in reduced size. This provides the teacher material for follow-up worksheets and seat work. An attractive and very useful teaching book.

Books By the Same Author: Four other concept books in this primer series are *Colors, Opposites, ABC* and *123,* all with a 1986 copyright.

ONE FISH, TWO FISH, RED FISH, BLUE FISH

by Dr. Seuss
New York: Random House, 1960, 1987 edition includes a cassette   63 pages

Grades: K-3   **ESL Level:** beginner
Genre: easy reader, picture book

Vocabulary: numbers, colors, opposites
Grammar: adjectives, present tense, questions
Patterns: rhyming, repeated word and sentence patterns

"From there to here, from here to there, funny things are everywhere." Dr. Seuss has creatively used humor and rhyming verse to delight young audiences for over two generations now. His books have been used to teach beginning readers, replacing more traditional basal readers. This one can also be used to teach the concepts of numbers (1-10), colors, opposites and modifiers.

This also makes a delightful read-aloud. However, lacking a unified story line, its singsong chants can become repetitious after a while. My beginning ESL students enjoy and learn from this book best when it is read aloud in small portions. Plan for a minimum of two sessions. This also allows time for short, frequent rereadings. Then, it is like candy—a little treat!

Books By the Same Author: See *Hop on Pop* (1963) in the RAL.

DEEP IN THE FOREST

by Brinton Turkle
New York: E.P. Dutton, 1976, 1987   31 pages

Grades: K-3   **ESL Level:** beginner, intermediate
Genre: wordless picture book

Vocabulary: natural environments—forest; household, family, animals—bears

This book gives a fresh twist to the "Goldilocks and the Three Bears" story by cleverly reversing the roles. Here, it is the bear cub who intrudes into the empty log cabin of Goldilocks's family. The sequence of events follows the same pattern as in the popular nursery tale. Brinton Turkle's use of earth colors lends authenticity to the picturesque early American setting. This is a charming book.

One purpose of wordless books is to give students the opportunity to tell the story themselves. Here, familiarity with the original tale is helpful. The three sizes of the bowls, chairs and beds allow practice in making comparisons, as well as using other descriptors.

Related Books: *Goldilocks and the Three Bears* (Galdone, 1972), *Blueberries for Sal* (McCloskey, 1948)

Books By the Same Author: *Do Not Open* (1981), *Thy Friend Obadiah* (1969) and other Obadiah stories.

HAILSTONES AND HALIBUT BONES

by Mary O'Neill   illustrated by Leonard Weisgard
New York: Doubleday, 1961, 1989   59 pages

Grades: 2-5, 4-8   **ESL Level:** intermediate, advanced
Genre: poetry

Vocabulary: colors, nature, animals, birds, fish, feelings
Grammar: auxiliary verb—*to be*, adjectives, nouns—count and mass, articles
Patterns: rhyming, repeated sentence patterns, metaphoric language

Beyond the beginner level, there is more to colors than simply identifying them. According to the poet/author, "Each has a taste, and each has a smell and each has a wonderful story to tell . . . " She weaves those stories in twelve color poems, from two to three pages each.

Poems benefit from being read-aloud. Each of these can be completed within 5-10 minutes. With their easy sing-song rhythms and vivid, fresh images, they are fun, stimulating and educational. Through them, students are introduced to new vocabulary, metaphors and the challenge of imagination. These poems also use clearly definable predictable patterns and poetic form. By modeling these, students can be led to create their own color poems.

OPPOSITES/MODIFIERS

IS IT ROUGH? IS IT SMOOTH? IS IT SHINY?

by Tana Hoban
New York: Greenwillow Books, 1984   30 pages

Grades: K-3, 4-8   **ESL Level:** beginner, intermediate
Genre: wordless picture book, concept book

Vocabulary: textures, everyday objects
Grammar: adjectives
Patterns: repeated format

All of the objects in these 30 colored photographs describe distinct and different textures. But they do even more than that. Each establishes a wordless scene awaiting description. A simple sentence using the verb *to be* with a single adjective can be generated by beginners (e.g. "the apples are red"), with more complex sentences using multiple adjectives created by intermediates. Many of these photos also work well as story starters, either for the oral or written medium. Because of the sophisticated layout and diversity of subjects, this book appeals to a wide age range, from K-8 and even beyond. It is a good teaching book and a visual pleasure. Another Hoban success!

Related Book: *Think About Touching* (Pluckrose, 1986)

Books By the Same Author: See *A, B, See* (1982) in the RAL.

QUICK AS A CRICKET

by Audrey Wood   illustrated by Don Wood
Sudbury, MA: Playspaces, 1982   32 pages

Grades: K-3   **ESL Level:** beginner, intermediate
Genre: picture book—concept book

Vocabulary: animals, emotions, opposites
Grammar: comparative adjectives, singular articles—indefinite, auxiliary verb—to be (I'm)
Patterns: short sentences, repeated sentence pattern

In this very clever book, a young child's emotions are compared to various members of the animal kingdom. Each of the 11 sets of similes uses the same sentence pattern and is given as a contrast. For example, "I'm as tough as a rhino, I'm as gentle as a lamb." The final pages encourage summarizing and synthesizing all these contrasting emotions within the child. It ends, "Put it all together, and you've got me!"

This is an absolute quality book. The large illustrations are both attractive and convincing. The book design is smart. Plus, the heavy quality of paper makes it practical for classroom use. Stunning and lovely!

Book By the Same Author: *The Napping House* (1984) in the RAL.

FAST-SLOW HIGH-LOW

by Peter Spier
New York: Doubleday, 1972, 1988   46 pages

Grades: 2-5, 4-8   **ESL Level:** beginner, intermediate
Genre: picture book—concept book

Vocabulary: opposites
Grammar: adjectives, nouns
Patterns: repeated format

Peter Spier cleverly uses over 500 drawings to illustrate 28 sets of common opposites. As in most other Spier books, the art predominates. Here, it explains the concept. The only writing is the opposite words themselves. This allows the students to generate sentences using the vocabulary and the modifiers. The complexity of the sentences will vary with the proficiency level of the individual students. Thus, the book can be successfully used with a multilevel class. Appealing to a wide age range, this attractive book both teaches and delights.

It is good for whole class oral practice and also, as a follow-up, for individual sentence writing. For that assignment it is helpful to have a few copies.

Related Book: *Push-Pull, Empty-Full* (Hoban, 1972)

Books By the Same Author: See *Bored-Nothing to Do* (1978) in the RAL.

FORTUNATELY

by Remy Charlip
New York: Macmillan (Four Winds), 1964, 1985   41 pages

Grades: K-3, 2-5   **ESL Level:** beginner, intermediate
Genre: picture book, modern fantasy

Vocabulary: transportation
Grammar: existential sentences—*there is/are*, past tense, prepositional phrases of place, verbs of physical activity
Patterns: simple sentences, repeated word pattern

Fortunately, in this story, all ends even better than it begins. Unfortunately, the hero has some close encounters on the way. This predictable pattern of near disaster followed by some dramatic escapes makes for an exciting read-aloud. The text on each two page spread is limited to one short sentence, which is clearly explained by the imaginative illustrations. The book also provides an excellent model for students to write their own adventure books. It's a lot of fun!

THINK ABOUT SMELLING

by Henry Pluckrose   illustrated by Chris Fairclough
New York: Franklin Watts, 1986   28 pages

Grades: K-3   **ESL Level:** beginner, intermediate
Genre: non-fiction picture book

Vocabulary: senses—smells
Grammar: adjectives, nouns

We often overlook our sense of smell. In this book, sharp, colorful photographs highlight a variety of smells from our everyday environment—from cut onions to polished shoes to freshly ironed clothes. The simple text identifies the vocabulary, using a variety of sentence patterns. The attractive book design and interesting photographs help maintain interest. This short book can be very useful for vocabulary building and to complement a science unit on the senses for primary age students. Although no sentence patterns are repeated in the text, the teacher could develop simple patterns for sentence building and vocabulary practice: for example, "I smell _____," "*Cut grass* smells like _____" or "I like the smell of _____." This book could also serve as a stimulus for a class "smell walk" to be followed up with a language experience story. Well-done and very practical for ESL classes.

Related Books by Same Author: This excellent series includes similar texts on the other senses—hearing, seeing, tasting and touching, all published in 1986. *Think About Tasting* is included in the RAL.

Clothing / Body

OLD HAT, NEW HAT

by Stan and Jan Berenstain
New York: Random House, 1970   28 pages

Grades: K-3   **ESL Level:** beginner
Genre: easy reader, picture book—concept book

Vocabulary: hats, modifiers
Grammar: adverbs of degree—*too*, adjectives
Patterns: repeated word patterns

   Papa Bear is very particular about a new hat. In fact, after trying on a whole store of them, he settles back with his old familiar one, much to the chagrin of the salesmen. The Berenstains create this amusing bear adventure with just 37 words (many of them repeated numerous times). Most of these words are adjectives, described humorously by hats, and reinforced in the repeated pattern— *too* _____. Great fiction this is not, but it does introduce 33 different adjectives in contextually meaningfully situations.

   After the students understand the modifiers and have heard them in a read-aloud context, this book makes an excellent beginning reader. As a follow-up, have students illustrate their favorite hats and describe them with either single adjectives, phrases (as in the book) or whole sentences.

Related Books By Same Author: See *Bears on Wheels* (1969) in the RAL.

HAND, HAND, FINGER, THUMB

by Al Perkins   illustrated by Eric Gurney
New York: Random House, 1969   29 pages

Grades: K-3   **ESL Level:** beginner
Genre: easy reader, picture book

Vocabulary: body, musical instruments, greetings
Grammar: nouns—singular and plural, present tense
Patterns: rhythmical chants, repeated word patterns and refrain

   This is a silly little nothing of a book that absolutely delights kids, but is likely to drive most adults crazy, especially its repeated refrain, "Dum ditty, dum ditty, dum dum dum." My students and own children continue to ask for it year after year. I think they enjoy the frivolity of it all, combined with its rhythmical chanting and repetitions. In its favor, it does a nice job of teaching body parts, simple greetings and present tense. It also provides a lot of practice on short vowel sounds and is a good easy reader. Guaranteed to get young children hooked on books!

Related Book by Same Author: *The Nose Book* (1970)

CAPS FOR SALE

by Esphyr Slobodkina
New York: Harper & Row, 1940, 1987; Scholastic, 1987 (big book)   42 pages

Grades: K-3   **ESL Level:** beginner, intermediate
Genre: picture book
Ethnic Identity: Russian

Vocabulary: clothing, body, colors
Grammar: past tense, adjectives
Patterns: repeated sentence and refrain

This tried and true story of a peddlar trying to retrieve his stack of colorful hats from a tree full of monkeys never fails to amuse its audience. Children and adults will long remember the peddlar/salesman's cheery refrain, "Caps! Caps for sale! Fifty cents a cap!" The choice of a peddlar as the happy central character provides a flavor of the author/illustrator's Russian origins. The monkeys are the hit of the story, however. And the peddlar's human struggles to "out monkey" them have kept this alive as classic children's literature for 50 years!

For additional reinforcement, have the children listen to this on cassette (Live Oaks Media, 1987).

YOU'LL SOON GROW INTO THEM, TITCH

by Pat Hutchins
New York: Greenwillow Books, 1983   26 pages

Grades: K-3   **ESL Level:** beginner
Genre: picture book

Vocabulary: clothing, family
Grammar: future tense—*will*, adjectives, contractions
Patterns: repeated sentence patterns, dialogue

Poor Titch. He always gets his two older siblings' hand-me-down clothes . . . until his dad takes him shopping to buy him his own new clothes. He then proudly passes on his old ones to the new baby.The story is brief, the patterns repeat and the illustrations are cheery. It carries an affirming family message. In sum, it is a good, short read-aloud for young beginners. Peppered with dialogues, it also lends itself to role playing and dramatization. It has five characters, just the right number for a group play.

Related Book: *Peter's Chair* (Keats, 1967)

Related Book By Same Author: *Titch* (1971)

Book By the Same Author: *Rosie's Walk* (1968) in the RAL.

LITTLE BEAR

by Else Holmelund Minarik   illustrated by Maurice Sendak
New York: Harper & Row, 1957, 1986 (with cassette)   63 pages

Grades: K-3   **ESL Level:** beginner, intermediate
Genre: easy reader, picture book

Vocabulary: clothing—winter; birthday, food—vegetables; animals, space
Grammar: present continuous tense, future tense—*will*, questions, conditionals
Patterns: repeated sentence patterns, dialogue

Little Bear has been loved by young audiences for over 30 years. This book includes four easy-to-read stories about him, each only 11-14 pages. The stories cover topics of interest to young children and thus, basic vocabulary. The last story, wishing about things he would like to do, conveniently reviews the adventures of the previous three. The soft illustrations, by award-winning artist Maurice Sendak, create a tender bond between mother and child. Because of the book's small size, the illustrations are best appreciated in groups under six children. An enduring childhood classic!

Related Books By Same Author: There are other, equally delightful, sequels. These include *Little Bear's Visit* (1961) about grandparents, *Little Bear's Friend* (1960) and *Father Bear Comes Home* (1959), a good choice for Father's Day.

THE ELVES AND THE SHOEMAKER

by Paul Galdone
New York: Clarion Books, 1984   30 pages

Grades: K-3, 2-5   **ESL Level:** intermediate, advanced
Genre: picture book—fairy tale

Vocabulary: clothing, household, tools
Grammar: adverbial clauses, conjunctions—*and*
Patterns: compound and complex sentences

Everyone loves the story of the poor shoemaker who is secretly helped to success by nimble elves and their nocturnal labors of love. It is reassuring to young and old alike how the shoemaker and his wife find a way to repay the elves' kindness.

While enjoying this classic Grimm fairy tale, students have an opportunity to practice basic clothing and household vocabulary while being exposed to fairly complex syntax. Galdone's warm illustrations, which fill each page, are of assistance here. They clearly explain each major action of the text, while capturing the emotions of the shoemaker and the magic of the elves. The specific vocabulary items are also distinctively drawn in detail. In sum, the pictures are both helpful and charming.

Books By the Same Author: Paul Galdone is a master at clearly retelling and dramatically illustrating fairy and folk tales. Those referred to in this RAL include *Rumplestiltskin* (1985), *Cinderella* (1978), *The Little Red Hen* (1973), *The Gingerbread Boy* (1975), *Henny Penny* (1968) and *The Three Billy Goats Gruff* (1973).

HOW AND WHY: A KID'S BOOK ABOUT THE BODY

by Catherine O'Neill   illustrated by Loel Barr
Mount Vernon, NY: Consumers Union, 1988   134 pages

Grades: 4-8   **ESL Level:** intermediate, advanced
Genre: non-fiction

Vocabulary: body, medical, health, feelings
Grammar: simple present tense, third person agreement, adverbial clauses, *wh*-questions
Patterns: question and answer sequence, repeated format

Fact can be as interesting as fiction, especially if it is written in an engaging style. Such is the case with this book, which explores how the body is made and how it functions. Questions such as "Why do I shiver?," "Why do I get bumps on my face?" and "Why do I have to get shots, anyway?" are aimed at middle school interests and are answered with enough information to satisfy their curiosity but not too much detail to bore them. That translates into about 1-3 pages per question. This allows the teacher to select one question/answer for a 5-10 minute read-aloud session, or to expand it proportionally. The questions are logically grouped into five chapter headings, which coordinate with traditional science topics. For example, one is labelled "Skin and Bones," and another "Sensational Senses."

It is not easy to simultaneously entertain, inform and assure a preteen audience. Catherine O'Neill, a former elementary school teacher and an experienced science writer, does this very well.

HOLIDAYS

MARTIN LUTHER KING DAY

MARTIN LUTHER KING, JR.

by Margaret Boone-Jones   illustrated by Rozel Scott
Chicago: Children's Press, 1968   28 pages

Grades: K-3   **ESL Level:** beginner, intermediate
Genre: biography, picture book, easy reader
Ethnic Identity: Black American

Vocabulary: occupations, values, human rights, politics
Grammar: conditionals, auxiliary verb—*to be*, past tense, imperatives
Patterns: simple sentence patterns

It is an art to simplify a complex life story and still capture its essence with accuracy. This author/kindergarten teacher has done it quite well. Written shortly after his death, her compassion for King's life and his life work is deeply felt throughout the text. The muted, black and white drawings which appear on nearly every page visually enhance the key experiences of King's life described in the text. By emphasizing his youth and by limiting the complexity of language, this short biography makes this famous Black American comprehensible to younger, elementary-age students and beginning SL learners. It is also good as a easy reader.

Related Books: *Martin Luther King, Jr. Free at Last* (Adler, 1986), *Martin Luther King* (Troll Associates, 1985). Also, *Rosa Parks* (Greenfield, 1973) is an easy reader for grades 2-5 (intermediate level) about "the mother" of the Civil Rights Movement.

VALENTINE'S DAY

BEE MY VALENTINE!

by Miriam Cohen   illustrated by Lillian Hoban
New York: Greenwillow Books, 1978; Dell, 1983   31 pages

Grades: K-3   **ESL Level:** intermediate
Genre: picture book
Ethnic Identity: multiethnic

Vocabulary: school, holiday customs, friendship
Grammar: exclamatory sentences
Patterns: dialogue

Poor Jim. He didn't get as many valentines as his other first grade classmates. But the same children who caused his problem also solve it by making him happy again . . . with music. It all ends happily with a school Valentine's Day party. Through this small picture book, students are introduced to the elementary school customs of valentine exchanges and holiday parties.

Miriam Cohen has a wonderful way of combining the best and worst of childhood and having it turn out OK. Her clever use of dialogue in picture books for primary age children creates authenticity in the characters. This also makes for a good read-aloud story. Students also enjoy looking at Lillian Hoban's colorful illustrations.

Related Books By Same Author: Cohen and Hoban have combined on five other books about Jim and his friends. One of them, *Best Friends* (1971) is in the RAL. Another, the easy reader, *When Will I Read* (1977) is also very affirming.

CHINESE NEW YEAR

GUNG HAY FAT CHOY

by June Behrens
Chicago: Children's Press, 1982   31 pages

Grades: K-3, 2-5   **ESL Level:** beginner, intermediate
Genre: non-fiction picture book
Ethnic Identity: Asian-Chinese, Asian American

Vocabulary: holiday customs, food, family, parade
Grammar: simple present tense, exclamatory sentences, auxiliary verb—*to be*
Patterns: passive voice

This book explains the significance of Chinese New Year and describes its celebration here in the United States as a giant communal birthday party, replete with feasting, presents and family celebrations. The highlight of all this is the Golden Dragon Parade which comes alive in numerous, color photographs. Do not be alarmed by the Chinese title—it is fully translated in the text, the rest of which is written in English.

Although the simple sentence patterns allow this to be read independently by most intermediate level SL students, the topic becomes more exciting when shared with a group. This can also lead to further discussion of how this holiday is celebrated in your own area. Perhaps even a trip could be planned to the local parade.

Related Books: *Chinese New Year* (Brown, 1987) is also a picture book, but with fewer photographs and those limited to black and white, the book seems less exciting. *Mei Lei* (Handforth, 1938) is a story about a young girl's experiences during Chinese New Year in China. This was the second recipient of the Caldecott Award. It is a little dated by today's standards, but still special during this holiday time.

Books By the Same Author: *I Can Be an Astronaut* (1984) in the RAL and *My Favorite Things* (1975).

PASSOVER

I LOVE PASSOVER

by Marilyn Hirsh
New York: Holiday House, 1985   31 pages

Grades: K-3   **ESL Level:** beginner, intermediate
Genre: non-fiction picture book
Ethnic Identity: Jewish American

Vocabulary: holiday customs, food, extended family
Grammar: action verbs, simple present tense, third person agreement, subject pronouns—first and third persons
Patterns: simple sentences

Passover celebrates the exodus of the Hebrews from Egypt. The Biblical story comes from the Old Testament (see related books). This story of freedom from bondage carries a universal message with a timeless appeal. This picture book both tells the historical Passover story and describes the contemporary holiday customs. The illustrations are clear and helpful. The main characters are a five and six year-old girl and boy, so the story is most age appropriate for grades K-3. However, the information is simply and objectively presented, and thus the book can stretch to older audiences as well.

A wonderful follow-up activity is to celebrate this holiday in your classroom with a food-based, mini-Seder. Don't forget to hide the "afikoman," the children's favorite Passover game. If there are no Jewish families in your classes, contact a local synagogue for volunteer help.

Related Book: *Exodus* (Chaikin, 1987) is a beautiful picture book version of the Bible story, for intermediates-advanced, grades 4-8.

Book By the Same Author: *I Love Hanukkah* (1984)

MOTHER'S DAY

ARE YOU MY MOTHER?

by P.D. Eastman
New York: Random House, 1960, 1989   63 pages

Grades: Pre K-1, K-3   **ESL Level:** beginner
Genre: easy reader, picture book

Vocabulary: animals, natural environment, transportation
Grammar: future tense—*will*, past tense, simple present tense, negative and interrogative sentences
Patterns: repeated refrain, repeated format

Mother bird leaves her nest to get some food for her baby, who is just about to hatch. When he does, he looks for his mother, all over the place. He asks everything from a dog to a bulldozer, "Are you my mother?" The comical quest and his amusing escapades are happily resolved when mother returns with a plump juicy worm. All is well, once again, in their cozy nest.

Children love this story and love to hear it over and over again. Why? Perhaps it is the basic underlying theme of maternal bonding. Perhaps it is the simple text in repeated patterns. Perhaps it is the ridiculous situations in which baby bird finds himself. Perhaps it is the funny drawings which accompany the text. Probably, it is the combination of all these. It works well both as a read-aloud and later, as an independent reader.

This popular book has been translated into French and Spanish (Macmillan, 1967), making it very useful for bilingual programs. Cassettes are available in both of these languages, plus English.

THE MOTHER'S DAY MICE

by Eve Bunting   illustrated by Jan Brett
New York: Clarion Books, 1986   32 pages

Grades: K-3   **ESL Level:** intermediate, advanced
Genre: picture book

Vocabulary: natural environments, household, clothing
Grammar: superlatives, adjectives, adverbs of manner
Patterns: dialogue

Three nicely-dressed mice children go out to the meadow at dawn, seeking presents for Mother's Day. The Biggest finds a dandelion fluff ball, good for making wishes, and the Middle chooses a luscious strawberry, symbolic of the coming summer. But Little Mouse comes up with the most unusual gift of all. All three are warmly appreciated by mother on her special day. The vocabulary and choice of modifiers make this a challenging listening experience for SL students. The illustrations of the large-sized mice, set in their natural environment, provide additional visual stimulation. This book can be comprehended at many different levels. It may not be easy, but it is satisfying.

Related Books By Same Author: Other holiday stories by the same author/artist/publisher combination: *The Valentine Bears* (1983) and *St. Patrick's Day in the Morning* (1980).

Book By the Same Author: *How Many Days to America?* (1988) in the RAL.

JOURNEY TO THE BRIGHT KINGDOM

by Elizabeth Winthrop   illustrated by Charles Mikolaycak
New York: Holiday House, 1979   38 pages

Grades: 4-8   **ESL Level:** intermediate, advanced
Genre: folk tale, short story
Ethnic Identity: Asian-Japanese

Vocabulary: family—mother-daughter; home, handicap—blindness
Grammar: adverbs of manner, adverbial clauses
Patterns: complex sentence patterns

A Japanese folktale is expanded into this short novel, enhanced by occasional, Oriental-style illustrations. The story is somewhat somber, yet infused with the hopeful magic of Kakure-sato, the underground kingdom ruled by mice. There is no sadness, sickness or blindness there, but only a trusted few are allowed to visit. Unknowingly, it is these mice that Kiyo befriends on her walks home from school. It is these same mice that Kiyo's mother beautifully sketched before she lost her eyesight, before her daughter's birth. And finally, it is to their kingdom that Kiyo finally leads her mother, who so yearns to see her daughter and the rest of life, at least one time.

This a Mother's Day story for middle school students and above. Through it, you feel the comfort a loving child can bring to a handicapped parent. It affirms the strength of children and their importance to their parents. It is a very touching book.

Book By the Same Illustrator: *The Perfect Crane* (Laurin, 1981) in the RAL.

FATHER'S DAY

JUST LIKE DADDY

by Frank Asch
Englewood Cliffs, NJ: Prentice Hall, 1981   30 pages

Grades: Pre-K-1, K-3   **ESL Level:** beginner
Genre: picture book

Vocabulary: daily activities, clothing, recreation — fishing
Grammar: action verbs, past tense, direct objects
Patterns: repeated refrain and format

This short simple story follows a little boy bear, who follows his Daddy . . . until the end, when he follows _____. Let your children guess the ending during the first read-aloud session. They will chuckle at it in each subsequent reading. There is something very basic and very satisfying about this unpretentious little story. It affirms not only the father-son bonding but also the nuclear family unit. The repeated refrain "Just Like Daddy" can be used as the theme for follow-up Father's Day activities.

The bright, but uncluttered pictures clearly demonstrate each of the activities described on the pages. They provide useful visual aids. Don't forget to watch for the bird. He's part of the family too!

Related Book: *Daddy, Play With Me!* (Watanabe, 1984)

Books By the Same Author: *Bear Shadow* (1985) and *Moon Game* (1984)

POEMS FOR FATHER

selected by Myra Cohn Livingston   illustrated by Robert Casilla
New York: Holiday House, 1989   32 pages

Grades: 2-5, 4-8   **ESL Level:** intermediate
Genre: poetry, picture book
Ethnic Identity: multiethnic

Vocabulary: family, emotions
Patterns: rhyming, repeated sentence patterns

These eighteen, mostly contemporary, poems describe many kinds of fathers, including stepfathers and fathers who have moved away. I find one called "Daddy," written by the compiler herself, Myra Cohn Livingston very poignant. In just 44 plain words, she captures the mixed emotions a boy feels for a father he loved, but who is no longer there. Certainly not all the poems are sad. Many recount humorous, shared experiences. Others talk with pride of father. All children can find some poem here with which to identify. Together, they create a modern kaleidoscope of fatherhood. To insure this, over half of the poems were commissioned especially for this volume.

Nearly all the poems fit comfortably on one page and each is movingly illustrated in the hues of blue, gray and white, with splashes of rosy orange for warmth. This is a lovely picture book of poems. Using these as models, encourage your students to write and illustrate their own poem/s as a Father's Day gift.

Related Book By Same Author: *Poems for Mother* (1988) is a similar volume, equally perfect for Mother's Day.

U.S. INDEPENDENCE DAY-FOURTH OF JULY

THE STAR-SPANGLED BANNER

illustrated by Peter Spier
New York: Doubleday, 1973, 1986   50 pages

Grades: 4-8   **ESL Level:** advanced
Genre: picture book—singable book
Ethnic Identity: European—British

Vocabulary: military, patriotic
Grammar: adjectives, adverbs of manner, questions
Patterns: repeated refrain, complex sentence patterns

Peter Spier has exquisitely illustrated the U.S. national anthem in this majestic, over-sized picture book. Although Francis Scott Key's poem was originally written in 1814, it has come to symbolize American independence from England, earned on July 4, 1776. The holiday is celebrated on that date each year with parades, pride and fireworks.

Although Spier's book does not describe this holiday, it captures the spirit of U.S. patriotism by visually detailing, phrase by phrase, the words of what has become the national anthem. He does this by blending both historical and contemporary images of the United States. Spier's illustrations help decipher the difficult language and vocabulary of Key's original poem. Historical notes and musical notation are provided at the back of the book. Another Spier masterpiece! Challenging but accessible.

Books By the Same Author: See *Bored-Nothing to Do!* (1978) in the RAL.

HALLOWEEN

IT'S HALLOWEEN

by Jack Prelutsky   illustrated by Marylin Hafner
New York: Greenwillow Books, 1977; Scholastic, 1987 (includes a cassette)   56 pages

Grades: K-3, 2-5   **ESL Level:** beginner, intermediate
Genre: poetry, easy reader, mystery

Vocabulary: holiday customs, clothing, numbers—10-1, animals—cats
Grammar: present tense—simple and continuous, conjunctions—*and, or*
Patterns: rhyming

This collection of 13 short poems about this special children's holiday delight and excite young listeners. Each poem focuses on one aspect of the holiday, be it costumes, trick or treating, jack-o-lanterns, ghosts or haunted houses. Collectively, they fully explain the holiday's customs. This is important for many ESL students, for whom this is a new cultural experience. The illustrations lend humor and the appropriate amount of scariness for its young audience. It's upbeat and bewitching!

Poems always work best when first introduced orally. This can be followed up by listening to them on cassette, available from the publisher. These are also intended for independent easy reading. This would be appropriate for intermediate ESL students.

Related Book: *Halloween* (Gibbons, 1984)

Book By the Same Author: *Nightmares* (1976) is a collection of scary poems for grades 4-8, advanced ESL level (an ALA Notable Book).

ESTEBAN AND THE GHOST

by Sibyl Hancock   illustrated by Dirk Zimmer
New York: Dial Books (E.P. Dutton), 1983, 1985   31 pages

Grades: K-3, 2-5   **ESL Level:** intermediate, advanced
Genre: picture book—folk tale, mystery
Ethnic Identity: European—Spanish

Vocabulary: body, places in the community—castle, small village
Grammar: adverbial phrases, exclamatory sentences
Patterns: dialogues

Modern Halloween derives from the European holiday of All Hallow's Eve, the night to frighten away the ghosts and evil spirits before all Saint's Day, the following morning. From this origin derives many of the holiday's stories, including this one.

This Halloween ghost story combines the traditional elements of scariness and gore, but injects it with a bit of bravado and a healthy dose of humor. Based on an old Spanish folk tale, it is actually set on all Hallow's Eve in a haunted castle of a small Spanish village. The wealthy owner has annually offered "a thousand gold reales" to drive the ghost away. But none have returned alive from this challenge. Esteban, a merry mender of pots seems undaunted by this history and offers to try his luck. So the drama begins! The black and white line drawings with full color wash authenticate the European village setting and also inject humor into the character of Esteban, a most engaging and earthy personality.

The rather long story (for a picture book), descriptive vocabulary and complicated sentence structures make it most appropriate for advanced ESL students. It presents them with both a challenging and a charming story! An ALA Notable Children's Book and Booklist Reviewer's Choice.

Related Books: *The Tailypo. A Ghost Story* (Galdone, 1977) is for grades 2-5, beginner-intermediate ESL proficiency level.

THANKSGIVING

THANKSGIVING DAY

by Gail Gibbons
New York: Holiday House, 1983   28 pages

Grades: K-3, 4-8   **ESL Level:** beginner, intermediate
Genre: non-fiction picture book
Ethnic Identity: Native American

Vocabulary: food, harvest, family, friendship, community, immigration
Grammar: auxiliary verb—*to be*, verbs of physical activity, past tense, existential sentences—
  there is/was
Patterns: simple sentences patterns, passive voice

Thanksgiving combines elements of the universal harvest festival with specifics of the first American immigrant experiences. As it is our most uniquely major U.S. holiday, nearly every ESL teacher struggles to explain it to her students.

In this book, Gibbons briefly traces Thanksgiving's origins and traditions from 17th century New England and concludes with a realistic description of a modern-day celebration. Her talent is her ability to synthesize vast amounts of non-fiction material into a simple picture-book format. Even with devoting only a sentence to two to each topic, she fills the succinct text with interesting information. Each colorful illustration clearly explains the text below, the importance of which cannot be underestimated for SL students. The author's straightforward style appeals to the entire elementary-age span. This is a very useful contribution.

Related Books By Same Author: *Halloween* (1984) and *Christmas Time* (1982)

Books By the Same Author: Gail Gibbons writes high-quality, picture book non-fiction. Her books, which have won numerous awards, are very useful in teaching content-based topics in a literature format. They usually appeal to a wide age-range. Others included in the RAL are *The Milk Makers* (1985), *Playgrounds* (1985), *Fill it Up! All About Service Stations* (1985), *Department Store* (1984), *Weather Forecasting* (1987), *Zoo* (1983), and *The Seasons of Arnold's Apple Tree* (1984).

OVER THE RIVER AND THROUGH THE WOODS

by Lydia Maria Child   illustrated by Brinton Turkle
New York: Putnam Publishing Group
(Coward, McCann & Geoghegan), 1974; Scholastic, 1987   28 pages

Grades: 2-5   **ESL Level:** intermediate
Genre: picture book—singable book

Vocabulary: seasons—winter; seasonal activities, food—holiday; household, family, animals—horse, dog
Grammar: prepositional phrases of place, simple present tense
Patterns: repeated sentence

This book captures the popular Thanksgiving song of the title's name through stunning illustrations. Some American children will be familiar with the first and last verses of this holiday song, marking the beginning and end of this wintertime family journey to grandfather's house, but how many know the other ten verses, each adding something special to the building excitement. As in most well-done singable books, the words and music are reprinted in full at the end. What makes this book so successful are Turkle's inviting illustrations and the clever book design, which capture not only the details but also the mood.

This is an idealized Thanksgiving of a wealthy, extended family of another century, but it is part of our heritage and as such, deserves to be shared with children unfamiliar with the historical celebration. A beautiful book!

Books By the Same Illustrator: *Obadiah* books (six separate titles), *Do Not Open* (1981) and *Deep in the Forest* (1976) in the RAL.

CHRISTMAS

PETER SPIER'S CHRISTMAS!

by Peter Spier
New York: Doubleday, 1983   38 pages

Grades: K-3, 4-8   **ESL Level:** beginner, intermediate
Genre: wordless picture book

Vocabulary: holiday customs, shopping, food, home, family, church, celebration

In over 90 color paintings, Peter Spier brings to life the spirit and joy (and also the work) of Christmas. Each picture, whether full page or one-quarter sized, is rich detailed. Through very effective sequencing, together they fully describe the holiday customs. Although there are church scenes, the religious story is not the focus here. This secular approach can be very useful for the book's use in a school setting.

For the read-aloud session, vocabulary and sentence patterns can be added by the teacher. The pictures provide enough visual complexity to span the beginner to intermediate range. Students, especially non and limited readers, also enjoy studying this wordless story book on their own. It is very attractive and appealing to a wide age range.

Related Book: *Christmas Time* (Gibbons, 1982)

Books by Same Author: See *Bored-Nothing to Do!* (1978) in the RAL.

THE NIGHT BEFORE CHRISTMAS

by Clement Moore
New York: Scholastic, 1985

illustrated by James Marshall
30 pages

Grades: K-3, 2-5   **ESL Level:** intermediate
Genre: narrative poem

Vocabulary: toys, household, holiday customs
Grammar: adjectives, nouns
Patterns: rhyming, metaphoric language

About the classic popularity of this famous Christmas poem there can be no doubt. For over 150 years now, children have delighted (and memorized) these poetic lines of Santa Claus's nocturnal visit. The only question can be which version to choose. Over the years, there have been hundreds, most of them with large, beautiful homes in idyllic settings.

As a change of pace, I recommend a modern, somewhat irreverent version. In Marshall's edition, the house is small and cramped, filled with children, pets and all their stuff. Santa, in cowboy boots, does his traditional stocking-filling thing, but then he raids the refrigerator for pickles and a soda. Kids find this version amusing because it adds new twists. For contemporary children, it offers easy identification.

Related Books: For more traditional illustrations, see the editions illustrated by dePaola (1980) and Gorsline (1975).

Books By the Same Illustrator: *George and Martha* books (1972)

Food/Nutrition

THE SUPERMARKET

by Anne Rockwell and Harlow Rockwell
New York: Macmillan, 1979

22 pages

Grades: Pre-K-1, K-3   **ESL Level:** beginner
Genre: picture book—concept book
Ethnic Identity: multiethnic

Vocabulary: supermarket, food
Grammar: simple present tense, third person agreement, plural nouns—count and mass
Patterns: simple sentences

This book allows the audience to observe the different stages of weekly grocery shopping with a boy and his mother. Set in a loose story format, the simple text covers basic foods and supermarket vocabulary. The pictures facilitate clear identification of the objects and scenes. While not great literature, it is a very useful book. If possible, coordinate its presentation with a field trip to a local supermarket.

Books By the Same Author: See *Happy Birthday to Me* (1981) in the RAL.

LET'S EAT

by Gyo Fujikawa
New York: Putnam Publishing Group, 1975, 1989   16 pages

Grades: Pre-K-1, K-3   **ESL Level:** beginner
Genre: picture book—concept book
Ethnic Identity: multiethnic

Vocabulary: food, animals
Grammar: nouns, indefinite articles
Patterns: question format

This book begins by stating simply, "Here are some delicious things to eat. What do YOU like best?" In the subsequent pages the pictures illustrate happy children enjoying their favorite foods. The final scene of a birthday party table filled with cake, ice cream and cookies, provides a fitting climax! Pause, to allow students to absorb it all.

This book is an easy way to introduce both food vocabulary and literature to primary age students. The multiethnic characters are an additional plus. The heavy cardboard pages allow students to pore over this book at their leisure, after it has been orally introduced. They will soon be reading the pictures, which is, after all, the first step to full reading. An ever popular book!

Related Book: *Think About Tasting* (1986, Pluckrose) in this section of the RAL.

Related Books By Same Author: *Let's Play* (1975) and *Let's Grow a Garden* (1978)

GREEN EGGS AND HAM

by Dr. Seuss
New York: Random House, 1960, 1987 edition includes a cassette   62 pages

Grades: K-3   **ESL Level:** beginner
Genre: easy reader, picture book

Vocabulary: food, animals, transportation
Grammar: conditionals, future tense—*will*, simple present tense, negative and exclamatory
     sentences, prepositional phrases of place, direct objects
Patterns: rhythmical chants, rhyming, repeated sentence patterns (!)

This well-known story delightfully tells of Sam's (aka "I-am-Sam" aka "Sam-I-am") attempts to get his friend to taste green eggs and ham. His friend repeatedly insists "I do not like green eggs and ham" and rebuffs all comical and rhyming combinations to try them. He eventually bows to the pressure, tries them, loves them, and thanks "Sam I am." The long-standing popularity of this book rests on its clever rhymes, effective repetitions and active, cartoon-like drawings.

Designed as an easy reader, it also works well as a read-aloud, especially for those SL students not yet reading independently. It uses and repeats numerous grammatical structures, which can be reinforced in follow-up activities. This is a tried and true winner!

Books By Same Author: See *Hop on Pop* (1963) in the RAL.

THE LITTLE RED HEN

by Paul Galdone
Boston: Houghton Mifflin (Clarion Books), 1973, 1987 edition includes a cassette
37 pages

Grades: Pre K-1, K-3   **ESL Level:** beginner, intermediate
Genre: picture book—fairy tale

Vocabulary: animals, house, baking
Grammar: past tense, action verbs, negation, future tense—*will*, direct objects, *wh*-questions
Patterns: short sentences, repeated sentence patterns and sentences

Comfortably established in a rustic farm house are three lazy animals and one hardworking one. The industrious hen does all the work necessary to produce a cake—from the planting of the wheat, to the grinding it into flour to baking it. All her requests for help are unheeded until the end, when the others are all there to help her eat it. They then get a rude awakening, which convinces them to change their ways.

Paul Galdone's version of this classic fairy tale is very satisfying to read aloud. The illustrations are colorful, dramatic and fully explanatory of the text, which is kept to a minimum on each page. For example, each of the various stages needed to develop grains of wheat into a baked good are individually drawn. He also makes the most of the numerous repetitions, which is good for SL learners. This provides ample opportunities for oral practice, role playing or even a small group play.

Books By Same Author: See *The Elves and the Shoemaker* (1984) in the RAL.

THE GINGERBREAD BOY

by Paul Galdone
Boston: Houghton Mifflin (Clarion Books), 1975, 1983   35 pages

Grades: Pre K-1, K-3   **ESL Level:** intermediate
Genre: picture book—fairy tale

Vocabulary: farm, animals, natural environments
Grammar: present perfect tense, contractions
Patterns: cumulative repetition

The folktale of the clever gingerbread boy who outsmarts everyone except the sly fox is a happy part of literary childhood. Galdone's rhythmical text and expressive illustrations make this a particularly charming edition. The repeated use of the present perfect tense in the cumulative refrain also provides an excellent opportunity to practice this difficult tense in a meaningful context.

Galdone's ending injects that it is all right to eat the gingerbread boy . . . after all that's what it's for. A perfect follow-up is for the class to bake and eat their own batch. Enjoy!

Books By the Same Author: See *The Elves and the Shoemaker* (1984) in the RAL.

THINK ABOUT TASTING

by Henry Pluckrose   illustrated by Chris Fairclough
New York: Franklin Watts, 1986   28 pages

Grades: K-3, 2-5   **ESL Level:** beginner
Genre: non-fiction picture book

Vocabulary: food
Grammar: questions, simple present tense, nouns, adjectives
Patterns: question format

This attractive picture book makes us aware of the diversity of tastes in the food we eat. It does this by asking leading questions about different foods, which are displayed in smartly designed, color photographs. They are large enough to be seen by a big group and look good enough to eat!

A natural extension is to gather an assortment of foods, have students sample them and try to describe the tastes. Not only is this an excellent vocabulary builder for food names but also for descriptors and adjectives! Such a project smoothly integrates primary-level science with language development.

Related Book: *Let's Eat* (Fujikawa, 1975) in the RAL.

Related Books By Same Author: See *Think About Smelling* (1986) in the RAL.

PANCAKES FOR BREAKFAST

by Tomie dePaola
New York: Harcourt Brace Jovanovich, 1978   31 pages

Grades: Pre K-1, K-3   **ESL Level:** beginner
Genre: wordless picture book

Vocabulary: food, cooking, places in the community—rural, farm

This talented artist uses pictures to tell the story of an old farm lady who dreams of eating *Pancakes for Breakfast*. With a lot of work and a little ingenuity, she gets her wish. From her own farm she gathers eggs, milks her cow and churns the butter. All of this is a healthy antidote to picking these ingredients off a supermarket shelf.

The book includes a recipe for the pancakes. Cooking and eating them as a class project makes a perfect follow-up activity. It also allows you to introduce nutritional information about breakfast, an important meal for children's success at school.

Books By the Same Author: See *Mary Had a Little Lamb* (1984) in the RAL.

THE GREY LADY AND THE STRAWBERRY SNATCHER

by Molly Bang
New York: Macmillan (Four Winds Books), 1980   48 pages

Grades: K-3, 2-5   **ESL Level:** beginner
Genre: wordless picture book, mystery
Ethnic Identity: Black American

Vocabulary: food, places in the community—small town, rural

This story begins innocently enough with an old black woman buying a delicious-looking basket of strawberries in a vegetable market. A mysterious creature also finds them attractive and thus begins the adventurous chase through the town, on a bus ride, into a forest and finally home. In the end, although the old woman outwits her would be "strawberry snatcher," they are both satisfied. It is an imaginative, win-win solution. This dramatic story line, complemented by richly detailed pictures, earned this book a Caldecott Honor.

This wordless picture book frees both the reader and listener to a very creative experience. The numerous illustrations and clear action sequence make it easy for either the teacher or students to tell this story. It also affords the opportunity to practice third person agreement in the simple present tense.

Books by the Same Author: *The Paper Crane* (1985) in this section of the RAL and *Ten, Nine, Eight* (1983), another Caldecott Honor Book.

STONE SOUP

by Ann McGovern   illustrated by Winslow Pels
New York: Scholastic, 1986   32 pages

Grades: K-3, 2-5   **ESL Level:** intermediate
Genre: picture book—folk tale; easy reader
Ethnic Identity: European

Vocabulary: food, cooking, places in the community—rural; gardening
Grammar: future tense, conditionals, imperatives, adjectives
Patterns: repeated word patterns, sentences and format, dialogue

In this old French folktale a hungry young man is refused food by a greedy village woman. He tricks her into cooking a delicious soup filled with vegetables and meat by telling her that he can make soup from a stone. It is a classic tale and one that lends itself well to a class project of cooking soup and writing about the experience.

This modern version can be compared to the 1947 edition, a Caldecott Honor Book, by Marcia Brown, which is also still in print. The newer one adds predictable and repeated patterns which are helpful learning tools. They make it possible, for example, to recommend the book as an independent reader, after a read-aloud session. The new edition also includes a variety of verb tenses, which can be used for grammar practice. It is basically a simpler version, both in language and in number of characters. Lost in the 1986 edition are the colorful soldiers and the vibrant French village setting with busy peasants. For your more advanced students, try introducing both editions and comparing. See which one they prefer!

Book by the Same Author: *If You Sailed on the Mayflower* (1969)

CLOUDY WITH A CHANCE OF MEATBALLS

by Judi Barrett   illustrated by Ron Barrett
New York: Scholastic Books, 1978; Live Oak Media, 1985 (includes cassette and guide)   30 pages

Grades: 2-5   **ESL Level:** intermediate
Genre: picture book, modern fantasy

Vocabulary: food, places in the community—small town; weather
Grammar: past tense, adverbs of time
Patterns: declarative sentences

Grandpa tells a whopper of a bedtime story about the town of "Chewandswallow," where food falls from the sky three times a day. Bad weather causes the daily food drop to take a nasty turn, and eventually the townsfolk are crowded out by food. This scenario creates a very imaginative story. Its humor appeals especially to older elementary students, who are usually quite intrigued with the idea of an ongoing, free food supply. This book works well as a light and lively break from a science unit on food and nutrition. It is very popular with children.

HANSEL AND GRETEL

by the Brothers Grimm   illustrated by Susan Jeffers
New York: E. P. Dutton (Dial Books), 1980   30 pages

Grades: K-3, 2-5   **ESL Level:** intermediate
Genre: picture book—fairy tale
Ethnic Identity: European

Vocabulary: family, natural environments—forest; food—bread, candy; animals
Grammar: future tense, imperatives, action verbs, past tense
Patterns: dialogue, complex sentences

This clear retelling of a classic fairy tale affirms the ingenuity of children and the archetypal triumph of good over evil. Susan Jeffers' handsome illustrations in this oversized picture book format recommend it as a read-aloud selection. Although many students will be familiar with the story, they will be drawn to it again through these large pictures and attractive book design. Hansel and Gretel are portrayed old enough to appeal to a wide age range of elementary age students. Details are precisely drawn with fine lines in a natural setting of forests and animals. Somehow, a sense of magic manages to permeate this woodland reality. An artistic masterpiece!

POEM STEW

by William Cole   illustrated by Karen Ann Weinhaus
New York: J.B. Lippincott, 1981   84 pages

Grades: 2-5, 4-8   **ESL Level:** intermediate
Genre: poetry

Vocabulary: food

This is an attractive collection of 57 humorous, mostly contemporary poems about food, written by such popular poets as Ogden Nash, Shel Silverstein, Myra Cohn Livingston and some by the compiler himself. Each poem is honored with its own page or two and its own whimsical illustration. The book concludes with the usual author and title indexes.

Short poems, such as these, make good read-alouds because two or three can be squeezed into a five-minute spot. This enjoyable volume doubly appeals to older elementary students—both in their stomachs and their funny bone! It's perfect for a light break from a more serious food unit.

THE PAPER CRANE

by Molly Bang
New York: Greenwillow Books, 1985   32 pages

Grades: K-3, 2-5   **ESL Level:** intermediate
Genre: picture book—folk tale; modern fantasy
Ethnic Identity: Asian-Japanese, multiethnic

Vocabulary: restaurants, food
Grammar: past tense, conjunctions
Patterns: compound sentences

A mysterious stranger comes to a lovely restaurant which has, alas, fallen on bad times. The kindly owner feeds him, even though the old Japanese man can repay him only with a paper crane. The man disappears, leaving behind his magical crane, which brings music, happiness and success to the restaurant. Bang's three-dimensional illustrations, filled with multiethnic people enjoying a good time together, breathe modern life into this ancient Japanese folktale.

It is fun to follow-up this story with some origami—Japanese paper folding. Start with a paper crane, of course! A different kind of reinforcement is to watch the eight-minute filmstrip while listening to the cassette. This is available from Random House/McGraw-Hill Educational Resources.

Related Book: *The Perfect Crane* (Laurin, 1981) in the RAL.

Books By the Same Author: See *The Grey Lady and the Strawberry Snatcher* in this section of the RAL.

HOW MY PARENTS LEARNED TO EAT

by Ina R. Friedman   illustrated by Allen Say
Boston: Houghton Mifflin, 1984   32 pages

Grades: K-3, 2-5   **ESL Level:** intermediate
Genre: picture book—concept book
Ethnic Identity: Asian-Japanese, Asian American

Vocabulary: food, manners, family, emotions
Grammar: auxiliary verb—*to be*, past tense, adjectives
Patterns: dialogues

A young American sailor and Japanese school girl meet and court in Japan. In order to please the other, each secretly learns the eating customs of the other's culture. All ends happily in a marriage proposal. The illustrations, done in muted watercolors, sensitively capture both the details and nuances of Japanese culture.

The story is warmly told from the perspective of their bicultural daughter, who begins the story eating Japanese food and ends it with an American meal. She is comfortable with both. As she says, "For me, it's natural."

This light story affirms bicultural marriages, while subtly portraying the cross-cultural misunderstandings that do arise between Asian and American customs. Enjoyable and thought provoking.

THE MILK MAKERS

by Gail Gibbons
New York: Macmillan, 1985   32 pages

Grades: 2-5, 4-8   **ESL Level:** beginner, intermediate
Genre: non-fiction picture book
Ethnic Identity: multiethnic

Vocabulary: farm, food production, food—milk products; animals—cows; transportation
Grammar: auxiliary verb—to be, present tense, adverbs of time, existential sentences—there is/
   are
Patterns: passive voice, academic language

This excellent book covers milk production from pasture to pasteurization to supermarket shelf. Award winning Gail Gibbons has once again thoroughly researched her topic, synthesized the information and presented it clearly. The bright pictures which cover ¾ of each page clearly explain the three to four sentences of text below. Some illustrations include diagrams with labels.

Neither the pictures nor the text are babyish, allowing the book to be used from kindergarten through 8th grade. Depending on the age and proficiency level of the class, you can vary the amount of text read per page. This is very good for content-based science lessons on milk production and milk products. Another star for Gibbons!

Related Book: *Milk* (Carrick, 1985)

Books By the Same Author: See *Thanksgiving Day* (1983) in the RAL.

NUTRITION

by Leslie Jean LeMaster
Chicago: Children's Press, 1985   48 pages

Grades: 2-5, 4-8   **ESL Level:** beginner, intermediate
Genre: non-fiction picture book, easy reader
Ethnic Identity: multiethnic

Vocabulary: food, nutrition, health
Grammar: simple present tense, third person agreement, nouns
Patterns: academic language

"Almost everyone will agree that eating is fun. Food tastes good . . . Here's to good nutrition." Sandwiched between these first and last sentences is your basic information about nutrition. This includes a one to three page description of each of the six nutrient groups and the four basic food groups. Because the photographs depict a wide age range of people, it can be used comfortably by older elementary and middle school students. The syntax, limited amount of text and abundance of pictures make it appropriate for an advanced beginner ESL level, both as a read-aloud and later for answering factual questions.

This is not great literature, but it is very useful for learning language through the content areas and for teaching or reinforcing the ubiquitous food unit. A *New True Book*.

Books in the Same Series: This *"New True Series"*, a primary series, includes over 75 non-fiction picture books. They cover a wide range of topics, from *Olympics* to *Television* to *Volcanoes*. Those in the RAL are *Weather Experiments* (Webster, 1982), *Your Heart and Blood* (LeMaster, 1984) and *Space Colonies* (Fradin, 1985).

Community

PLACES

ODD ONE OUT

by Rodney Peppe
New York: Penguin (Viking Books), 1974   26 pages

Grades: Pre K-1, K-3   **ESL Level:** beginner
Genre: picture book—concept book

Vocabulary: places in the community
Grammar: past tense, action verbs, conjunctions, prepositional phrases of place
Patterns: short, simple sentences, compound sentences

This cheerful book follows little Peter in his walk around the town and countryside. Everything is fine, except that in each of the eleven scenes something doesn't belong. Discerning the *Odd One Out* requires careful looking, and explaining it provides opportunities for natural language use. The clear and detailed illustrations help this game, which also develops the concept of similar and different. The book helps vocabulary building and communication; it's both fun and practical!

BEARS IN THE NIGHT

by Stan and Jan Berenstain
New York: Random House, 1971   32 pages

Grades: K-3   **ESL Level:** beginner
Genre: easy reader, picture book—concept book

Vocabulary: natural environment—woods
Grammar: prepositional phrases of place, definite article, singular nouns
Patterns: repeated word patterns, cumulative repetitions

This easy reader succeeds where most basals fail. It does so by infusing simple words with dramatic conflict. The illustrations further enhance the suspense. What's out there? What has frightened the bears out of their beds in the dark of night? Like other Berenstain beginning readers, this one also uses phrases, rather than complete sentences and each phrase is separately illustrated. In addition, one or two phrases from the previous page are repeated on the next to provide continuity and additional reading practice. Plus, the book is filled with prepositional phrases, which are usually difficult to explain to young children. This book nicely does it for you—isolating one grammar point while integrating it into literature.

A read-aloud introduction will generally stimulate the students to try to read the book themselves. Even if they are only reading the pictures, they still feel successful.

Related Book: *Klippity Klop* (Emberly, 1974)-prepositions

Books By the Same Authors: See *Bears on Wheels* (1969) in the RAL.

PLAYGROUNDS

by Gail Gibbons
New York: Holiday House, 1985   32 pages

Grades: K-3   **ESL Level:** beginner
Genre: picture book—concept book
Ethnic Identity: multiethnic

Vocabulary: games, recreation, toys
Grammar: existential sentences (*there is/are*), countable nouns—plurals, adjectives
Patterns: repeated format

Playgrounds are part of every community and for many children, it is their favorite part. This book provides a colorful guide to every possible playground equipment and activity. It also contains a simple text, with a word label attached to each vocabulary item.

When read-aloud, it is a wonderful stimulus for students to talk about their playground preferences and play experiences. Students also enjoy studying the pictures themselves. It is the next best thing to being there!

This happy book deserves to be followed up (or preceded) with a trip to neighborhood or school playground. Story writing and/or drawings can complete this mini-unit on outdoor play.

Books By the Same Author: See *Thanksgiving Day* (1983) in the RAL.

THE FIRE STATION BOOK

by Nancy Bundt
Minneapolis, MN: Carolrhoda Books, 1981   29 pages

Grades: 2-5, 4-8   **ESL Level:** intermediate
Genre: non-fiction picture book

Vocabulary: transportation—fire trucks; vehicles, places in the community—fire station; clothing, equipment
Grammar: simple present tense, nouns, adverbial clauses
Patterns: passive voice

Over 80 black and white photographs and a descriptive text follow a "regular" day in the life of a fire station, including, of course, a big fire. Because the photographs concentrate on adults and machines doing "grown-up" things, this book spans a wide age range.

Be forewarned that this does read somewhat like a science text. While this makes it useful for follow-up, content-based activities, it distracts from its read-aloud qualities. For example, it does not dramatize the fire station or fire fighting. A supplemental field trip to the fire station or to a fire will have to do that. This is a good primer or reinforcement for such a trip.

Related Books: *Fire! Fire!* (Gibbons, 1984) and *Fire Trucks* (Marston, 1984)

THE LITTLE HOUSE

by Virginia Lee Burton
Boston: Houghton Mifflin, 1942, 1978   40 pages

Grades: K-3, 4-8   **ESL Level:** beginner, intermediate
Genre: picture book

Vocabulary: places in the community—urban, rural; seasons, seasonal activities
Grammar: direct objects, adverbial clauses, adverbs of time
Patterns: repeated words and sentence patterns

This is the classic story of a little house, whose environment changed from country to city, while she stood still. Even back in 1942, people were sensitive to the issues of development! It was awarded one of the first Caldecott Medals. This book endures because its message lives on.

Because it is a theme story, it has a wide age range. For example, it integrates well with either a primary social studies unit on country and city differences, or a middle school one on urban development. For ESL classes K-8, it provides community and seasonal vocabulary in a meaningful context.

It makes a good read-aloud because of its predictable patterns and full illustrations. Although the language is at the intermediate ESL level, the detailed artwork, which independently tells the story, extends its proficiency range. This also makes it useful for both multi-level and multi-age classes.

Book By the Same Author: *Mike Mulligan and his Steam Shovel* (1939)

FILL IT UP! ALL ABOUT SERVICE STATIONS

by Gail Gibbons
New York: Harper & Row (Thomas Y. Crowell), 1985   32 pages

Grades: K-3, 4-8   **ESL Level:** intermediate
Genre: non-fiction picture book
Ethnic Identity: multiethnic

Vocabulary: transportation—cars; service stations, tools, occupations
Grammar: simple present tense, third person agreement, prepositional phrases of place
Patterns: passive voice

Gail Gibbons tells young people most everything they would want to know about service stations. She covers their diverse functions, including gas and repairs and the related jobs, from attendant to mechanic. Most of this information is conveyed in simple sentences, with no more than three per page. She goes into more detail a few times to explain more complex procedures, such as how to change a tire. This all might sound boring, but it is not. The bright illustrations clearly explain the text and the information is contained in a story format, using cartoon captions. The detailed sections are even designed to not interfere with the story line, and thus can be skipped for reading aloud.

For SL students especially, this and most other Gibbons' books are a real find. She has mastered the art of communicating practical information in a simple, readable style with descriptive illustrations. This book effectively spans the entire elementary age range.

Related Book: *Cars and How They Go* (Cole, 1983). This book looks similar because it was illustrated by Gail Gibbons.

Books By the Same Author: See *Thanksgiving Day* (1983) in the RAL.

THE RED BALLOON

by Albert Lamorisse
New York: Doubleday, 1956, 1978   47 pages

Grades: K-3, 4-8   **ESL Level:** intermediate, advanced
Genre: fiction—short story, modern fantasy
Ethnic Identity: European—French

Vocabulary:places in the community, town
Grammar: adverbial clauses, adjectives, past tense, conjunctions
Patterns: complex sentence patterns

This is a modern childhood classic about how a simple balloon, a magic balloon, brings joy to a lonely French school boy. His adventures take him throughout his town, from his apartment, to the school yard, bakery, bus, church and playing fields. Although the story is charming, the language is challenging, with a lot of text per page. It is definitely for experienced listeners.

The story is perhaps best known as an Academy Award winning movie (now available in video from the Janus Collection). However, the book by itself is also powerful. It also works well as an introduction to the movie version. The two are unified by the book's illustrations, which are the original photographs for the movie. Set in a small French city in the 1950s, they seem somewhat quaint by today's standards. But the magic of the story lives on! A treasure for all times and all ages!

ENCYCLOPEDIA BROWN, BOY DETECTIVE

by Donald Sobol   illustrated by Leonard Shortall
New York: Bantam Books, 1963, 1978   111 pages

Grades: 4-8   **ESL Level:** intermediate, advanced
Genre: fiction—short story, mystery

Vocabulary: places in the community—small town; friendship, children's activities
Grammar: past tense, interrogative and exclamatory sentences
Patterns: dialogue

Leroy Brown got the nickname "Encyclopedia" because his head was full of facts. This most unusual ten-year old boy uses this talent to help solve small town mysteries. He is a big help to his father, the police chief of Idaville. He is also a friend to a wide assortment of preteens, who are engaged in typical adolescent activities, many of them mildly mischievous. This all translates into good, adventurous mysteries.

When read-aloud, this collection of 10 short stories, each only 4-8 pages, challenges SL students to listen carefully for the clues. Sobol sets up each story so his audience can guess the answer. This guessing usually stimulates a lively class discussion. The solution is then given in full in the back of the book. If time allows, it is helpful to read the story aloud a second time, either before or after the solution. This book is also a popular choice for independent reading.

Related Books By Same Author: This is the first of 16 books in the *Encyclopedia Brown* series. The others follow a similar format, can be read in any order and do not significantly increase in difficulty.

SHOPPING

CORDUROY

by Don Freeman
New York: Penguin (Viking Books), 1968, 1976 includes a cassette, 1988 (Spanish edition); Live Oaks, 1982 (school edition includes 4 paperbacks, a cassette and a teacher's guide)   32 pages

Grades: K-3   **ESL Level:** intermediate
Genre: picture book
Ethnic Identity: Black American

Vocabulary: shopping, department store, household items, emotions
Grammar: present perfect tense, contractions
Patterns: repeated word pattern

Corduroy is an endearing little bear. He lives in a toy department of a big store, but he dreams of a home. Lisa is an attractive, young girl who falls in love with Corduroy and fulfills both of their wishes. The story provides a good literary vehicle to introduce the present perfect tense and contractions, plus store and shopping vocabulary. It also lends itself well to oral story retelling. A much loved, picture-book classic!

Related Book By Same Author: *A Pocket for Corduroy* (1978)

THE OX-CART MAN

by Donald Hall   illustrated by Barbara Cooney
New York: Penguin (Puffin Books), 1979, 1983; Live Oaks Media, 1989 (school edition includes 4 paperbacks, a cassette and teaacher's guide)   38 pages

Grades: K-3, 4-8   **ESL Level:** beginner, intermediate
Genre: picture book, historical fiction

Vocabulary: places in the community—rural, small town; months, seasons, buying/selling, farming
Grammar: past tense, relative clauses, nouns
Patterns: compound sentences, repeated word and sentence patterns

In a simple fashion, this book quietly captures the natural rhythm of nineteenth century, rural farm life—the producing on the farm, and then the buying and selling in town, all of it linked with the cycle of the seasons. It is especially appropriate for SL learners because of the masterful repetition of the basic sentence patterns and main verbs (*bought* and *sold*). Plus, each of the products referred to in the text is included in the drawings.

This is a book that children ask for time after time. It is more than pretty; its rhythm and repetitions make it deeply reassuring. It also integrates well with many social studies topics. Winner of the Caldecott Medal and a *Reading Rainbow* Book.

A CHAIR FOR MY MOTHER
SOMETHING SPECIAL FOR ME
MUSIC, MUSIC FOR EVERYONE

by Vera B. Williams
New York: Greenwillow Books, 1982, 1983, 1984;
Morrow, 1988 (includes a cassette)   31 pages each

Grades: K-3, 2-5   **ESL Level:** intermediate
Genre: picture book
Ethnic Identity: multiethnic

Vocabulary: money, shopping, stores, extended family, home
Grammar: adjectives, adverbial clauses, subject pronouns
Patterns: dialogue

This is a tender trilogy of a three generation family of strong working women: Grandma, Mama and daughter Rosa. You feel their struggles through Rosa, who tells the story in the first person. The focus in all three stories is on the money they save, bit by bit, in their big glass jar and how they spend it. In the first, they buy *A Chair for My Mother* to replace the one lost in the fire. Mama is tired after her long hours as a waitress and Rosa wants her to be comfortable. In the second, the money goes for *Something Special for Me*. After many attractive choices in numerous stores, Rosa settles on an accordion, which her great grandmother loved to play. In the third, the money is needed for grandma's medical bills.

All the stories speak of compassion and love for one's extended family. They also cover the useful vocabulary of money, shopping and stores, which is difficult to find in picture books. Williams illustrates her stories in bright full page pictures which balance half pages of text. Each two page spread is framed by a distinctive border. *A Chair for My Mother* was deservedly named a Caldecott Honor Book. The books grow on you.

Related Book: *The Giving Tree* (Silverstein, 1964) in the RAL.

Book By the Same Author: *Three Days on a River in a Red Canoe* (1981) in the RAL.

DEPARTMENT STORE

by Gail Gibbons
New York: Harper & Row (Thomas Y. Crowell), 1984   32 pages

Grades: K-3, 4-8   **ESL Level:** beginner
Genre: non-fiction picture book
Ethnic Identity: multiethnic

Vocabulary: shopping, household, clothing
Grammar: simple present tense, countable nouns—plurals
Patterns: passive voice

Department store shopping is a common way of life in the United States. These large stores, however, can be very confusing to newcomers, because of both the language and the concepts. This book helps to unlock some of these mysteries in its brief explanations and clear pictures. Because the drawings contain people of all ages, the book can be used from K-8, and beyond.

When read-aloud, it is best to read just the text beneath the pictures. Save the cartoon captions in the above sections for follow-up, independent reading. There are so many visuals and consumer products that most students enjoy perusing the book on their own. This book also integrates well into a unit on shopping. It provides the basic vocabulary to develop dialogues for further practice.

Books By the Same Author: See *Thanksgiving Day* (1983) in the RAL.

TRANSPORTATION/SAFETY

SCHOOL BUS

by Donald Crews
New York: Greenwillow Books, 1984   32 pages

Grades: Pre K-1, K-3   **ESL Level:** beginner
Genre: picture book—concept book
Ethnic Identity: multiethnic

Vocabulary: transportation—school busses, traffic, safety
Grammar: simple present tense, adjectives
Patterns: declarative sentences, repeated word patterns and sentences

Single school busses on the street intrigue young children. This whole book about them does too. Maybe it is the big, authentic drawings. Maybe it is the simple, declarative text, or the school busses' commanding presence as they drive through town together. Or just maybe, it is the fun of coming and going to school with friends, without actually working there all day long.

This entire short book can be read aloud slowly within five minutes. It deserves a second reading and time for independent looking, as well. It also does a subtle job of reinforcing traffic safety rules. Another star for this award-winning author/illustrator for young children.

Books by Same Author: *Parade* (1983) and *We Read: A to Z* (1984)

Related Books By Same Author: *Truck* (1980) and *Freight Train* (1978), both Caldecott Honor Books and *Harbor* (1982).

TRAFFIC: A BOOK OF OPPOSITES

by Betsy and Giulio Maestro
New York: Crown, 1981   31 pages

Grades: Pre K-1, K-3   **ESL Level:** beginner
Genre: picture book—concept book

Vocabulary: vehicles, places in the community—urban, rural
Grammar: adjectives, imperatives
Patterns: simple sentences, repeated format

A pink little car travels the highways and byways to reach its home in the country. It passes numerous other vehicles as well as different settings, from urban to rural. The authors cleverly use this journey to introduce 14 pairs of opposites related to traffic and travel. Each of the opposite pairs receive a full page spread and each is presented in a simple sentence, usually an imperative. In addition, each opposite word is highlighted in bold for easy identification. The bright colors, flat paint and big pictures create a dazzling, happy effect. All of this allows the listener to combine learning with pleasure. An ALA Notable Book.

Related Books: *Fast-Slow, High-Low* (Spier, 1972) in the RAL, and *Push-Pull, Empty-Full* (Hoban, 1972).

Books By the Same Authors: See *Where is my Friend?* in the RAL.

I READ SYMBOLS

by Tana Hoban
New York: Greenwillow Books, 1983   29 pages

Grades: K-3, 4-8   **ESL Level:** beginner
Genre: wordless picture book, concept book

Vocabulary: traffic safety, places in the community

Clear color photographs of traffic safety and community information signs fill each page. A full page is devoted to each of the 27 symbols. From these international symbols, students can generate the words, in either their native language or in English. This can be expanded to simple sentence making. No words accompany the photographs until the last two pages, where all the signs are reduced and accompanied by labels. This serves as a helpful review and an introduction to the associated words. All these qualities make this book appropriate for use with older students and also in bilingual classes.

Related Book: *Harriet Reads Signs and More Signs* (Maestro, 1981)

Related Book By Same Author: *I Read Signs* (1983) covers the similar topic with word signs. This can be used as a more intermediate, companion text for those who are already reading and with beginners for important sight word vocabulary.

Books By the Same Author: See *A, B, See* (1982) in the RAL.

WE'RE TAKING AN AIRPLANE TRIP

by Dinah Moche   illustrated by Carolyn Bracken
Racine, WI: Western (Golden Book), 1982   23 pages

Grades: K-3, 2-5   **ESL Level:** intermediate
Genre: non-fiction picture book
Ethnic Identity: multiethnic

Vocabulary: transportation—airplane
Grammar: past tense, nouns
Patterns: passive voice

Today, children over five are allowed to fly on commercial airlines without their parents. This book about two such children, who fly independently to meet their grandparents, prepares children for that experience. By describing all the stages of airplane travel, from check-in to luggage pick-up, it also prepares all children for an airplane flight. Although the book is filled with factual information, it strings it together with a loose and satisfying story line. The bright, color illustrations also maintain that balance between fiction and non-fiction. Some of the pictures describe the story's actions, others identify in labeled diagrams parts of the airplane and the airport. For a small book, it does a lot and does it well.

After a read-aloud introduction, this book is bound to lead to discussions of students' own flying experiences. For a social studies unit on transportation, coordinate this book with a field trip to an airport.

Book By the Same Author: See *Astronomy Today* (1982) in the RAL.

RECREATION/SPORTS

CURIOUS GEORGE RIDES A BIKE

by H.A. Rey
Boston: Houghton Mifflin, 1952, 1973   48 pages

Grades: Pre K-1, K-3   **ESL Level:** intermediate, advanced
Genre: picture book

Vocabulary: transportation—bicycles, paper boats, circus
Grammar: past tense, action verbs, adjectives
Patterns: compound sentences

This is a fun-filled adventure about curious George, the lovable monkey who has appealed to over two generations of avid, young fans. Here he receives a bicycle from his friend, the man with the yellow hat, and rides it all over town, innocently getting into trouble. His good nature saves him and lands him a job, as star of the traveling circus.

Along the way, George transforms a stack of newspapers he was supposed to have delivered into paper boats. The author includes clear, step-by-step directions for how to do this. This allows the teacher to integrate a practical lesson on functional reading/following directions with recreation vocabulary and a delightful classic of children's literature.

Related Books By Same Author: There are MANY other *Curious George* books. Start with the original (1941) and expand from there. *Curious George Goes to the Hospital* (1966) is included in the RAL.

PLAY BALL, AMELIA BEDELIA

by Peggy Parish   illustrated by Wallace Tripp
New York: Harper & Row, 1972, 1985 (includes a cassette)   64 pages

Grades: K-3, 2-5   **ESL Level:** intermediate
Genre: easy reader, picture book

Vocabulary: baseball
Grammar: action verbs—transitive, direct objects, exclamatory and interrogative sentences
Patterns: short, simple sentences, dialogues, idiomatic expressions

Beware! Amelia Bedelia is out of the house and onto the ball field. She has agreed to fill in for a sick player. It doesn't bother her that she doesn't know how to play the game. Humor reigns as she follows directions literally to "steal the base" and "run home," among other things. It's good fun! Listeners unfamiliar with baseball will get a novel introduction to the sport and seasoned Little League vets will gain a fresh appreciation.

This book, unlike the original *Amelia Bedelia*, is written as an easy reader. Although it still warrants a read-aloud presentation, it can also double as an independent reader.

Related Books By Same Author: See *Amelia Bedelia* (1963) in the RAL.

YAGUA DAYS

by Cruz Martel   illustrated by Jerry Pinkney
New York: E.P. Dutton (Dial books), 1976, 1987   35 pages

Grades: K-3, 2-5   **ESL Level:** beginner, intermediate
Genre: picture book
Ethnic Identity: Hispanic-Puerto Rican

Vocabulary: extended family, food, natural environments, farming, travel
Grammar: past tense, imperative and exclamatory sentences
Patterns: dialogue

A Hispanic boy from New York City visits his extended family in Puerto Rico for the first time. There he learns about his large, fun-loving family, and his uncle's farm—the source for some of the produce his father sells in the city. But best of all, he experiences the joys of a "yagua day." I won't spoil the fun. Read the book and discover it for yourself.

Although this is not a bilingual book, it is liberally laced with Spanish words and phrases. A Spanish word list with definitions and pronunciations is included. Runner-up for the Council on Interracial Books, Children's Competition.

THREE DAYS ON A RIVER IN A RED CANOE

by Vera B. Williams
New York: Greenwillow Books, 1981   31 pages

Grades: K-3, 2-5   **ESL Level:** intermediate
Genre: picture book

Vocabulary: travel, camping, natural environments, places in the community—rural
Grammar: present continuous tense, direct objects, prepositional phrases of place and location
Patterns: complex sentences, repeated sentence pattern

Camping and canoeing seem fun and exciting from Vera Williams' portrayal of them. Although this is a fictional story, a lot of factual information is provided about buying supplies, setting up a tent, building a fire and cooking over it (including recipes). It is also affirming of women's ability to handle the outdoors, as the two adults are both female. Because the informative drawings are small with soft colors, this book is appreciated best in groups no larger than five to six.

This is a perfect story to read aloud as an introduction to an overnight camping trip, a single day canoeing trip or even for a hike in a state park. Even if no outdoor education plans are in the future, reading about it is the next best thing to doing it yourself (and it's certainly easier!).

Books By the Same Author: *A Chair for my Mother* trilogy (1982-84) in the RAL.

STRANGE BUT TRUE BASKETBALL STORIES

by Howard Liss
New York: Random House, 1972   133 pages

Grades: 4-8   **ESL Level:** intermediate, advanced
Genre: non-fiction, short stories
Ethnic Identity: multiethnic

Vocabulary: sports
Grammar: adverbial clauses, conjunctions, past tense
Patterns: compound and complex sentence patterns

Did you know that more people watch soccer than any other sport but that more people play basketball? Did you care? Or do you think some of your students will? If so, this collection of eighteen true stories about unique events and personalities in the history of basketball will satiate your/their curiosity. They capture the excitement of the game—its off beat moments and zany players. The ample action-packed black and white photographs lend additional excitement. The style is journalistic, much like the daily sports page and the text moves quickly.

With each story separate and only 5-10 pages in length, readers/listeners can enjoy a complete episode in 10 minutes. The book is enhanced by its table of contents but lacks an index. Recommended for youthful sports lovers, likely to bore others.

This is currently out of print but still available on many library shelves. *The Giant Book of More Strange but True Sports Stories,* also written by Liss (1983) uses the same format and style but is slightly longer.

Related Books: *Strange but True Baseball Stories* (Bisher, 1966) and *Strange but True Football Stories* (Hollander, 1967)

CASEY AT THE BAT

by Ernest Thayer   illustrated by Keith Bendis
New York: Workman, 1987; Raintree, 1984 (includes a cassette)   68 pages

Grades: 4-8   **ESL Level:** intermediate, advanced
Genre: narrative poem, picture book

Vocabulary: sports—baseball
Grammar: adverbial clauses, prepositional phrases, past tense
Patterns: rhyming, complex sentences, metaphoric language

Even those students who don't understand, or don't care about, baseball will be smitten with this narrative poem. Written over 100 years ago, in 1888, it remains the most famous American sports poem. It makes baseball as big as life, if not bigger, by capturing Casey's quintessential pride. The poem magnificently builds dramatic conflict, which holds the reader until the very last word . . . and beyond.

Be warned that this poem is linguistically difficult and 52 lines long. Its wonderfully rich descriptions use complex syntax and challenging vocabulary. Yet the story line is clear and the marvelous rhythm and rhymes make it flow smoothly. The numerous black and white drawings in this paperback edition both capture the spirit and help explain the text. Students seem to enjoy the cartoon-like style.

Casey lends itself to a dramatic, oral presentation. It is thus a great read-aloud and perfect for a group of advanced, middle-school students to perform for a spring assembly. They will become part of American baseball history!

Related Book: *Casey at the Bat* (Thayer, 1964). This Prentice Hall edition with illustrations by Paul Frame is more aesthetically uplifting. It is unfortunately out of print, but still appears on many library shelves.

Role Models

HEROES

AMELIA EARHART, ADVENTURE IN THE SKY

by Francene Sabin   illustrated by Karen Milone
Mahwah, NJ: Troll Associates, 1983   48 pages

Grades: 2-5, 4-8   **ESL Level:** intermediate
Genre: biography

Vocabulary: childhood activities, transportation—airplanes
Grammar: negation, modals, past tense
Patterns: passive voice

Amelia Earhart became a famous pilot, the first one to make several long distance solo flights. She has also become a female role model of courage and strong spirit. This biography emphasizes her childhood and then touches briefly upon her adult achievements. The reader comes to appreciate her independence and her intelligence. She loved adventure and she also loved to read and to learn.

This book gives a flavor of her life, but does not bog down in details. Its length and complexity make it very appropriate for intermediate SL students in the middle school grades.

Related Books: *Amelia Earhart* (1982) by her sister, Muriel Earhart Morrissey, is a very exciting biography, but a step more comprehensive. It does, however, include better and more drawings than the one annotated above.

Books By the Same Publisher: Troll publishes numerous other biographies of approximately the same length and difficulty.

JOHN HENRY, AN AMERICAN LEGEND

by Ezra Jack Keats
New York: Random House, 1965; Knopf, 1987   28 pages

Grades: 4-8   **ESL Level:** intermediate, advanced
Genre: picture book—legend, singable book
Ethnic Identity: Black American

Vocabulary: transportation—trains; safety, tools—hammer
Grammar: past tense, verbs of physical activity—transitive, contractions
Patterns: dialogues, nonstandard language

John Henry—big, brawny and black—commands a powerful presence among our American legendary heroes. This picture book does that image justice, with its large pages, strong illustrations and dramatic text, much of it punctuated with enlivened dialogue and some Black English. (For comprehension purposes, you may want to reword some of this language.)

The real John Henry was a "steel driving" railroad man in the American 19th century rural South. This book touches upon his entire life from birth to death, stringing together episodes demonstrating not only his physical prowess but also his bravery and courage. He was a strong hero and this is an empowering book.

This is a real find because it is a relatively short picture book which, because of both the topic and its treatment, seems most appropriate for older elementary-age students and above. SL students, even at the advanced intermediate level, find the illustrations helpful and the size manageable.

As an additional reinforcement, listen to the traditional folksong of "John Henry" on *The Wabash Cannonball* (National Geographic, 1977). Words are included on the record jacket.

Books By the Same Author: See *A Letter to Amy* (1968) in the RAL.

SAINT GEORGE AND THE DRAGON

by Margaret Hodges   illustrated by Trina Schart Hyman
Boston: Little Brown, 1984   32 pages

Grades: 2-5, 4-8   **ESL Level:** intermediate, advanced
Genre: picture book—legend

Vocabulary: royalty, monsters
Grammar: adjectives, past perfect tense, action verbs
Rhetorical Patterns: complex sentences, literary language

This classic legend of merry old England offers an attractive male hero, Saint George. He bravely slays the fierce dragon and rescues the beautiful princess and her kingdom from death. Students enjoy the dramatic illustrations and also depend on them to help explain the intricate language. This stunning edition challenges SL learners with rich descriptions and literary prose. The staying power of the story makes it worth the effort. It is difficult to find a picture book complex enough for advanced, older students. This one is a gem!

Book By the Same Illustrator: *Little Red Riding Hood* (1983) in the RAL.

GREEK GODS AND HEROES

by Alice Low   illustrated by Arvis Stewart
New York: Macmillan, 1985   185 pages

Grades: 2-5, 4-8   **ESL Level:** intermediate
Genre: myths, anthology
Ethnic Identity: European—Greeks

Vocabulary: family, extended family, natural environments
Grammar: past perfect tense, relative clauses
Patterns: dialogue

"In the beginning there was no earth or sea or sky. There was only a mass of confusion in darkness called Chaos." So begins the Greek stories of the creation of heaven and earth and of the numerous gods, heroes and constellations therein.

This handsome edition serves as an illustrated introduction to Greek mythology for elementary-age children. With each of the 37 stories only 3-4 pages of large print, it provides a comprehensive overview. At times, however, the drama of the myths suffer from oversimplification. The book is quite impressive, with large pages, heavy paper and ample white space. The numerous illustrations, although somewhat lifeless, do add color. A table of contents, foreword, afterword and thorough index frame the stories and provide helpful user guides.

ROBIN HOOD, HIS LIFE AND LEGEND

by Bernard Miles   illustrated by Victor Ambrus
New York: Hamlyn, 1979; Rand-McNally, 1984   127 pages

Grades: 4-8   **ESL Level:** intermediate, advanced
Genre: myths/legends

Vocabulary: places in the community, natural environment
Grammar: past tense, past perfect tense
Patterns: dialogue, complex sentences, nonstandard language—old English

Robin Hood was the old English champion of the poor and the underdog. His life, by today's standards, seems glamorous. His adventures survive in a gray area between fairy tale, legend, and popular social history. There are many books written about this famous character. This particular one is recommended as a read-aloud for many reasons. First, it is handsomely illustrated with large art work on nearly every page. Students need these pictures to not only help explain the stories but also the historical era. Second, the author is a sophisticated story teller. The text reads quickly, with excitement and a sense of impending danger. Third, the book is divided into 15 chapters of about 5-10 page pages each. This provides material for self-contained, read-aloud sessions. There is also a helpful introduction and epilogue.

In addition, the book is comprehensive, covering all the main events and people of Robin Hood's life. It also attempts to authenticate the historical rather than the mythical. The author details his stories with dates and by identifying places on large, attractive maps. This can generate follow-up activities for social studies skill development. Highly recommended.

SPORTS STAR, FERNANDO VALENZUELA

by S.H. Burchard
New York: Harcourt Brace Jovanovich, 1982   64 pages

Grades: 2-5, 4-8   **ESL Level:** intermediate
Genre: biography, easy reader
Ethnic Identity: Hispanic-Mexican

Vocabulary: baseball, family
Grammar: past tense, past perfect tense, adverbial clauses

This biography chronicles the meteoric rise to fame of a young Mexican baseball pitcher. Born into a large family of poor Mexican farmers, Fernando Valenzuela's baseball talent is realized early and he becomes a professional player in Mexico at age 15. The story concentrates on his outstanding rookie year for the Los Angeles Dodgers, topped with a World Series victory and with the most prestigious awards in baseball. At age 21, Fernando had become a hero both to his native Mexico and to his enthusiastic American fans.

The style here is more journalistic than literary. Nevertheless, the story moves chronologically in unembellished prose. If read aloud, it can be understood by advanced beginners and can be read independently by intermediates. As a follow-up research project, have students investigate and report on Valenzuela's career and life after his rookie year.

Related Book: *The Pride of Puerto Rico, The Life of Roberto Clemente* (Walker, 1988) in the RAL.

Books in the Same Series: This biographical series includes 21 other contemporary sport stars, including Pele.

THE STORY OF JACKIE ROBINSON, BRAVEST MAN IN BASEBALL

by Margaret Davidson   illustrated by Floyd Cooper
New York: Parachute Press, 1988   92 pages

Grades: 4-8   **ESL Level:** intermediate
Genre: biography
Ethnic Identity: Black American

Vocabulary: sports—baseball, human rights
Grammar: auxiliary verb—*to be*, past tense, adjectives
Patterns: dialogue, passive voice

Jackie Robinson is famous because he broke the color barrier in professional baseball. This well-written biography captures his courageous fight to be treated equally as an athlete. It is not easy to be the first, but Jackie Robinson, with his great athletic ability and the help of a few supporters, was up to the challenge. His struggle in the 1940s and 50s allows other minority people to freely compete in all professional sports today.

The author, who specializes in biographies for children, has thoroughly researched both the man and the era. She has skillfully synthesized a lot of information without diluting it. This is a powerful story that reads quickly and easily.

THE PRIDE OF PUERTO RICO, THE LIFE OF ROBERTO CLEMENTE

by Paul Robert Walker
San Diego, CA: Harcourt Brace Jovanovich, 1988   136 pages

Grades: 4-8   **ESL Level:** intermediate, advanced
Genre: biography
Ethnic Identity: Hispanic-Puerto Rican

Vocabulary: sports—baseball; emotions
Grammar: past tense, action verbs, adjectives
Patterns: dialogue

Roberto Clemente was talented, proud and sensitive. His baseball skills allowed him to win all the major awards of professional baseball. His pride in himself and in his country, Puerto Rico, led him to return many times over what was given to him. His concern for others led ultimately to his tragic death. This well-written biography weaves together Clemente's entire life—from his boyhood baseball games in the Barrio San Anton to his impressive baseball career to the airplane accident that took his life.

This biography contains many elements of a good read-aloud. It reads quickly, uses dialogue and is divided into chapters that can be completed in 15 minute intervals. A full page of his career baseball statistics are included, providing numerous opportunities for math problems. The book would be enhanced by photographs.

This biography appeals to an audience larger than baseball fans. Roberto Clemente's entire life offers all youth a positive role model, but especially Hispanics from Puerto Rico.

Related Book: *The Story of Jackie Robinson, Bravest Man in Baseball.* (Davidson, 1988), annotated in the RAL, directly above. Robinson broke the color barrier in professional baseball about 10 years before Roberto Clemente entered. However, prejudice still existed. By reading Robinson's biography first, you better understand Clemente's dilemmas. Both books can also be appreciated independently.

CAREERS

AMELIA BEDELIA'S FAMILY ALBUM

by Peggy Parish
New York: Greenwillow Books, 1988

illustrated by Lynn Sweat
48 pages

Grades: 2-5   **ESL Level:** intermediate
Genre: easy reader, picture book

Vocabulary: occupations, extended family
Grammar: simple present tense, third person agreement, auxiliary verb—*to be*, indefinite
   article-singular
Patterns: repeated format, idiomatic expressions

After 25 years, Peggy Parish has not lost her magic touch! Her newest Amelia Bedelia book serves as a delightful introduction to occupations. Mr. and Mrs. Rogers, Amelia's bosses, want to give her a party and meet her family. Amelia tries to describe them by their work. The humor ensues with her literal use of words. For example, there is Uncle Dan, who "takes pictures." Mrs. Rogers thinks of him as a photographer, but Amelia describes him as a thief (one who literally takes the pictures)! In this way, we are briefly introduced to 14 different occcupations. Sweat's cheery drawings capture both Amelia's definition and the more traditional one.

This is a light-hearted way to introduce a unit on occupations! It works well both as a read-aloud and afterwards, as an easy reader.

Related Books By Same Author: See *Amelia Bedelia* (1963) in the RAL.

I CAN BE A CARPENTER

by Dee Lillegard
Chicago: Children's Press, 1986

32 pages

Grades: K-3, 4-8   **ESL Level:** beginner, intermediate
Genre: non-fiction picture book

Vocabulary: tools, construction
Grammar: present tense
Patterns: passive voice

Carpentry is an occupation that children can relate to. They like the tools and can see the work. This book elevates this "working man" to a skilled professional. Its clear simple text explains the various aspects of the trade and the training required of a modern carpenter. Its attractive color photographs and diagrams, most of them labelled, further explain the text. Both sexes are represented in these photographs. The print is large and limited to no more than four sentences per page. This makes it accessible as an easy reader as well as a read-aloud. A glossary and index are included as study guides. This book is appropriate to a wide age-span and is especially useful for older, beginner SL learners.

Books in the Same Series: Over 35 occupations, from *Animal Doctor* to *Zoo Keeper*, are covered in this excellent *I Can Be A* Series. Two others that appear in this RAL are *I Can Be a Doctor* (1985) and *I Can Be an Astronaut* (1984).

I CAN BE A DOCTOR

by Rebecca Hankin
Chicago: Children's Press, 1985   32 pages

Grades: 2-5, 4-8   **ESL Level:** beginner
Genre: non-fiction picture book
Ethnic Identity: multiethnic

Vocabulary: medical, health, hospitals, body
Grammar: simple present tense, third person agreement
Patterns: simple sentences

This book describes the medical profession in clear, simple language. The key vocabulary is further explained in color photographs and small drawings. A picture dictionary, glossary and index add to the book's usefulness as a science resource.

A read-aloud introduction allows for class discussion of the concepts and medical terminology. Its large, boldface print facilitates its being read independently for follow-up assignments. For example, information gathered could prepare students for a visit by a (retired) doctor or for a field trip to a medical clinic, thus expanding this into a mini-unit on health careers.

This book is part of the large, *I Can Be A* career series. It fills an important niche for beginning SL students in the middle grades by providing basic information easily and with ample illustrations.

Books in the Same Series: See *I Can Be A Carpenter* (1986), in the RAL.

WEATHER FORECASTING

by Gail Gibbons
New York: Macmillan (Four Winds), 1987   32 pages

Grades: 2-5, 4-8   **ESL Level:** intermediate
Genre: non-fiction picture book
Ethnic Identity: multiethnic

Vocabulary: weather, seasons
Grammar: adjectives, simple present tense, third person agreement, auxiliary verb—*to be*
Patterns: passive voice, scientific language

We all depend on weather forecasts to warn us of upcoming natural phenomenon and, more mundanely, to advise us how to dress appropriately for the coming day. Behind the 60 second weather spot is the fascinating career of meteorology, with its diverse jobs and different instruments. Once again, Gail Gibbons has done a superb job of explaining factual material in an interesting style and an attractive format. She does this through a behind-the-scenes look at a modern weather station.

Basic weather vocabulary appears early in most ESL curriculum and texts. This book serves as an excellent intermediate level expansion of this vocabulary and general topic, including seasons and seasonal changes. A teacher can introduce the book as a read-aloud and leave the students to read independently the scientific definitions in smaller print, for follow-up assignments.

Related Books: *Summer Is . . .* (Zolotow, 1983), *Weather Experiments* (Webster, 1982) and *Sunshine Makes the Seasons* (Branley, 1974) all in the RAL.

Related Book By Same Author: *The Seasons of Arnold's Apple Tree* (1984) in the RAL.

Books By the Same Author: For others, see *Thanksgiving Day* (1983) in the RAL.

History/Geography

UNITED STATES

WHEN I FIRST CAME TO THIS LAND

by Oscar Brand   illustrated by Doris Burn
New York: Putnam Publishing Group, 1965, 1974   42 pages

Grades: 2-5, 4-8   **ESL Level:** beginning, intermediate
Genre: picture book—singable book; historical fiction
Ethnic Identity: European

Vocabulary: animals, farm, family
Grammar: past tense, auxiliary verb—to be, adjectives, conjunctions
Patterns: rhyming, repeated refrain, cumulative repetitions

This popular folk song, written in 1948, tells of a 19th century European immigrant's struggles to develop the land and find happiness in the U.S. He first appears as a bedraggled but appealing adolescent. Through hard work, he gains one thing at a time, from farm to family. All is not easy, but he ends each addition with the upbeat refrain, "But the land was sweet and good and I did what I could."

This book fills that hard-to-find category of being mature enough thematically for beginner middle school SL learners, yet simple enough grammatically. Because of the rhymes and catchy melody, students easily memorize the entire book, without being asked! The music and words are reprinted in full at the end. The book is officially out of print, but many libraries still have it in circulation.

Although most 20th century immigrants have a more urban experience, this connection with the American pioneer, rural immigrant past is a positive link to the American Dream. Through follow-up activities, students can modernize the story. Highly recommended to immigrant and non-immigrant children of all ages!

THE ERIE CANAL

by Peter Spier
New York: Doubleday, 1970   38 pages

Grades: 2-5, 4-8   **ESL Level:** intermediate
Genre: picture book—singable book; historical fiction

Vocabulary: transportation—canalboat; travel, places in the community, buying and selling
        (trading), animals—mules
Grammar: contractions, present perfect tense, modal auxiliary, verbs—can
Patterns: repeated refrains, repeated word and sentence patterns

History comes alive in this traditional folksong of 19th travel along the Erie Canal in upstate New York. Peter Spier visually authenticates what words in history texts can only describe. Based on thorough research, he recreates not only the canal transportation but also the entire canal trading life. Plus, it is a fun song to sing. Each line of the song is fully illustrated on its own page, making it appropriate for advanced beginners. The repeated patterns and simple tune provide additional learning tools. Yet the vocabulary and sentence structures mark it more clearly for the intermediate level. To aid the adults, Spier includes two helpful endnotes: the musical notation and detailed historical notes.

This is more than just a picture book for children. It is a vivacious slice of Americana — toiling, trading, laughing and living — 150 years ago. Enjoy!

Books By the Same Author: See *Bored-Nothing to Do* (1978) in the RAL.

DEBORAH SAMPSON GOES TO WAR

by Bryna Stevens   illustrated by Florence Hill
Minneapolis, MN: Carolrhoda Books, 1984   48 pages

Grades: 2-5, 4-8   **ESL Level:** beginner, intermediate
Genre: biography, easy reader, picture book

Vocabulary: military, occupations, patriotic
Grammar: action verbs
Patterns: short, simple sentences, passive voice

In 1781 the American Revolution was in full gear. At 21, many young people were patriotic and eager to join the fight for freedom. Some of them were tall and strong, just what the Army wanted. The fact that Deborah happened to be female wasn't going to stop her. So, she disguised herself as a man and joined the army. This is both her story and that of a proud young nation.

This and other *On Your Own* books are written as easy readers. The sentences are short, the syntax simple and the print large. They also benefit from a read-aloud presentation, with their rudimentary illustrations serving as a baseline introduction to the revolutionary era. It is a good, easy story with a strong female model.

Books in the Same Series: The six other titles in this *On My Own* series cover little known stories of early American history.

WAGON WHEELS

by Barbara Brenner   illustrated by Don Bolognese
New York: Harper & Row, 1978, 1984   64 pages

Grades: 2-5   **ESL Level:** beginner, intermediate
Genre: easy reader, picture book, historical fiction
Ethnic Identity: Black American, Native American

Vocabulary: pioneer, travel, family — father and sons
Grammar: simple present tense, past tense
Patterns: dialogue, short, simple sentences

Did you know that there were thousands of black Americans who left the South after the Civil War to settle the West? The Homestead Act of 1878 promised free land to all Americans willing to relocate. This *I Can Read History Book* documents the pioneer adventures of one black family, with nary a mention of racial antagonism. Young people identify with the eleven, eight and three year old sons, who bravely travel 150 miles on foot to meet up with their father.

This easy reader works well as a read-aloud. The dramatic adventures make for exciting reading, which is not the case in many easy readers. The episodes are also conveniently divided into four chapters. As many SL students are not familiar with the American pioneer era, a read-aloud introduction allows the teacher to fill in some background information. In this way, this can be used as part of a content-based social studies unit. It is important for new immigrants and refugees to know that America historically was a land of opportunity for many.

Related Book: *The Courage of Sarah Noble* (Dalgliesh, 1954), an earlier pioneer story, in the RAL.

Book By the Same Author: *The Three Little Pigs* (1983)

AND THEN WHAT HAPPENED, PAUL REVERE?

by Jean Fritz   illustrated by Margot Tomes
New York: Putnam Publishing Group
(Coward, McCann & Goeghegan), 1973   48 pages

Grades: 2-5, 4-8   **ESL Level:** intermediate, advanced
Genre: biography

Vocabulary: historical—colonial era; occupations, military, occupations, family
Grammar: action verbs, past tense, past perfect tense
Patterns: informal language

Paul Revere was an early American patriot—a true freedom fighter. Many SL students come from countries currently engaged in their own fights for freedom. Paul Revere serves as an American model of whom all can be proud.

He comes alive in the able hands of this famous American biographer, who specializes in the upper elementary/middle school age. She has a real pulse on what will intrigue this age reader. For example, she regularly spices up the text with off-beat facts. She writes humorously and with a light touch, which makes this an excellent choice for a read-aloud. Jean Fritz is well-grounded in American history, and thus one can be assured of the accuracy of her information.

This biography also serves as an excellent orientation to the entire colonial period. The cartoon-like illustrations on nearly every page further help the reader to envision this time period. Highly recommended!

Related Books: *Paul Revere's Ride* (Longfellow). The most dramatic retelling of this narrative poem in picture book form is the one illustrated by Galdone (1963). Unfortunately, it is out of print, but still available in many libraries.

Related Books By Same Author: Others of hers that relate specifically to the colonial era include *Shh! We're Writing the Constitution* in the RAL, *George Washington's Breakfast* (1984) and *What's the Big Idea, Ben Franklin?* (1976).

Books by the Same Author: All of Jean Fritz's biographies are highly recommended. One other in the RAL is *Where Do You Think You're Going, Christopher Columbus?* (1980).

SHH! WE'RE WRITING THE CONSTITUTION

by Jean Fritz   illustrated by Tomie dePaola
New York: Putnam Publishing Group, 1987   64 pages

Grades: 4-8   **ESL Level:** intermediate, advanced
Genre: non-fiction

Vocabulary: government, geography—U.S.
Grammar: interrogative and exclamatory sentences, conditionals
Patterns: complex sentence patterns

Once again, Jean Fritz has taken the facts of history and woven them together with the skill of a master story teller. One gains a new appreciation of the Constitution of the United States by hearing the human drama of how it was written. Through this book, you experience history as a melange of events and personalities. You feel present at an historic happening.

Fritz's engaging writing skill makes this an excellent choice for a read-aloud. It is also a perfect complement to a social studies unit on this early American era. Historical notes and the complete Constitution are included at the end.

Related Book: *A More Perfect Union: The Story of Our Constitution* (Maestro, 1987)

Books By the Same Author: See *And Then What Happened, Paul Revere?* (1973) in the RAL.

WORLD

WHERE THE FOREST MEETS THE SEA

by Jeannie Baker
New York: Greenwillow Books, 1987   29 pages

Grades: 2-5   **ESL Level:** beginner, intermediate
Genre: picture book—concept book
Ethnic Identity: Australian

Vocabulary: natural environment—sea, reef, rain forest; animals, birds, fish
Grammar: simple present tense
Patterns: simple and compound sentences, reported speech

With a simple story line, the author/artist captures both the beauty of the Australian rain forest and its endangered status. The debates about development of wilderness areas moves this book beyond young children while the simple language and picture book format with limited text make it available to beginner SL learners. Plus, it is a good (although short) read-aloud within the social studies content area. And if all this was not sufficient to recommend it, add also the unusual illustrations. They are reproductions of relief collages, constructed from a variety of materials, including preserved natural objects, gathered during field trips to the site. They provide a wonderful stimulus for students to create their own collages.

Related Books: *Take a Trip to Australia* (Truby, 1981) and *A Family in Australia* (Gunner/McConky, 1984)

Book By the Same Author: *Home in the Sky* (1984), an ALA Notable Book.

MAPS AND GLOBES

by Jack Knowlton   illustrated by Harriett Barton
New York: Harper & Row, 1985   42 pages

Grades: 2-5, 4-8   **ESL Level:** beginning
Genre: non-fiction picture book
Ethnic Identity: multiethnic

Vocabulary: geography
Grammar: simple present tense, third person agreement, existential sentences—*there is*
Patterns: simple sentences, passive voice

This book gives a brief history of map making, a simple explanation of how to read maps and globes, and an introduction to the many different kinds of maps. This might sound dry, but the success of the book lies in its interesting story telling style, its colorful drawings and, of course, its numerous maps and globes.

The book design highlights each "topic" or question in bold print on one page and completes that presentation on the same or facing page. The print is large, encouraging students to read the book independently. However, because of the density of content, students benefit from a read-aloud introduction. Its objective presentation also makes it age-appropriate for older beginning SL learners. Well-done! A *Reading Rainbow* Book.

TAKE A TRIP TO NIGERIA

by Keith Lye
London: Franklin Watts, 1983   32 pages

Grades: 2-5, 4-8   **ESL Level:** intermediate
Genre: non-fiction picture book
Ethnic Identity: African

Vocabulary: places in the community, natural environments, geography
Grammar: simple present tense, auxiliary verbs—*to be, to have*
Patterns: simple sentences, passive voice, academic language

This book, part of the *Take a Trip to* Series, introduces elementary-age students to modern Nigeria. In addition to basic geographical information, it includes a variety of topics that appeal to young people, including sports, school and home life. The text is simply written and limited to four to five sentences per page. The rest of each page is filled with color photographs that help to tell the story. A short one-page index is included. Overall, this book presents a realistic portrayal of Nigeria today. Well done.

Books in the Same Series: This *Take a Trip* series is excellent. It includes 23 countries from A (for Australia) to W (for West Indies).

A FAMILY IN CHINA

by Peter Otto Jacobsen and Preben Sejer Kristensen
New York: Bookwright Press, 1986   32 pages

Grades: 2-5, 4-8   **ESL Level:** intermediate
Genre: non-fiction picture book
Ethnic Identity: Asian-Chinese

Vocabulary: travel, family, household, occupations
Grammar: simple present tense, third person agreement, auxiliary verb—*to be*
Patterns: passive voice, repeated format

This book combines basic information about China with a report about a "typical" Chinese family. The authors/photographers write as tourists, which is the way most westerners will also be introduced to China. With them, we visit Bejing and the Great Wall, before flying to Guangzhou, a southern city, to meet the Chen family. A two-page "chapter" is devoted to each family member, taking you through their day and also explaining their family life. The information presented is accurate, as verified by other Chinese, although it is written in a rather uninteresting, non-fiction style. It is the crisp, descriptive photographs which enliven the text and imbue it with character. Useful study guides included are a table of contents, glossary, "Facts about China" and an index.

Everything here seems clean and rosy, giving the book a slight tinge of propaganda to the West. But it is a well-done, personalized introduction to a distant land and culture.

Related Book: *Take a Trip to China* (Mason, 1981), a simpler presentation.

Books in the Same Series: The 14 other countries/areas included in this *Families Around the World* series follow the same pattern. Some of the titles are *A Family in Japan, Mexico, The Persian Gulf, Thailand, U.S.S.R.* and *West Africa.*

INDIA (MY COUNTRY SERIES)

by Bernice and Cliff Moon   illustrated by Chris Fairclough
New York: Marshall Cavendish, 1986   64 pages

Grades: 2-5, 4-8   **ESL Level:** beginner, intermediate
Genre: picture book, non-fiction
Ethnic Identity: Asian-Indian

Vocabulary: occupations, places in the community—rural, urban
Grammar: simple present tense, auxiliary verb—*to be*, subject pronoun—*I*
Patterns: repeated sentence patterns and format

In this book, 28 people from all over India tell about their work, their community and their families. Their occupations range from police officer to student to movie star to Member of Parliament. Each person receives his or her own two-page spread and three color photographs. The text is simply written and part of it describes the photos, much like in a family album.

This people-oriented approach personalizes a foreign country. Read-aloud, ideally in segments, it serves as a good introduction to a social studies unit or as a more general, cross-cultural sharing. The study aids—two pages of facts, a short glossary and an index—help students locate specific information for report writing. However, this is not primarily a reference book. It is a glossy story of some of India's people.

Books in the Same Series: This British series includes 20 different countries.

THE LAND I LOST: ADVENTURES OF A BOY IN VIETNAM

by Huynh Quang Nhuong   illustrated by Vo-Dinh Mai
New York: Harper & Row, 1982, 1986   116 pages

Grades: 4-8   **ESL Level:** intermediate, advanced
Genre: autobiography, short stories
Ethnic Identity: Asian-Indochinese

Vocabulary: animals—jungle; extended family, community, friendship
Grammar: past tense, adverbial clauses, adverbs of time—*first, next, then*
Patterns: simple and compound sentence patterns

In this series of true stories, the author shares his exciting childhood adventures of his village hamlet in the central highlands of Vietnam before the Vietnam War. He writes clearly and simply, without nostalgia or bitterness. His experiences are rich with dramas of exotic animals and cultural customs.

The book is divided into 15 stories of about 6-10 pages each, unified by the author's involvement and his family's pet, his water buffalo, "Tank." The full page black and white illustrations, which appear, unfortunately only once in each story, provide helpful visual explanations of these adventures.

This book does for Vietnamese village life what Laura Wilder's *Little House* books did for American pioneer life. It is an important part of Vietnam's social history. And as the Vietnamese become Vietnamese-Americans, their history becomes part of America's as well. This is a book well worth sharing in grade-level as well as ESL classes, for enhancing cross-cultural awareness. Recognized as an ALA Notable Children's Book. Highly recommended.

Related Books: *Little House On the Prairie* books (Laura Wilder, 1973), a nine-volume set. Original copyrights were in the 1930s.

Books by the Same Illustrator: *The Brocaded Slipper and Other Vietnamese Tales* (Vuong, 1982) and *Angel Child, Dragon Child* (Surat, 1983), both in the RAL.

WHERE DO YOU THINK YOU'RE GOING, CHRISTOPHER COLUMBUS?

by Jean Fritz   illustrated by Margot Tomes
New York: Putnam Publishing Group, 1980   80 pages

Grades: 4-8   **ESL Level:** intermediate, advanced
Genre: biography
Ethnic Identity: European, Native American

Vocabulary: natural environments—ocean; travel—ship
Grammar: *wh*-questions, negation, contractions past perfect tense
Patterns: complex sentences, informal language

Christopher Columbus was that famous Italian explorer who "discovered" America for the Queen of Spain, while searching for the gold of the Indies and China. Columbus was a more interesting character than the annual Columbus Day celebrations depict him to be, and the tales of his daring explorations are much more dramatic.

All this makes for a great read-aloud story, especially under the able pen of Jean Fritz, that talented author of early American history. She targets her preteen audience with accuracy. She writes informally, infusing the story with stimulating questions and details, but above all with humor. She also includes additional notes and an index, so that the book can easily be used as a historical resource.

Books By the Same Author: See *And Then What Happened, Paul Revere?* (1973) under this topic in the RAL.

IMMIGRATION/CROSS-CULTURAL ADJUSTMENT

MOLLY'S PILGRIM

by Barbara Cohen   illustrated by Michael J. Deraney
New York: Lothrop, Lee & Shepard, 1983   29 pages

Grades: K-3   **ESL Level:** intermediate
Genre: picture book, historical fiction
Ethnic Identity: Jewish American

Vocabulary: school, classroom, friendship, holiday—Thanksgiving; immigration, emotions
Grammar: past tense, questions
Patterns: dialogue

Molly doesn't like her school in Winter Hill. The other children laugh at her because she is different. She speaks imperfect English and wears old-country clothes. Third-grade Molly wants to return to New York City, where there are other Jewish children or to Russia, but no, says her mother, this is now their home. She offers to help Molly, but she speaks little English, only Yiddish. Through a Thanksgiving homework assignment to make a Pilgrim doll, Molly's Mom communicates that "it takes all kind of Pilgrims to make a Thanksgiving." Molly's sensitive teacher affirms that Molly and her Mom are indeed "modern day Pilgrims who came to American to worship God in their own way, in peace and freedom." In the end, Molly makes her first friend.

This touching story, lovingly told, is based on a true incident from one of the author's older relatives. The dress and classroom style, convincingly captured in the black and white illustrations, set the story in older times, but the message and appeal are universal.

Related Books: *How Many Days to America? A Thanksgiving Story* (Bunting, 1988), and *The Night Journey* (Lasky, 1981), a Russian immigration novel for grades 6-8, both in the RAL.

HOW MANY DAYS TO AMERICA? A THANKSGIVING STORY

by Eve Bunting   illustrated by Beth Peck
Boston: Houghton Mifflin (Clarion Books), 1988   30 pages

Grades: 2-5   **ESL Level:** intermediate
Genre: picture book, contemporary realistic fiction
Ethnic Identity: Caribbean, Black American

Vocabulary: transportation—boat; family, immigration, emotions, holidays—Thanksgiving
Grammar: past tense, questions
Patterns: dialogues, repeated refrain and sentence

A black family from an unnamed Caribbean island, but presumably Jamaica, flees their home at night in fear of their lives. They leave all their belongings behind to join many others on a small, crowded boat, bound for freedom in America. The two children are frightened but comforted by their parents. After many harrowing adventures, they do arrive safely. With a fictional flourish, they just happen to arrive on Thanksgiving Day to a welcoming feast. This conveniently allows the author to share the Thanksgiving message that America is a land of freedom for immigrants seeking a better life.

Author and illustrator have skillfully blended a modern immigration story into the picture book genre. They have reduced the generally long immigration saga to a single, powerful experience—the boat trip to freedom. The somber illustrations powerfully express the range of emotions experienced by the refugee family, from fear, to anger to relief and finally joy.

Related Book: *Molly's Pilgrim* (Cohen, 1983), in the RAL.

Book by Same Author: *The Mother's Day Mice* (1986) in the RAL.

THE LONG WAY TO A NEW LAND

by Joan Sandlin
New York: Harper & Row, 1981   63 pages

Grades: 2-5, 4-8   **ESL Level:** intermediate
Genre: easy reader, picture book, historical fiction
Ethnic Identity: European-Swedish

Vocabulary: farm, transportation—boat; immigration
Grammar: past tense, action verbs
Patterns: simple sentences

In 1868 and 1869, over 50,000 Swedes emigrated to America seeking a better life. These were the "hunger years" in Sweden, and life was hard. This book tells of one Swedish family's immigration experience, from their failing farm in Sweden via numerous forms of transportation to their welcome to America by their Swedish friends.

Written as an easy reader, it uses easy syntax and short sentences. Because the plot has intrinsic drama, it also works well as a read-aloud. The ample illustrations visually express the mood, as well as explain the historical setting. Honored as an ALA Notable Children's Book and as a *Reading Rainbow* selection.

Related Book: *Watch the Stars Come Out* (Levinson, 1985) is a picture book about another immigrant experience of the same era.

THE WITCH OF FOURTH STREET AND OTHER STORIES

by Myron Levoy   illustrated by Gabriel Lisowski
New York: Harper & Row, 1972   110 pages

Grades: 4-8   **ESL Level:** intermediate
Genre: short stories, mystery/suspense
Ethnic Identity: multiethnic

Vocabulary: friends, home, family, places in the community — urban; occupations
Grammar: exclamatory sentences
Patterns: dialogue

The Lower Side of New York City in the early 1900s became the new home for a melange of recent immigrant families. There were Russians, Italians, Irish, Greeks and Lithuanians, all living together, all different, yet all striving to build a better life for themselves and their children. These eight short stories are about the children, their dreams, their fears, and their pride. Levoy spins a wonderful yarn, with crisp dialogue, surprise endings and more than a touch of magic. The stories, which average about 12 full pages each, take about 20 minutes to read, and require good listening skills. The single, black and white illustration for each story provides a pleasant visual focus.

IN THE YEAR OF THE BOAR AND JACKIE ROBINSON

by Bette Bao Lord   illustrated by Marc Simont
New York: Harper & Row, 1984   169 pages

Grades: 4-8   **ESL Level:** intermediate, advanced
Genre: fiction — long novel, historical fiction
Ethnic Identity: Asian-Chinese, Asian American

Vocabulary: school, home, family, sports — baseball; emotions
Grammar: adverbial clauses, exclamatory and interrogative sentences
Patterns: informal language, idiomatic expressions, dialogues

In 1947, a nine-year old Chinese child comes to Brooklyn, bewildered. She gradually starts to feel at home and make friends in her 5th grade class at school, especially when she discovers baseball and the Brooklyn Dodgers. Shirley Temple Wong's adventures, which touch a range of emotions, are based on the author's own immigrant experiences. Imaginative pen and ink drawings that blend the Chinese and American cultures introduce each of the 12 chapters.

This makes an excellent read-aloud because of its fast pace and humor. If read aloud a few pages daily, it can easily be completed in a month. When shared in this way, it also serves as a stimulating model for SL students to write their own autobiographies.

It is highly recommended for both immigrant and non-immigrant children alike because it so sensitively captures the cross-cultural adjustment through the eyes of a child. A real contribution!

Book By the Same Author: *Spring Moon* (1981) for adults

A JAR OF DREAMS

by Yoshiko Uchida
New York: Macmillan, 1981   131 pages

Grades: 4-8   **ESL Level:** intermediate, advanced
Genre: fiction—long novel, historical fiction
Ethnic Identity: Asian American, Asian-Japanese

Vocabulary: family, household, occupations, prejudice
Grammar: adverbial clauses
Patterns: dialogue, complex sentences

Eleven-year old Rinko and her two brothers were all born in the United States, to Japanese parents. The children speak English fluently and are comfortable with American ways. That doesn't mean, however, that they are fully acculturated or accepted by other Americans. This story recounts the bravery of the Tsujimura family when threatened with prejudice in Depression-torn California. They don't back down. Rather, they move forward with their dreams—mother of her home laundry business, father of his garage and repair shop, older brother Cal (short for California) of pursuing engineering at the university and Rinko of becoming a teacher. Their jar of dreams is impressive, as is their whole family's story. Modern bicultural students can relate to these struggles, as they seek to make their own way in their new homeland.

Related Book By Same Author: *Journey Home* (1978) is about a Japanese-American family, after their release from an American prison camp during World War II.

A BOAT TO NOWHERE

by Maureen Crane Wartski   illustrated by Dick Teicher
Philadelphia: Westminster John Knox, 1980   189 pages

Grades: 4-8   **ESL Level:** intermediate, advanced
Genre: fiction—long novel, contemporary realistic fiction
Ethnic Identity: Asian-Indochinese

Vocabulary: places in the community—rural; natural environments—sea;
    transportation—fishing boat; emotions
Grammar: past tense
Patterns: dialogue

This gripping novel documents the harrowing adventures of three Vietnamese children and their honored grandfather, who flee from the Communists on a small fishing boat. Their long voyage to freedom is treacherous, but they are fighters and lucky. Finally they are rescued. The dialogue moves the story quickly and the plot is dramatic but not depressing.

This is an important book to share in communities with Vietnamese refugees, even if the particular Vietnamese have not emigrated in this manner. It also gives a sense of Vietnamese village life before the Communist takeover in 1976. The children, ages about 4 to 14, quickly gain the audience's admiration. How would any of us have fared under similar circumstances?

Related Book: *The Land I Lost: Adventures of a Boy in Vietnam.* (Nhuong, 1982) in the RAL.

Related Book By the Same Author: *A Long Way from Home* (Wartski, 1980) in the RAL.

A LONG WAY FROM HOME

by Maureen Crane Wartski
Philadelphia: Westminster John Knox, 1980   155 pages

Grades: 6-8   **ESL Level:** intermediate, advanced
Genre: fiction—long novel, contemporary realistic fiction
Ethnic Identity: Asian-Indochinese

Vocabulary: family—adopted, extended; household, school, prejudice, places in the
    community
Grammar: past tense
Patterns: dialogue

This book is the sequel to *A Boat to Nowhere*, annotated above. It takes the children from a refugee camp in Hong Kong to their new American family in California. Reading the books in sequence provides insights into the difficulties of cross-cultural adjustment, especially for the fifteen year-old boy/man, Kien. The book concentrates on two major incidents involving prejudice towards the Vietnamese. The author couches them in concrete, school and community-based situations with which the audience can easily identify. As with much adolescent literature, it has an upbeat resolution. The incidents can stimulate class discussions of creative ways to handle prejudice.

The Japanese author has done a superb job on both books. They are hard to put down. She deserves an award and all your students deserve to hear them!

Related Books: *My Best Friend, Duc Tran* (Macmillan and Freeman, 1987), about Vietnamese-American friendship and *The Story of Jackie Robinson, Bravest Man in Baseball* (Davidson, 1988) about prejudice. Both are in the RAL.

LUPITA MAÑANA

by Patricia Beatty
New York: William Morrow, 1981   192 pages

Grades: 6-8   **ESL Level:** intermediate, advanced
Genre: fiction—long novel, contemporary realistic fiction
Ethnic Identity: Hispanic-Mexican, Hispanic American

Vocabulary: travel, places in the community, occupations
Grammar: adverbial clauses, adverbs, questions, exclamatory sentences
Patterns: dialogue

This is Lupita's and Salvador's story, a thirteen and fifteen year old brother and sister. Their life in rural Mexico collapses when their father dies in a fishing accident. Their poor family needs money to survive, but there is no work in the village for them.

Lupita and Salvador are real people and Beatty tells their story knowledgeably and with compassion. She infuses her characters with youthful spirit and hope. Writing for an adolescent audience, she moves the novel with action and suspense. For example, one is struck by the illegal immigrants' constant fears, even after they have crossed the border.

This fast-moving novel make a gripping read-aloud to older, more advanced students. Read by chapters, it can easily be completed in two to three weeks. But be forewarned: it is hard to put down. The book's ending leaves one wondering how life unfolds for these young people. As a follow-up, have your students orally discuss the possibilities and then write their own final chapter (or prologue).

THE NIGHT JOURNEY

by Kathryn Lasky
New York: Frederick Warne, 1981

illustrated by Trina Schart Hyman
150 pages

Grades: 6-8   **ESL Level:** advanced
Genre: fiction—long novel, historical fiction
Ethnic Identity: Jewish American, Russian

Vocabulary: travel, places in the community, family, household
Grammar: past tense, past perfect tense
Patterns: dialogue

Twelve year-old Rachel lives comfortably with her parents, grandmother and great grandmother in Minnesota until she discovers, with horror, that her great great grandparents were murdered in their beds by the Tsar's henchmen in Russia over 100 years ago. That events launches her driving desire to understand her family's Jewish heritage. It also develops a strong bond between the great grandmother who wants to tell and her great granddaughter who wants to hear.

The tales of nine year-old Sasha's dramatic plan for a night time escape from Tsarist Russia with her extended family of seven makes a gripping read-aloud story. Using the flash-back technique, the novel interweaves the family's contemporary life dilemmas with the historical immigration saga. It subtly instills Jewish cultural pride, and also appeals to that universal spirit that yearns for freedom. Well-written for advanced, older students. Highly recommended!

Related Book: *Molly's Pilgrim* (Cohen, 1983), a Russian-American, cross-cultural adjustment story, for K-3, annotated earlier in this section.

 # ANIMALS

BIRDS

OWLS IN THE FAMILY

by Farley Mowat
Boston: Little Brown, 1961; Bantam, 1981

illustrated by Robert Frankenberg
91 pages

Grades: 2-5   **ESL Level:** intermediate
Genre: short novel

Vocabulary: animals—owls, other birds, dogs, gophers, snakes, skunks, horses, foxes;
seasons—spring, summer
Grammar: past tense, action verbs

In this adventure story, the author relives his happy childhood experiences in the prairies of Western Canada. He lovingly tells of his pets, especially Wol and Weeps, his owls, but also of Mutt, his dog, and his 30 gophers. They certainly had some amusing experiences!

This book makes a good read-aloud. It introduces contemporary urban children to a simpler era, when leisurely exploring the nearby countryside was a safe childhood pastime. The eleven chapters are short enough, about six pages each, to be completed within a 10-15 minute read-aloud session. Each chapter is also conveniently self-contained. The prose style reads quickly and the black and white line drawings contribute by clearly capturing the most amusing scenes.

This modern Canadian classic rings with authenticity!

Related Book: *Winnie-the-Pooh* (Milne, 1926). Wol, Mowat's owl, is named after the owl in Milne's famous story.

Related Book By Same Author: *The Dog Who Wouldn't Be* (1957) is about Mutt, the dog.

THE UGLY DUCKLING

by Hans Christian Andersen   illustrated and retold by Lorinda Bryan Cauley
New York: Harcourt Brace Jovanovich, 1979   44 pages

Grades: 2-5, 4-8   **ESL Level:** intermediate
Genre: picture book—fairy tale

Vocabulary: animals, natural environments—ponds, marshes, swamps, woods, farmyard
Grammar: exclamatory sentences, action verbs
Patterns: dialogue

The ugly duckling is a misfit, unable to please his peers or fit into an often harsh world . . . until, at the end, he changes into a beautiful swan, admired by all. Such is the plot summary of this popular fairy tale by Hans Christian Andersen.

Lorinda Cauley has not only dramatically illustrated the tale, but has retold it. Her modern version deepens the original, making you really feel the despair of the unwanted duck. This makes it very appropriate for middle school students, whose emerging adolescence often makes them feel like "ugly ducklings." Those new to this culture and additionally struggling with the awkwardness of another language can further identify with the ugly duckling's alienation. But he does find his place and does emerge into a graceful swan. Read as an allegory, this tale can be very reassuring. It can also be enjoyed as a pleasant animal fairy tale by younger listeners.

Books By the Same Author: Hans Christian Andersen has written many fairy tales. Eighteen of his most popular ones can be found in the collection, *Hans Andersen—His Classic Fairy Tales* (1978). Many of these have also been beautifully recreated in individual picture books.

Related Book By Same Illustrator: *The Elephant's Child* (1983) in the RAL.

FARM

THE FARMER IN THE DELL

illustrated by Diane Stanley Zuromskis
Boston: Little Brown, 1978   30 pages

Grades: Pre-K-1, K-3   **ESL Level:** beginner
Genre: picture book—nursery rhyme, singable book; easy reader

Vocabulary: home, family, pets, food—cheese
Grammar: simple present tense, third person agreement, singular articles—definite and indefinite, nouns
Patterns: simple sentence patterns, repeated phrases and sentences

This is the traditional American singing game about a farmer and the amusing sequence of events that happens once he "takes a wife." Young children love to play this in a circle. Each is assigned a different character and gets taken into the family circle in turn. The remaining children sing as they walk around the outside of the circle.

This small book reflects the simplicity of the nursery rhyme. Each illustration clearly explains the few lines of text on the opposite page. The text pages are uncluttered, making it possible for first or second graders to use it as an easy reader as well.

Unfortunately, this is not still in print, although it is still available on many library shelves. Look for a newer edition (Fay, 1988).

BABY FARM ANIMALS

by Merrill Windsor
Washington, DC: National Geographic Society, 1984   32 pages

Grades: K-3, 2-5   **ESL Level:** beginner, intermediate
Genre: non-fiction picture book

Vocabulary: farming, animals
Grammar: simple present tense, third person agreement, adverbs of time
Patterns: passive voice, definitions

"Have you ever been to a farm?" the author asks. For those who haven't, this book provides a pleasant armchair visit. In keeping with National Geographic standards, the photographs are beautiful: sharp, alive and full of action. The simple text strings the pictures together and tells their story in words. The focus is *baby* farm animals. They are very endearing. Through them, the working life of a dairy farm is explained.

This is a quality book that students will enjoy perusing on their own, after the benefit of a read-aloud introduction. Use it independently or as part of a social studies unit on farming or animals.

Related Books: *Baby Animals on the Farm* (Isenbart, 1981) and *The Milk Makers* (Gibbons, 1985), both in the RAL.

Related Books in the Same Series: *Animals Helping People* (1983) is one of the many nonfiction picture books about animals in this excellent series, *Books for Young Explorers*.

ROSIE'S WALK

by Pat Hutchins
New York: Macmillan, 1968, 1971   27 pages

Grades: K-3   **ESL Level:** beginner
Genre: picture book, easy reader

Vocabulary: farm, animals
Grammar: prepositional phrases of place, definite article, count nouns
Patterns: repeated word patterns

Rosie the hen is innocently out for her morning walk. She doesn't realize the hungry fox is stalking her, but the children do. They delight as the fox's evil intentions come to no good. The book consists simply of one long sentence (only 32 words) strung together by prepositional phrases. Each of the 14 places Rosie goes (for example, "under the beehives") is brightly illustrated on its own page. Good for beginning language learners, beginning listeners and also beginning readers. An ALA Notable Book.

Related Book: *Three Little Pigs* (Galdone, 1970)

Book By the Same Author: *You'll Soon Grow Into Them, Titch* (1983) in the RAL.

OLD MACDONALD HAD A FARM

by Tracey Campbell Pearson
New York: E.P. Dutton (Dial Books), 1984   22 pages

Grades: Pre K-1, K-3   **ESL Level:** beginner
Genre: picture book—singable book

Vocabulary: animals, farming
Grammar: auxiliary verb—*to have*, past tense, direct objects, indefinite articles-singular and plural
Patterns: rhyming, repeated word phrases, cumulative repetitions

The predictable patterns and cumulative verses of this popular childhood song make it an excellent language learning source. Many illustrators have converted it into picture books. I recommend this one because it is particularly zany, creative and still filled with the complete repetitions. Pearson has taken the liberty to add her own verses and encourages her audience to do the same. Children like it because it includes all the animals and noise sounds, adding many that weren't in the original. The comical and cartoon-like illustrations help SL students to easily identify each newly added animal. My only criticism is that it does not include the musical notation, usually a standard feature for singable books. Otherwise, it's a great song and a delightful book. Once read-aloud, it quickly transforms into a sing-along! Enjoy!

HENNY PENNY

by Paul Galdone
Boston: Houghton Mifflin (Clarion Books), 1968, 1984   32 pages

Grades: Pre-K-1, K-3   **ESL Level:** beginner, intermediate
Genre: picture book—fairy tale

Vocabulary: animals—rooster, hen, duck, goose, turkey, fox
Grammar: present continuous tense, conjunctions—*and, so;* relative clauses
Patterns: rhyming, dialogue, repeated word patterns and sentences, cumulative repetitions

The premise for this tale, that an acorn falling from a tree means that the sky is falling, is quite silly, but terribly amusing to young listeners. One farm animal tells another the news and then joins the group, as they go off to tell the king. The sly fox tricks them all and enjoys a good meal at their expense.

This makes a good read-aloud because of the numerous predictable patterns which repeat often during the story. One of these, the animals' names, also rhyme and can be used as aids in phonetic reading. Galdone's large and attractive illustrations provide another read-aloud asset. They also clearly identify each of the animals.

Related Book: *Little Red Riding Hood* (Hyman, 1983) and *The Fox Went Out on a Chilly Night* (Spier, 1961), both in the RAL.

Related Books By Same Author: *The Gingerbread Boy* (1975), about a clever fox and *The Little Red Hen* (1973), about a hard-working hen, both in the RAL.

Books By the Same Author: See *The Elves and the Shoemaker* (1984) in the RAL.

THE FOX WENT OUT ON A CHILLY NIGHT

illustrated by Peter Spier
New York: Doubleday, 1961   46 pages

Grades: 2-5, 4-8   **ESL Level:** intermediate
Genre: picture book—singable book

Vocabulary: animals, farm
Grammar: past tense, prepositional phrases—of place, manner and instrument, subject
    pronouns
Patterns: rhyming, repeated word patterns and sentences

Here is another example of a traditional song transformed into a successful picture book through the palette of a talented artist. This engaging folk song, written in 1945, tells of a likeable fox who steals some farm animals for his family's dinner. And so, the chase begins! It is nice to see the much maligned fox as a family man. Because there are no young children as protagonists, the book's appeal is ageless. Music and verses are included inside the back cover.

Peter Spier's setting in a 19th century New England farm and town adds a rich historical dimension. His detailed pen and ink illustrations lend character and warmth. These full illustrations are accompanied with only a line of text per page. Plus each two lines is repeated in full. Nevertheless, the vocabulary and syntax puts it beyond the reach of most beginners. A challenging fun picture book for older, more advanced students! It is a treat, sure to please, plus a great way to teach the past tense!

Related Book: *Henny Penny* (Galdone, 1968) in the RAL.

Books By the Same Author: See *Bored-Nothing to Do* (1978) in the RAL.

OUR ANIMAL FRIENDS AT MAPLE FARM

by Alice and Martin Provensen
New York: Random House, 1974, 1984   57 pages

Grades: 2-5   **ESL Level:** beginner, intermediate
Genre: picture book

Vocabulary: farm animals
Grammar: present tense—simple and continuous, adjectives
Patterns: repeated format

This is a very personal farm story. It lovingly tells of the different animals on the Provensen's own farm and makes it seem like one big happy family! Each animal, from Max the cat to Lovelace the rooster has an affectionate name, like a pet. You learn not only about the general characteristics of farm animals, but about the personalities of these particular ones.

The humorous stories and sophisticated artwork make this a good read-aloud choice for older elementary students still at the beginning to intermediate level. The text is ample and detailed, but not difficult. This big book is too long to be completed in one read-aloud setting, but it divides easily into smaller units by animals.

Book by the Same Author: *The Glorious Flight* (1983) awarded the Caldecott Medal.

PETS

WHERE IS IT?

by Tana Hoban
New York: Macmillan, 1974   29 pages

Grades: K-3   **ESL Level:** beginner
Genre: picture book

Vocabulary: natural environment, vegetables, numbers—1–10
Grammar: questions, imperatives, prepositional phrases of place
Patterns: repeated sentence

Through a series of 16 black and white photos, Tana Hoban recreates a bunny's hunt. This cute white rabbit is looking for something special. Encourage the children to guess what that might be. The soft photographs are accompanied by a minimal text, 46 words altogether, with as few as one or two words on some pages. Within this short, small gem, beginner students can hear a wide variety of basic syntax, plus visually follow an exciting chase. The entire book can be read-aloud, slowly, within five minutes. As a follow-up, ask students to talk about and draw something special that they would seek out for themselves.

Books By the Same Author: See *A, B, See* (1982) in the RAL.

WHERE'S SPOT?

by Eric Hill
New York: Putnam Publishing Group, 1980   22 pages
(Spanish edition also available)

Grades: Pre K-1   **ESL Level:** beginner
Genre: picture book, easy reader

Vocabulary: animals—dogs; household, furniture
Grammar: questions, auxiliary verb—*to be,* prepositional phrases of place, contractions
Patterns: repeated sentence pattern and format, question and answer sequence, initial s
    sound

Where's Spot? His mother is looking for him throughout the house. Young children love this peek-a-boo book, as they try, with mother, to find him. Children quickly get involved, as they lift up the flaps and find different animals. In nine separate scenes, the same yes/no question pattern is used, giving the students multiple opportunities for question and answer practice. Although the written answer is simply "No," students can be encouraged to give fuller responses (e.g. *No, he isn't. It's a monkey.*). In the end, there is the happy reunion when Mother Sally finds her puppy Spot.

Although this was written primarily as a read-aloud picture book, it also works well as a beginning reader. Most of the words are simple, the patterns repeat and the bold black print is large. For many reasons, then, this is a very popular book.

Related Books By Same Author: There are many other Spot sequels, some of which have also been translated into Spanish. They include *Spot at the Circus* (1986) and *Spot's Birthday Party* (1982). I still find the original (annotated above) the most useful for language teaching.

A BAG FULL OF PUPS

by Dick Gackenbach
Boston: Houghton Mifflin (Clarion Books), 1981   30 pages

Grades: K-3   **ESL Level:** beginner, intermediate
Genre: picture book

Vocabulary: places in the community, occupations, numbers—1-12
Grammar: indefinite articles—singular, simple present tense, future tense—*will*
Patterns: repeated sentence patterns and format

Mr. Mullin has a litter of 12 adorable puppies to give away. One by one they are claimed by adults with different occupations, each with a practical reason for wanting a dog . . . until only one pup remains. Who will get him? Let the children guess. The repeated patterns and format make this very useful for beginning SL students. The story moves predictably in simple sentences. Any child who would like a puppy (isn't that nearly all of them!) will enjoy this book.

To practice expanded prediction skills before the read-aloud session, ask the children how dogs can be used by different people. Develop a list together. Then, let them see how many of these things they discover dogs doing in the story. At the end, they may want to expand the book with their own ideas.

MILLIONS OF CATS

by Wanda Gag
New York: Putnam Publishing Group (Coward, McCann & Geoghegan) 1928, 1988
29 pages

Grades: K-3   **ESL Level:** intermediate
Genre: picture book

Vocabulary: animals—cats; household, numbers—large
Grammar: superlatives, adjectives
Patterns: repeated word patterns and refrain

It all begins "once upon a time." This original fairy tale about a good-hearted man with too many cats to care for has been delighting young audiences for over 60 years. Happily, it shows no signs of tiring. In fact, its small size, calligraphy print and simple black and white drawings provide a charming alternative to the more slick, modern productions. In addition to these qualities, its catchy and often repeated refrain strongly etches the entire story in one's childhood memory. It is hard to forget, "Cats here, cats there, cats and kittens everywhere. Hundreds of cats, thousands of cats, millions and billions and trillions of cats." In recognition, it was named one of the first Newbery Honor Books, in 1929.

On a more practical level, the book's introduction of large numbers provide a liaison between literature and math. These mathematical concepts and vocabulary fascinate children far more than the manageable 1, 2 3s.

PREHISTORIC

DINOSAUR TIME

by Peggy Parish   illustrated by Arnold Lobel
New York: Harper & Row, 1974, 1983   30 pages

Grades: K-3, 2-5   **ESL Level:** beginner
Genre: non-fiction, easy reader

Vocabulary: dinosaurs, body, food
Grammar: auxiliary verbs—*to be, to have*, action verbs, adjectives, plural nouns
Patterns: short sentences, repeated sentence patterns and format

This easy-to-read book provides five to ten sentences of brief information about 11 different dinosaurs. Included for each is how to pronounce the name, a short physical description, what it ate and a distinguishing characteristic. Plus, there is a clear drawing of each dinosaur set in its natural habitat.

This is a very useful book for beginning SL students who want factual information about dinosaurs. Read aloud, it allows the teacher to introduce and also further discuss this topic. Read independently, it can be used to answer basic content-based questions. It is a good, very simple resource.

Related Book: *Prehistoric Monsters Did the Strangest Things* (Hornblow, 1974). This provides similar, but more detailed information. It is part of the *Step-Up Book Series*, intended for independent reading (2nd-5th grader).

DANNY AND THE DINOSAUR

by Syd Hoff
New York: Harper & Row, 1958, 1978   64 pages

Grades: K-3   **ESL Level:** beginner, intermediate
Genre: easy reader, picture book

Vocabulary: places in the community, children's activities
Grammar: imperatives (*Let's go!*)
Patterns: repeated sentence patterns, dialogue

Danny and the friendly dinosaur from the local museum spend a great day together, and so do we, as their reading audience. Together, they explore the town, visiting the zoo and a baseball game and playing games with other friends. It's all quite unreal, but that doesn't seem to bother anybody. This is high fantasy, illustrated in a simple cartoon style and set in the 1950s. Danny's dress and style is reminiscent of Dennis the Menace.

This book works extremely well as a read-aloud for the entire beginning to intermediate range because of its short amount of text per page (3 sentences each) and its clear, humorous drawings. Although it was intended as an easy reader, its varied and somewhat complex sentence patterns limit that use to intermediate SL students.

Related Book: *Patrick's Dinosaurs* (Carrick, 1983), is a more contemporary story about the size of dinosaurs in comparison to zoo animals and how frightening it would be if they actually existed. (K-3, intermediate)

Books By the Same Author: Syd Hoff has written many other easy readers about animals. They include *Chester* (1961) about a horse, *Oliver* (1960) about an elephant, and more recently, *Walpole* (1977) about a walrus.

TYRANNOSAURUS WAS A BEAST

by Jack Prelutsky
New York: Greenwillow Books, 1988

illustrated by Arnold Lobel
32 pages

Grades: 2-5   **ESL Level:** intermediate, advanced
Genre: poetry

Vocabulary: dinosaurs
Grammar: past tense, action verbs, adjectives
Patterns: rhyming, repeated word patterns (within each poem), metaphoric language

These award winners (both poet and illustrator) have combined to create a very inviting volume of poems about dinosaurs. Fourteen different species spring to life in Prelutsky's rhyming verses and Lobel's bright illustrations. One is initially attracted by the distinctive drawings. One's interest is held by the clever verses and repeated patterns. Although the poems are challenging because of vocabulary and literary metaphors, none is longer than 16 lines, and many are as short as eight. The first one has only four lines! This makes it a nice introduction.

While this collection provides some light relief from the more serious study of animal behavior, it is also a source of information about the individual dinosaurs. Additional factual data is provided in the table of contents and time line of the dinosaur eras. What a nice blend of science and poetry!

Related Book: *Dinosaurs* is a collection of poems selected by Hopkins (1987). It includes interesting poems but the rhymes aren't as catchy nor the illustrations as colorful.

Book by the Same Illustrator: *On Market Street* (1981) in the RAL.

STRANGE CREATURES THAT REALLY LIVED

by Millicent Selsam
New York: Scholastic, 1987

illustrated by Jennifer Dewey
32 pages

Grades: 2-5, 4-8   **ESL Level:** intermediate
Genre: non-fiction picture book

Vocabulary: animals—prehistoric; natural environments, numbers—large
Grammar: comparatives, past tense, adjectives, conditionals
Patterns: definitions

The concept of extinction intrigues modern man. This attractive picture book fulfills our curiosity with information about dozens of animals that lived from millions to hundreds of years ago. Written by a veteran science writer for children, the book devotes about a page to each of the extinct animals. It attempts to make them understandable through verbal comparisons with other animals and by drawing them in their natural environment.

Although the book adequately covers how these creatures lived, it does not explore why they died. Use this weakness to your advantage by encouraging the children to hypothesize what might have happened. Extend this for older students by initiating a cooperative research project to investigate.

Related Books: For some answers to the extinction question, see *The Monsters Who Died* (Cobb, 1983), in the RAL.

Related Book By Same Author: *Sea Monsters of Long Ago* (1977).

Books By the Same Author: Millicent Selsam has written over 100 science books for children, many about animals, including *Night Animals* (1979).

THE MONSTERS WHO DIED. A MYSTERY ABOUT DINOSAURS.

by Vicki Cobb   illustrated by Greg Wenzel
New York: Putnam Publishing Group (Coward, McCann and Geoghegan), 1983
63 pages

Grades: 4-8   **ESL Level:** intermediate, advanced
Genre: non-fiction

Vocabulary: dinosaurs, body
Grammar: *wh* questions, simple present tense, third person agreement
Patterns: repeated format

This book asks the big questions about dinosaurs: "Why are they all dead?" and "What killed them all?" It then involves the audience in the scientific detective work of the paleontologist. In the search for clues, the author investigates the earth's surface, the dinosaur fossils and the exciting process of reconstructing dinosaur bones. Like true scientific discovery, it poses as many questions as it answers. It also engages the reader, especially through its informal, well-written prose. Black and white scientific drawings and diagrams enhance the text.

This is an interesting book to share as part of a middle school science unit on the prehistoric era. By reading it aloud, the students can concentrate on the scientific quest rather than the reading process. Follow it up with the option of independent reading for further study.

Related Book: *Dinosaurs, Asteroids and Superstars: Why the Dinosaurs Disappeared* (Branley, 1982).

SEA

HUMPHREY: THE LOST WHALE

by Wendy Tokuda and Richard Hall   illustrated by Hanako Wakiyama
Union City, CA: Heian, 1986   33 pages

Grades: K-3, 4-8   **ESL Level:** intermediate
Genre: non-fiction picture book

Vocabulary: places in the community—country; natural environments—bay, river, ocean
Grammar: adjectives, adverbs

Huge Humphrey somehow managed to lose his traveling companions in the San Francisco Bay and get himself trapped. For 26 days he traveled 64 miles up the Sacramento River before scientists could free him. This book clearly retells this dramatic true story, with the last page providing additional information about the event. Each major action is further explained with large illustrations. This contributes to its success as a read-aloud. The large print and straightforward syntax also recommend it as an independent reader. This exciting story appeals to a wide age-range. *A Reading Rainbow* selection.

Related Book: *Humphrey the Wayward Whale* (Callenbach and Leefeldt, 1986)

WILD

A CROCODILE'S TALE

by Jose and Ariane Aruego
New York: Charles Scribner, 1972; Scholastic, 1976   31 pages

Grades: K-3, 2-5   **ESL Level:** intermediate
Genre: picture book—folktale
Ethnic Identity: Asian-Philippine

Vocabulary: natural environments—jungle; animals—crocodile, monkey
Grammar: questions, adverbial clauses
Patterns: dialogue, informal language, repeated sentences and refrain

Gratitude can be an abstract concept for children to grasp, yet it is an important one for values education. This Philippine folktale of a monkey who saves a boy from a crocodile's hungry jaws illustrates gratitude concretely. It does so through story telling (embedded in the tale itself) and by specific examples. With this format as a model, students can create their own stories to illustrate other pro-social behaviors (e.g. generosity). This appealing tale lends itself well to reading aloud because of its predictable patterns and numerous repetitions.

GIFT OF THE SACRED DOG

by Paul Goble
Scarsdale, NY: Bradbury Press, 1980, 1984   27 pages

Grades: 2-5, 4-8   **ESL Level:** intermediate, advanced
Genre: picture book—legend
Ethnic Identity: Native American

Vocabulary: animals—buffalo, horse; nature, weather—lightning, thunder; extended family,
     community, food
Grammar: modal auxiliary verbs, past perfect tense
Patterns: complex sentence patterns

This book presents a positive, historical portrayal of Native Americans. This particular legend spins the fascinating tale of how horses came to the Native Americans of the Great Plains. An adolescent boy, seeking relief for his hungry tribe of buffalo hunters, approaches the Great Spirit, who responds to his prayerful cries with the gift of the "sacred dog" (i.e. horses). Although the language patterns are complex, the amount of text per page is relatively short, about 6–10 lines (4–8 sentences). The strong colorful artwork is aesthetically exciting, visually clear and helpfully detailed.

Teachers should be aware that this legend does refer to a spiritual power and includes short prayers of petition and thanks, recognizing the Spirit's power in granting these requests. A teacher's decision to choose this book for her/his class should include sensitivity to the issues of prayer and religion in the individual school district. A *Reading Rainbow* selection.

Book By the Same Author: *Her Seven Brothers* (1988)

Related Book By Same Author: *The Girl Who Loved Wild Horses* (1978) in the RAL.

THE GIRL WHO LOVED WILD HORSES

by Paul Goble
Scarsdale, NY: Bradbury Press, 1978; Macmillan, 1986   32 pages

Grades: 2-5, 4-8   **ESL Level:** intermediate
Genre: picture book—legend
Ethnic Identity: Native American

Vocabulary: animals—horses, buffalo; natural environments, weather—thunder, lightning, wind
Grammar: past continuous tense, past perfect tense, action verbs-intransitive
Patterns: complex sentence patterns

This legend is a masterful blend of animal story, fantasy, mystery and romance. It tells of an adolescent girl who so loved wild horses that she ran with them. Its ending is somewhat unexpected but very satisfying. It appeals especially to young adolescent girls, whose attraction to horses appears to be an international quality.

This book expands Native American awareness, also present in *The Gift of the Sacred Dog* by the same author. *The Girl Who Loved Wild Horses* serves as a good follow-up. While it is approximately the same level of language difficulty, text per page and book length, it has a slightly more complex story line, challenging the intermediate learner to a higher level of comprehension. It is also "safer" because it contains no religious references.

Highly recommended for older, elementary students because of the age of the protagonists, mature themes and sophisticated art work. Winner of the Caldecott Medal.

Related Book By Same Author: *The Gift of the Sacred Dog* (1980) in this section of the RAL.

THE ELEPHANT'S CHILD

by Rudyard Kipling   illustrated by Lorinda Byran Cauley
New York: Harcourt Brace Jovanovich, 1983   43 pages

Grades: 2-5, 4-8   **ESL Level:** intermediate, advanced
Genre: picture book—folk tale

Vocabulary: animals—jungle, elephant, ostrich, giraffe, baboon, hippopotamus, snake, crocodile
Grammar: conditional sentences, adjectives, *wh*-questions, future tense
Patterns: repeated sentences, compound and complex sentence patterns, dialogue

This is the original "pourquoi" story, "O Best Beloved," of how the elephant got its trunk. Its availability as a fully illustrated picture book makes it more accessible to ESL learners than the same story in the full Kipling anthology. Some of its complex structures and vocabulary, while charming, will probably need to be simplified, even for advanced students.

Children particularly enjoy the "insatiable curiosity" of the young elephant and laugh at his naivete in asking everyone, including the crocodile, what the crocodile eats for dinner. Children identify with youthful heroes, especially when they outwit their elders. They find especially satisfying the revenge of the elephant child in returning the spankings to his older and larger relatives. This is a memorable myth for experienced listeners.

Related Books: Another classic animal character with an "insatiable curiosity" is George, the monkey. In the RAL, see *Curious George Rides a Bike* (Rey, 1952) and *Curious George Goes to the Hospital* (Rey, 1964).

Related Books By Same Author: *Just So Stories* (1912) is the original anthology. Many of these tales have been made into individual picture books: *The Beginning of the Armadillos* (1983), *How the Camel Got His Hump* (1985), *The Butterfly that Stamped* (1983), *The Cat that Walked by Himself* (1983), *The Crab that Played by the Sea* (1983).

ZOO

DEAR ZOO

by Rod Campbell
New York: Macmillan (Four Winds Books), 1982   17 pages

Grades: Pre K-1   **ESL Level:** beginner, intermediate
Genre: picture book

Vocabulary: animals—zoo
Grammar: adjectives, auxiliary verb—*to be*
Patterns: repeated sentence patterns and sentences

This is a cute peek-a-boo book about eight different animals the zoo sends to the young narrator. He returns them all, with explanations about why they don't qualify as his special pet. This provides a good introduction to adjectives. Finally they send him the perfect pet. Before the first reading, ask the children what their perfect zoo pet would be and what they think the narrator might have asked for.

Children love to guess what's under the picture and then to pull down the flap, even after they have read the book numerous times. With the repeated and predictable patterns, they will be reading it aloud with you after the first few times. This is very popular with the young set!

Book By the Same Author: *Henry's Busy Day* (1984)

A CHILDREN'S ZOO

by Tana Hoban
New York: Greenwillow Books, 1985   22 pages

Grades: K-3, 4-8   **ESL Level:** beginner
Genre: non-fiction picture book

Vocabulary: animals—zoo
Grammar: action verbs, third person agreement, adjectives
Patterns: repeated format

This is a stunning and very useful book. It includes 11 color photographs of zoo animals attractively displayed on black pages with white print. Each photograph receives its own page and the writing, its own. The text is limited to four words per animal. One is the animal's name in capital letters, one is a verb that defines a characteristic, and the other two are modifiers. (For example, for the seal, there is *SEAL swims, sleek* and *black.*) From these four words and the photograph, numerous sentences can be constructed.

I don't know why the author calls this *A Children's Zoo.* It does not include pictures of baby animals, nor is the text or design in any way immature. Quite the contrary, this book is very appropriate for older beginner, SL students. Of course, its perfect complement is a trip to the zoo on a warm spring day. For a simple zoo assignment have the students find and write/draw about different animals, using the same pattern of picture, name, verb and modifiers. Don't forget the picnic lunch! Enjoy!

Books By the Same Author: See *A, B, See* (1982) in the RAL.

ZOO

by Gail Gibbons
New York: Harper & Row (Thomas Y. Crowell), 1987   32 pages

Grades: 2-5   **ESL Level:** beginners, intermediate
Genre: non-fiction picture book
Ethnic Identity: multiethnic

Vocabulary: animals—zoo; food, health, occupations
Grammar: simple present tense, third person agreement, direct objects, auxiliary verb—*to be*
Patterns: passive voice

Zoos are more than animals in exhibit areas. There is a large behind the scenes network to support what we see as we stroll around. In this book, Gail Gibbons systematically introduces us to a modern day zoo: a work place with food vendors, zoo keepers, veterinarians, feeding schedules, kitchens, and hospitals. Her pictures are clear and her text simple, but explanatory. Reading this book before a trip to the local zoo will expand awareness and enrich the students' experience there. However, because she tries to be comprehensive, not all she describes will be present at every zoo.

This is an excellent book for older students who are tired of just animal pictures, yet are still intrigued by the zoo. It also provides a brief look at diverse zoo-related occupations.

Books By the Same Author: See *Thanksgiving Day* (1983) in the RAL.

KOKO'S KITTEN

by Francine Patterson   photographs by Ronald Cohn
New York: Scholastic, 1985, 1987 edition includes a teacher's manual   31 pages

Grades: 2-5, 4-8   **ESL Level:** intermediate
Genre: non-fiction picture book

Vocabulary: animal behavior, animals—gorillas, kittens
Grammar: questions, imperatives, action verbs
Patterns: dialogue, short simple sentences

Koko is the gorilla who has learned to communicate in sign language. Dr. Francine Patterson, the author, is also Koko's trainer. She has worked with him since 1972 and he has become her "life's work." This book communicates not only Koko's story but Patterson's love and devotion as well. She is really Koko's mother.

This book also spins a good story. In tenderly telling of Koko's love for a pet kitten, it incorporates many of the elements of good fiction—action, suspense, emotion and dialogue. The large color photographs, which document the events, create a further bond with the audience. All of this combines to recommend this as a non-fiction read-aloud.

Another interesting dimension is Koko's learning sign language, which is analogous to learning a second language. Insights can be gleaned from the story's dialogue, which records the actual words Koko signs.

Related Book By Same Author: *Koko's Story* (1986)

MISCELLANEOUS

A RHINOCEROS WAKES ME UP IN THE MORNING

by Peter Goodspeed   illustrated by Dennis Panek
Scarsdale, NY: Bradbury Press, 1984)   29 pages

Grades: Pre K-1, K-3   **ESL Level:** beginning, intermediate
Genre: picture book

Vocabulary: animals, childhood activities, household
Grammar: simple present tense, third person agreement, indefinite articles—singular, direct
    objects
Patterns: simple sentences, repeated sentence pattern

A small boy meanders through a day in the pleasant company of 28 animal friends. From sunrise to bedtime, he enjoys typical childhood activities, each with a different animal. A playful picture fills each page and a single sentence below clearly describes each picture and action.

The large, colorful illustrations allow the book to be easily seen by a large group, and the simple sentence pattern allows it to be easily understood. Plus, the book provides 28 opportunities to practice third person agreement, a tenacious error for most ESL students. Additionally, children find it amusing to see large animals intertwined in the daily life of a small boy. All these qualities recommend this as a good read-aloud.

OH, A HUNTING WE WILL GO

by John Langstaff   illustrated by Nancy Winslow Parker
New York: Macmillan (Antheneum), 1974   26 pages

Grades: K-3   **ESL Level:** beginner, intermediate
Genre: picture book—singable book, easy reader
Ethnic: multiethnic

Vocabulary: animals, household
Grammar: future tense—*will*, contractions—*we'll*, indefinite articles—singular, prepositional
    phrases of place, conjunctions—*and*
Patterns: short vowel sounds, rhyming, repeated sentences

This is a delightful singable book with 13 rhyming verses about animals and the amusing places they can go. The text is predictable, with only the rhyming words changing in each verse. Some of my favorites include "We'll catch a pig and put him in a wig" and "We'll catch an armadillo and put him in a pillow." Such fun nonsense encourages the creation of more humorous verses by the children. An amazing amount of language gets transmitted in the process. Plus kids love it! All the verses and musical notation are included at the end. The illustrations are multiethnic and clear. Great fun! Enjoy!

Books by Same Author: *Over in the Meadow* (1957) and *Frog Went A-Courting* (1956 Caldecott Award Winner).

THE STORY OF FERDINAND

by Munro Leaf   illustrated by Robert Lawson
New York: Viking Press, 1936; Penguin, 1977   70 pages

Grades K-3, 2-5   **ESL Level:** beginner, intermediate
Genre: picture book
Ethnic Identity: European-Spanish

Vocabulary: animals, sports—bullfighting
Grammar: action verbs, comparatives, superlatives, prepositional phrases of place
Patterns: repeated word patterns and refrain

Ferdinand is a bull who marches to his own drummer. No, he doesn't like to snort, butt heads or fight with the other bulls. He prefers to "sit just quietly and smell the flowers," thank you. Accidentally, Ferdinand gets selected to be the fiercest bull for the big bullfight in Madrid. How does he handle it? Does he fight? Leaf's creative answer affirms the power of passive resistance and the value of pacificism. For older students, it can be used as a model for conflict resolution.

This book was the highlight of Munro Leaf's writing career and has stood the test of time. Over 50 years young, it continues to be enjoyed as a read-aloud by both adults and children alike.

THE KNEE-HIGH MAN AND OTHER TALES

by Julius Lester   illustrated by Ralph Pinto
New York: E. P. Dutton (Dial Press), 1972, 1985   31 pages

Grades: 2-5, 4-8   **ESL Level:** intermediate
Genre: folk tales, fables, short stories, anthology
Ethnic Identity: Black American

Vocabulary: animals—dog, cat, bear, rabbit, owl, horse, bull, snake; farm, natural
          environments—ocean; weather—wind
Grammer: possessive adjectives, comparative adjectives
Patterns: short sentences, simple sentence patterns, dialogues, informal language

This collection of six Black American folktales, each briefly retold, includes animal tales, fables and "pourquoi" stories. The tales are quite short, from 1-4 pages of text each, and use simple language and brief dialogues. Nevertheless, they deliver powerful life messages. My favorite is the title story, "The Knee–High Man," who learns, after numerous attempts to be taller than he is, that with a little ingenuity, he can do all he really needs to just the way he is. The book concludes with a helpful note from the author, explaining the development of black folklore in general and these stories in particular. Pinto's descriptive illustrations, including minority characters, visually enrich the stories, creating a picture book-folktale anthology.

This book is especially good for a busy intermediate class with only a few minutes of read-aloud time available.

Related Book: *The People Could Fly: American Black Folktales* (Hamilton, 1985)

Related Book By Same Author: *To Be a Slave* (1968)

SEASONS/WEATHER

SUMMER IS . . .

by Charlotte Zolotow   illustrated by Ruth Lercher Bornstein
New York: Harper & Row (Thomas Y. Crowell), 1983   27 pages

Grades: K-3, 2-5   **ESL Level:** beginner, intermediate
Genre: picture book—concept book

Vocabulary: seasons, seasonal activities, home, natural environments
Grammar: nouns, noun phrases, adjectives, auxiliary verb—to be, present tense
Patterns: repeated sentence patterns and format

This book celebrates the seasons and invites you in to enjoy them too. It also makes you feel good about nature, seasons and life in general. The minimal text defines each season in short, almost poetic phrases. It captures the nicest qualities of each. Through this, seasonal vocabulary and its activities are introduced. Warm, pastel drawings create soft mood pieces of each season, in which the separate vocabulary is also easily identified. Further language can be generated from the illustrations themselves.

THE SEASONS OF ARNOLD'S APPLE TREE

by Gail Gibbons
New York: Harcourt, Brace, Jovanovich, 1984   32 pages

Grades: K-3, 2-5   **ESL Level:** beginner
Genre: picture book—concept book

Vocabulary: seasons, seasonal activities, weather
Grammar: simple present tense, third person agreement, nouns—singular and plural, verbs of physical activity—transitive
Patterns: simple sentence patterns

Arnold has his "very own secret place." It is a big, beautiful apple tree that keeps him very busy all through the year. This includes building a tree house in it during spring time, enjoying its shade in summer, harvesting apples from it in fall and building a snow fort to protect it during the winter. Also included is "Arnold's Apple Pie Recipe" in four easy steps. This provides a nice follow-up cooking activity.

Gail Gibbons the author has ingeniously woven the basic vocabulary of the seasons and accompanying weather into an engaging story of pleasurable childhood pastimes. Gail Gibbons the illustrator has clearly detailed each activity with bright colors. With each scene a separate page containing only a single sentence, even beginning ESL students can understand the text. Another Gibbons success!

Related Books: The Giving Tree (Silverstein, 1964) in the RAL and Seasons (Podendorf, 1981).

Related Book by Same Author: Playgrounds (1985) in the RAL.

Books By the Same Author: See Thanksgiving Day (1983) in the RAL.

THE SNOWY DAY

by Ezra Jack Keats
New York: Viking Press, 1962; Penguin, 1976   32 pages

Grades: K-3   **ESL Level:** intermediate
Genre: picture book
Ethnic Identity: Black American

Vocabulary: seasons—winter; seasonal activities—winter; weather—snow
Grammar: adverbial clauses, past tense
Patterns: repeated word and sentence patterns

This Caldecott Medal winner lightly chronicles the pleasant experiences of a young black boy during a pretty snowstorm. Although the text is limited, the syntax is complex, making it most appropriate for intermediate ESL students. However, the pictures can carry the story, even for beginners. Their unusual design of part water color and part collage create a sparkling atmosphere. There is enough detail so that one can identify the events described, but this is more of a mood book.

It is perfect to read either before an anticipated snowfall or right after. It provides English vocabulary for things the students will likely have experienced. It would be more difficult to use in environments without winter weather or snow.

Related Book: *The Snowman* (Briggs, 1978)

Books By the Same Author: See *A Letter to Amy* (1968) in the RAL.

THE BOY WHO DIDN'T BELIEVE IN SPRING

by Lucille Clifton   illustrated by Brinton Turkle
New York: E. P. Dutton, 1973, 1988   25 pages

Grades: K-3   **ESL Level:** intermediate
Genre: picture book
Ethnic Identity: Black American, multiethnic

Vocabulary: seasons—spring; places in the community—urban
Grammar: action verbs, past tense, direct objects
Patterns: nonstandard and informal language, dialogue

King Shabazz and Anthony Polito are young, tough city kids. They don't believe their teachers and mothers, when they tell them that Spring is coming. They need to discover evidence of it themselves, and they do, in the most unlikely places. Their quest takes them throughout their urban, multiethnic community.

This book portrays a positive interracial friendship. You will notice that some of the dialogue uses nonstandard English. It can be read, as is, to authenticate the characters' culture, or easily modified into standard speech. This story is especially popular when read during those cold, raw days just prior to the outburst of Spring.

Book By the Same Illustrator: *Deep in the Forest* (1976) in the RAL.

GILBERTO AND THE WIND

by Marie Hall Ets
New York: Viking Press, 1963; Penguin, 1978   32 pages

Grades: Pre K-1, K-3   **ESL Level:** beginner, intermediate
Genre: picture book
Ethnic Identity: Hispanic American

Vocabulary: weather—wind; childhood activities, feelings, seasons—spring
Grammar: simple present tense—first and third person agreement
Patterns: s and z final sounds

A young Hispanic boy joyfully experiences the wind and springtime activities. Written as a first person narrative, Gilberto talks simply about his wind-related adventures, what he likes and how he feels. Interesting illustrations emerge from a palette limited to shades of browns, grays and black, lightened with splashes of white. It is not as dull as it sounds; actually, it is quite effective.

The science theme of how wind affects various objects emerges from this book. This allows it to be integrated into a science unit on wind, weather or seasons. Listening to the book also entices the children to enjoy an outside walk on a windy day. A whole class story can later emerge from their own experiences.

TOAD IS THE UNCLE OF HEAVEN

by Jeanne M. Lee
New York: Holt, Rinehart & Winston, 1985   33 pages

Grades: K-3, 2-5   **ESL Level:** intermediate, advanced
Genre: picture book—folk tale
Ethnic Identity: Asian-Indochinese

Vocabulary: weather—drought, rain; animals, royalty
Grammar: past tense, future tense, action verbs, adjectives
Patterns: reported speech, repeated format

Throughout the world, folktales share common elements, while distinctly representing their own culture of origin. This Vietnamese tale follows the universal "pourquoi" strand by telling how the toad has become a symbol of rain in Vietnam. It also shares a familiar format in which more and more animals join along in search of something important. This allows repetition of information, a useful strategy for SL listeners. In keeping with the culture, it honors royalty and explains the custom of showing respect by calling someone "Uncle."

Numerous other qualities help maintain young listeners' attention. They include the diverse drawings and unusual page designs and also a series of fights in the plot. In sum, this is an attractive, action-filled ethnic tale.

Related Books: *Henny Penny* (Galdone, 1978), *The Elephant's Child* (Kipling, 1983) and *The Brocaded Slipper and Other Vietnamese Tales* (Voung, 1982), all in the RAL.

THE SEASIDE

by Maria Ruis and J. M. Parramon
Woodbury, NY: Barron's Educational Series, 1986   26 pages

Grades: K-3   **ESL Level:** beginner, intermediate
Genre: picture book—concept book
Ethnic Identity: European-Spanish

Vocabulary: natural environments, seaside
Grammar: adverbial clauses, present continuous tense, nouns—count and mass, definite article
Patterns: repeated sentence pattern

With large print and bright illustrations, this book introduces the vocabulary and activities of the seaside. It also mentions the geography, employment and recreation associated with the sea. The brief text is spread out in single phrases or single sentences on each page. Written originally in Spanish by a well-known Spanish children's author, it has been smoothly translated into English. For bilingual programs, the Spanish version is also available from the publisher.

The book works well either as a text for a social studies unit or as a preparation for summer vacation. A two-page guide for parents and teachers is included at the end.

Related Books By Same Author: There are three other titles in this *Let's Discover Series: The Mountains, The City* and *The Countryside.* All were published in 1986, both in English and Spanish.

Books by the Same Author: *Los Cuatro Elementos* (The Four Elements), 1985 is a series of four books. *Los Cinco Sentidos (The Five Senses),* 1985 is a series of five books. These are concept/picture books, in a format similar to *The Seaside.*

A DAY ON THE RIVER

by Reinhart Michl
Woodbury, NY: Barron's Educational Service, 1985   30 pages

Grades: 2-5, 4-8   **ESL Level:** advanced
Genre: picture book
Ethnic Identity: European—German

Vocabulary: natural environment—river; animals
Grammar: simple present tense, multiple adjectives, adverbial phrases
Patterns: complex sentences

Three boy friends play hooky from school and set off to spend the warm spring day with another friend of theirs, the local, meandering river. Well prepared with a fishing pole, an inner tube and two paddles, they explore their favorite river haunts. They also encounter some surprises, including a renegade girl. This adds to the wholesome fun of it all. The book excels in creating an inviting recreational adventure for preteens, away from urban life and parental authority.

This is the first book that this German draftsman/artist has written, and it reads like that—a little stiff and over written. It also suffers from translation. The illustrations are stronger than the text. In fact, they carry the story. They are fully detailed, environmentally rich and very appealing. This is a river trip that many of us can only experience through literature. Enjoy it vicariously!

STOPPING BY WOODS ON A SNOWY EVENING

by Robert Frost   illustrated by Susan Jeffers
New York: Dutton, 1978   27 pages

Grades: 4-8   **ESL Level:** intermediate
Genre: poetry, picture book

Vocabulary: winter, seasonal activities—winter; natural enviornment—woods
Grammar: nouns, adjectives, prepositional phrases of place
Patterns: literary language, rhyming, repeated sentence

This oft-quoted poem, written back in 1923 by the famous American poet Robert Frost, evokes the quiet delights of winter. In 16 short lines, it verbally invites us "to watch the woods fill up fill up with snow," but then pulls us onward: "I have promises to keep and miles to go before I sleep."

Artist Susan Jeffers has made a wonderful contribution by transforming this poem into a single volume picture book. Her soft, mostly black and white drawings explain what is explicit. In addition, she invitingly creates the mood of a frosty New England woods and the pilgrimage of the single traveler.

This edition of the poem serves as an excellent component of a winter and/or poetry unit for older beginner, SL students. It is a treat for both the ears and eyes.

Book By the Same Illustrator: *Hansel and Gretel* (1980) in the RAL.

FLASH, CRASH, RUMBLE, AND ROLL

by Franklyn M. Branley   illustrated by Barbara and Ed Emberly
New York: Harper & Row (Thomas Y. Crowell), 1985   32 pages

Grades: K-3, 2-5   **ESL Level:** intermediate
Genre: non-fiction picture book

Vocabulary: weather—thunder, lightning, storms; places in the community
Grammar: imperatives, modal auxiliaries—*may*, adverbial clauses, comparatives
Patterns: repeated sentence patterns—*if* clauses

Most children are intrigued with thunderstorms, many are frightened of them, yet few understand them. This book by Dr. Branley, a prolific science writer for children, carefully explains how and why thunderstorms happen. In addition, it details how to stay safe from lightning and addresses fears and myths about this weather pattern. It is very readable, yet the full explanations benefit from additional classroom reinforcement. It works well integrated into a science unit on this topic. The lively illustrations by the Emberlys add lightness and humor.

In sum, this book is scientifically accurate and visually attractive. For safety reasons, it is also an important one to share.

Books in the Same Series: This is part of the excellent, elementary *Let's Read-and-Find-Out Science Books.* This somewhat folksy series, of which Dr. Branley is the editor, includes over 100 titles. A few of the recent ones are *How to Talk to Your Computer, Why I Cough, Sneeze, Shiver, Hiccup & Yawn* and *Is There Life in Outer Space?*

Books By the Same Author: *Sunshine Makes the Seasons* (1974) and *The Planets in Our Solar System* (1987), both in the RAL.

SUNSHINE MAKES THE SEASONS

by Franklyn M. Branley   illustrated by Shelley Freshman
New York: Harper & Row (Thomas Y. Crowell), 1974   33 pages

Grades: 2-5   **ESL Level:** intermediate
Genre: non-fiction picture book, easy reader

Vocabulary: seasons, weather
Grammar: auxiliary verbs—to have, to be; simple present tense, third person agreement
Patterns: short sentences, simple and compound sentence patterns

This book describes how sunshine and the tilt of the earth's axis are responsible for the changing seasons. Dr. Branley explains the intriguing childhood questions of why the seasons change during the year and around the globe and why days are not always the same length. The author, an Astronomer Emeritus, writes in a scientifically clear, yet almost story-like manner. The language is fairly easy, yet the concepts are not diluted.

The illustrations mix clear and helpful diagrams with pleasant drawings of people enjoying the season. The distinctive design of each page helps create a very inviting book. The science "lesson" is pleasantly absorbed. It is part of the excellent *Let's Read-and-Find-Out Science Books*.

Even though it is currently out of print, its information is still accurate. It also remains available on many library shelves.

Related Books: *Sun up, Sun down* (Gibbons, 1983), for K-3 and *Wonders of the Seasons* (Brandt, 1982)

Books By the Same Author/Editor: See *Flash, Crash, Rumble and Roll* (1985), in the RAL.

WEATHER EXPERIMENTS

by Vera Webster
Chicago, IL: Children's Press, 1982   47 pages

Grades: 2-5   **ESL Level:** intermediate
Genre: non-fiction picture book

Vocabulary: weather
Grammar: simple present tense, third person agreement, imperatives, questions
Patterns: repeated format

This book briefly explains the basic components of weather. It also includes ten easy, weather-related experiments that demonstrate these principles. The language here is straightforward. Short declarative sentences are used throughout, with only three to four sentences per page and only two to three pages per topic. The difficulty of the material and the amount of information increases gradually. The color photographs and drawings of the experiments are helpful components, as are the page long study guides (table of contents, glossary and index).

The large, bold face type facilitates this being read for independent reading. But it will reach more students when integrated into a social studies or science unit as a read-aloud/do-together introductory text. Part of the *New True Books Series*.

Books in the Same Series: See *Nutrition* (LeMaster, 1985) in the RAL.

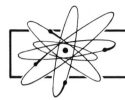

SCIENCE

GROWTH

THE CARROT SEED

by Ruth Krauss   illustrated by Crockett Johnson
New York: Harper & Row, 1945   25 pages

Grades: Pre-K-1, K-3   **ESL Level:** beginner, intermediate
Genre: picture book

Vocabulary: gardening, family
Grammar: future tense—*will*, conditionals, negation, contractions
Patterns: repeated word patterns and sentences

Some books seem to live on forever and this is one of them. Everyone in his family doubts the little boy's ability to grow a carrot. Like all children, he is active, always wanting to do something, but it also takes time for a seed to sprout. Both his work and his patience are rewarded in the end and another gardener is born! The author effectively used predictable patterns (long before they were in vogue) and limits the text to a sentence per page. Be warned however, that some of the syntax is at the intermediate level. The simple pictures carry the story though, even for beginners.

This book is perfect to use in conjunction with a springtime unit on gardening. This hands-on learning generates a lot of language, which can be later synthesized in a language experience story.

Book By the Same Author: *A Hole is to Dig: A First Book of Definitions.* (1952)

THE VERY HUNGRY CATERPILLAR

by Eric Carle
New York: Putnam Publishing Group (Philomel), 1970, 1989   30 pages

Grades: Pre-K-1, K-3   **ESL Level:** beginner, intermediate
Genre: picture book

Vocabulary: days, numbers—1-5; food
Grammar: prepositional phrases of place, nouns—mass and count, conjunctions, past tense
Patterns: repeated sentence pattern, repeated refrain

This story follows the metamorphosis of a small but appealing caterpillar into a big and colorful butterfly. Along the way he amazingly eats his way through a wide variety and quantity of food. Carle's brilliant collages and clever sequencing of days and numbers make you laugh and, in the end, smile in awe of nature. It is a perfect example of how literature can be used to teach basic concepts. All this combines to make this an absolutely wonderful read-aloud. Also extremely popular, it has sold over 4 million copies and has been translated into numerous languages. Very few children's picture books achieve quite this success. Congratulations Eric Carle!

Related Book By Same Author: *The Very Busy Spider* (1984)

Books By the Same Author/Illustrator: See *The Hole in the Dike* (1975) in the RAL.

THE LADY AND THE SPIDER

by Faith McNulty   illustrated by Bob Marshall
New York: Harper & Row, 1986   45 pages

Grades: K-3   **ESL Level:** intermediate
Genre: picture book

Vocabulary: gardening, insects
Grammar: prepositional phrases of place, possessive adjectives, nouns, third person subject
  pronoun
Patterns: simple and compound sentences

A spider innocently makes her home in the hills and valleys of a lettuce leaf. For her, it is a perfect den, with just the right amounts of dew drops for water and insects for food. Then enters the dramatic tension, known to the reader but not the spider: this lettuce is part of a tended garden and one day will be picked and eaten for lunch. The author sensitively resolves the conflict, affirming both the gardener, gardening and the life of the spider.

It is refreshing that the spider is not endowed with human feelings: she, indeed, acts like a spider. The illustrations accurately portray the insects, lettuce and humans and in approximately correct proportions. This reinforces the scientific information, which is gently intertwined with the story. A lovely small book, selected by the *Reading Rainbow* program.

Related Books: *Charlotte's Web* (White, 1952), the classic spider novel and *The Very Hungry Caterpillar* (Carle, 1970), both in the RAL.

A CHICK HATCHES

by Joanna Cole   photographs by Jerome Wexler
New York: William Morrow, 1976   47 pages

Grades: K-3, 2-5   **ESL Level:** beginner, intermediate
Genre: non-fiction picture book

Vocabulary: animal—chicken; birth
Grammar: simple present tense, present perfect tense, auxiliary verb—*to be*, comparatives
Patterns: passive voice

This books tells of a chick's birth from incubation to hatching to independence. The text is simple, yet it is also scientific and informative. Each stage of the three week process is documented with realistic photographs, six of them colored. Some of the photographs are taken inside the egg and others show a fetus in various stages of development. These pictures, combined with the clear text, document a fascinating life experience and make for a good story.

Often in the spring, elementary classes observe this process of eggs hatching as part of life science. This book integrates perfectly with this content-based unit.

Related Books By Same Author: *A Calf is Born* (1975) and *My Puppy is Born* (1973)

Books By the Same Author: *The Magic School Bus Inside the Earth* (1987) in the RAL and *Cars and How They Go* (1983)

HEALTH/HOSPITAL

MY DOCTOR

by Harlow Rockwell
New York: Harper & Row, 1973; Macmillan, 1985   20 pages

Grades: K-3   **ESL Level:** beginner
Genre: picture book—concept book

Vocabulary: body, medical
Grammar: simple present tense, third person agreement, auxiliary verb—*to have*, nouns—
 singular and plural, indefinite article, possessive adjectives—*my, her*
Patterns: simple sentences

A visit to a doctor's office can be frightening for children, especially if they are not familiar with the routine, instruments and/or language. This easy, non-fiction book helps dispel some of those fears by explaining a routine office visit of a young boy. The author uses the child as narrator. This has a reassuring effect on the reader and also provides helpful practice in the difficult third person present agreement.

The book is appropriately designed for young children. The type is large, only a sentence or two appears on each page, and clear illustrations explain each instrument or procedure. Because some of the words are long, this works best as a read-aloud rather than a beginning reader. Altogether, it is a very useful book.

Related Books By the Same Author: *Emergency Room* (1985), in the RAL, and *My Dentist* (1975).

Books By the Same Author: See *Happy Birthday to Me* (1981) in the RAL.

THE EMERGENCY ROOM

by Anne and Harlow Rockwell
New York: Macmillan, 1985   22 pages

Grades: K-3   **ESL Level:** beginner
Genre: picture book—concept book
Ethnic Identity: multiethnic

Vocabulary: hospitals
Grammar: existential sentences-*there is*, plural nouns

A young boy has hurt his leg and needs to go to the emergency room. Through his personally narrated experience, children are introduced to the procedure used to treat broken bones and repair cuts. Since most children encounter the emergency room at least once, this concept book will give them a painless first visit. It does not, however, address the emotional trauma of the experience. This will likely emerge in follow-up discussions of children's own experiences with injuries.

This book follows the same simple format and uses the same style of illustration as *My Doctor*, also by Harlow Rockwell, annotated just above. This one adds multiethnic people in the artwork.

Books By the Same Author: See *Happy Birthday to Me* (1981) in the RAL.

CURIOUS GEORGE GOES TO THE HOSPITAL

by Margaret and H.A. Rey
Boston: Houghton Mifflin, 1966, 1973   48 pages

Grades: Pre K-1, K-3   **ESL Level:** intermediate, advanced
Genre: picture book

Vocabulary: hospitals, medical, children's activities
Grammar: past tense, auxiliary verb–*to be*, countable nouns, adjectives
Patterns: compound sentences

There are more modern books about hospitals and health care today than this one. And these should be shared with children. (See other books in this topic for suggestions). But never has there been a funnier picture book about a childhood experience at a hospital. It's in a class by itself! It all begins innocently enough when George, a very curious monkey, notices a jigsaw puzzle. He knows he shouldn't touch it, but well, how can a curious monkey resist. He swallows a piece, thus touching off a hospital stay, tests and a successful operation. During his recovery period, he innocently causes much commotion. This brings spontaneous laughter to the sick children, which infectiously spreads to the listening audience. Curious George scores again!

Because this and other Curious George books are longer than most picture books and also contain more text, they are best reserved for experienced listeners.

Related Book By Same Author: *Curious George Rides a Bike* (1952) in the RAL.

YOUR HEART AND BLOOD

by Leslie Jean LeMaster
Chicago: Children's Press, 1984   48 pages

Grades: 2-5, 4-8   **ESL Level:** intermediate
Genre: non-fiction picture book, easy reader

Vocabulary: health, body
Grammar: adverbial clauses, simple present tense, third person agreement
Patterns: academic language

This *New True Book* looks more like an elementary science text than literature. For example, it contains the helpful textbook tools of a table of contents, glossary and an index. Nevertheless, its picture book format with clear diagrams and color photographs make it more attractive than a standard text.

Its large size print encourages students to try to read it themselves. It can still be recommended as a read-aloud because this (and other books in this series) can be somewhat dry. It benefits from an oral introduction and is especially useful when integrated with a science unit or for beginning research reports.

Related Books in the Same Series: *New True Books* that relate to health include *Bacteria and Viruses, Cells and Tissues, Health, Your Brain and Nervous System* and *Your Skeleton and Skin*.

Books in the Same Series: See *Nutrition* (1985) in the RAL.

SPACE/SOLAR SYSTEM

THE PLANETS IN OUR SOLAR SYSTEM

by Franklyn M. Branley   illustrated by Don Madden
New York: Harper & Row (Thomas Y. Crowell), 1987   34 pages

Grades: 2-5   **ESL Level:** beginner, intermediate
Genre: non-fiction picture book

Vocabulary: solar system, planets
Grammar: imperatives, comparatives, superlatives, simple present tense, auxiliary verb—*to be*
Patterns: informal language

This book is a friendly introduction to the planets and solar system. It provides basic information about their names, sizes, functions and locations. It also includes clear step-by-step directions for how to make two models about the solar system. These work well as cooperative classroom science projects. The text strikes a nice balance between folksy and factual. It speaks directly to the children, avoiding the passive voice, which is commonly used in more formal science texts.

The illustrations vary from cute drawings of children engaged in pseudo-scientific activities to labeled diagrams of the solar system to black and white photos. This combination allows the students to feel comfortable with the educational material. Children generally enjoy this topic and this book. It is part of the *Let's Read-and-Find-Out Series*.

Books in the Same Series: See *Flash, Crash, Rumble and Roll* (Branley, 1985) in the RAL.

I CAN BE AN ASTRONAUT

by June Behrens
Chicago: Children's Press, 1984   32 pages

Grades: 2-5, 6-8   **ESL Level:** beginner, intermediate
Genre: non-fiction picture book

Vocabulary: space
Grammar: simple present tense, third person agreement, future tense—*will*
Patterns: simple sentences

Many children dream of flying in space as an astronaut. It is very glamorous, yet it requires dedication, long hours and special training. This book, part of the occupational *I Can Be A . . .* series clearly introduces the career with simple text and attractive color photographs. The large print encourages the students to read the book independently. Readers benefit from the helpful study guides—a picture dictionary, glossary and index. Either read independently or heard as a read-aloud, this book is especially good for older students with limited English proficiency who are interested in factual information about this adventurous career.

Books in the Same Series: See *I Can Be A Carpenter* (Lillegard, 1986) in the RAL.

SPACE COLONIES

by Dennis B. Fradin
Chicago: Children's Press, 1985   48 pages

Grades: 2-5, 4-8   **ESL Level:** beginner, intermediate
Genre: non-fiction picture book, easy reader

Vocabulary: space
Grammar: auxiliary verb—*to be,* future tense—*will,* conditionals
Patterns: passive voice

Life in space always sounds like science fiction, but here it is presented as a matter-of-fact science book. It still seems unbelievable, but it is fascinating to explore and ponder. Discerning fact from fiction can lead to many interesting follow-up assignments, either in the realm of science or science fiction. Grammar plays a part in this, as the book alternates between the simple present (what is), the future (what will be) and the conditional (what would and could happen). *A New True Book.*

Books in the Same Series: See *Nutrition* (LeMaster, 1985) in the RAL.

ASTRONOMY TODAY

by Dinah L. Moche   illustrated by Harry Naught
New York: Random House, 1982   96 pages

Grades: 4-8   **ESL Level:** advanced
Genre: non-fiction

Vocabulary: space, solar system, planets, stars, seasons
Grammar: adverbial clauses
Patterns: academic language, passive voice

This is a good source for report writing on a variety of topics relating to space and the solar system. The text, written by a Professor of Astronomy and Physics, is clear and current. Yet each topic in this large and attractive book receives only a two-page spread. So, the amount of material, while detailed, is manageable. The material is additionally explained with numerous diagrams, pictures and charts. A detailed table of contents and index are included.

Space is fascinating, and so is this book! That helps qualify it as a recommended read-aloud. In addition, each topic can be completed within 10-15 minutes. Use this material to teach academic skills or integrate it more fully with a content-based science unit. Or, just read it aloud for stimulation and enrichment.

Book By the Same Author: *We're Taking an Airplane Ride* (1982) in the RAL.

MISCELLANEOUS

THE MAGIC SCHOOL BUS INSIDE THE EARTH

by Joanna Cole
New York: Scholastic, 1987

illustrated by Bruce Degen
40 pages

Grades: 2-5   **ESL Level:** intermediate
Genre: non-fiction picture book, science fiction
Ethnic Identity: multiethnic

Vocabulary: natural environments, school, transportation—school bus; rocks
Grammar: comparative adjectives, exclamatory sentences
Patterns: passive voice, dialogue

Who ever thought that someone could make earth science interesting, let alone transform it into an exciting children's adventure story? Joanna Cole, award-winning children's science writer, deserves the honor. She creates Ms. Frizzle, a rather unconventional science teacher, who takes her surprised class on an action-packed field trip, to, literally, the center of the earth! Along the way, the students experience the different kinds of rocks that compose the earth's surface. The comical illustrations and creative book design also contribute to the book's success.

To create this adventure, the author has liberally mixed fiction with fact. At the end, she cleverly acknowledges this and begins to help the student discern what actually is true. Continuing this provides a good way to review the book's content.

Related Books By Same Author: *The Magic School Bus Inside the Body* (1989) and *The Magic School Bus at the Waterworks* (1986)

Books By the Same Author: *Cars and How They Go* (1983) and a *Chick Hatches* (1976), both in the RAL.

TOP SECRET

by John Reynolds Gardiner
Boston: Little Brown, 1984

illustrated by Marc Simont
110 pages

Grades: 4-8   **ESL Level:** intermediate, advanced
Genre: fiction—long novel, science fiction

Vocabulary: science, school, family
Grammar: questions, past tense
Patterns: dialogues, informal language

Like many creative students, nine-year old Allen Brewster yearns to do something unusual for his annual science fair project. He is determined to duplicate plant photosynthesis in humans, with himself as the first experiment. Despite the disapproval of his teacher and family (except his supportive grandfather), he succeeds beyond his wildest imagination! And so does this pre-adolescent foray into science fiction. It is hilarious, serious and frightening!

It works well as a read-aloud for many reasons. The dialogue makes it fast-paced, it is divided into short chapters and Marc Simont's funny illustrations provide visual relief. Enjoy!

Book By the Same Author: *Stone Fox* (1980) in the RAL.

𝕴𝖒𝖆𝖌𝖎𝖓𝖆𝖙𝖎𝖔𝖓/𝕸𝖔𝖓𝖘𝖙𝖊𝖗𝖘/𝕸𝖆𝖌𝖎𝖈

RAIN MAKES APPLESAUCE

by Julian Scheer
New York: Holiday House, 1964

illustrated by Marvin Bileck
32 pages

Grades: Pre K-1, K-3   **ESL Level:** intermediate
Genre: picture book

Vocabulary: animals, weather
Grammar: simple present tense, third person agreement, prepositional phrases of place
Patterns: repeated sentence pattern, refrains and format

This is a nonsense book that children just love. It is made up of 13 self-contained scenes, unified by refrains. It revels in its own silliness. The illustrations also participate in the humor. They are, however, rather delicately drawn and in soft hues. This makes them difficult to be appreciated by large groups.

Because humor requires a more sophisticated understanding of language, this book can be difficult for SL learners, especially beginning ones, to understand. Happily, the repeated format and predictable patterns help comprehension.

As a follow-up, cook applesauce and discuss the role of rain in this process. Then, encourage the students to create their own nonsense drawings and sentences. Decide as a class either to keep the book's refrain or create your own. In either case, you will very quickly have a cooperative class book which can be bound, "published" and shared. This is a fun learning project!

THE THREE BILLY GOATS GRUFF

by Paul Galdone
Boston: Houghton Mifflin (Clarion Books), 1973   30 pages

Grades: K-3   **ESL Level:** intermediate
Genre: picture book—fairy tale

Vocabulary: numbers—ordinals, natural environment—countryside, stream
Grammar: adjectives, comparative adjectives, future tense—*going to*
Patterns: short vowel sounds, repeated word patterns and sentences, dialogue

"Once upon a time there were three Billy Goats . . . and their name was Gruff. The wanted to go up the hillside and get fat." But there was this little problem of a creaky bridge and the ugly troll who lived under it. You probably know the rest and so may the children you read it to. Yet they never seem to tire of it, especially when the biggest billy goat battles the mean troll. Of course, the good guy wins and the goat family lives happily ever after, on the hillside, eating grass.

There are many versions of this classic fairy tale. This one, illustrated by award-winner Paul Galdone, has large pages and dramatic illustrations. Much of the tale's charm lies with the original language, by its Danish author, Asbjorsen. Galdone retains most of this, including the repeated patterns, with some simplification added. Well done!

Related Book By Same Author: *The Three Little Pigs* (1970)

Books By the Same Author: For others in the RAL see *The Elves and the Shoemaker* (1984).

ABIYOYO

by Pete Seeger
New York: Macmillan, 1986

illustrated by Michael Hays
47 pages

Grades: K-3, 2-5   **ESL Level:** beginner, intermediate
Genre: picture book—folk tale; mystery/suspense
Ethnic Identity: African

Vocabulary: feelings, monster, places in the community-small town
Grammar: past tense, simple present tense, third person agreement, imperatives
Patterns: repeated refrain, dialogue

Pete Seeger created this "songstory" (as he calls it) from an old South African tale about a monster who eats people. In his version, there is a young African boy who plays the ukulele and his father who makes things disappear with his magic wand. They are both ostracized from their town but are welcomed back as heroes when they slay the feared monster, "Abiyoyo" through song, dance and magic.

The exciting story with its repeated chorus makes for a dramatic read-aloud. The expressive illustrations help capture the feelings, as well as the visual details. It could be developed into a challenging dramatization or play for a small group of intermediate-advanced students.

Related Books: *Do Not Open* (Turkle, 1981) and *Wiley and the Hairy Man* (Bang, 1976)

THE PERFECT CRANE

by Anne Laurin
New York: Harper & Row, 1981

illustrated by Charles Mikolaycak
31 pages

Grades: 2-5, 4-8   **ESL Level:** intermediate
Genre: fiction—short story, modern fantasy
Ethnic Identity: Asian-Japanese

Vocabulary: family, friendship
Grammar: present perfect tense, future tense, superlative adjectives
Patterns: dialogues

Gami, a Japanese magician, was lonely until he discovered that he could breathe life into his origami paper folding. He started with a flower, then a lantern and finally he created a "perfect" crane, one who called him "father." He was lonely no more, until his bird flew away. From the crane's going and his return, the author reveals much of the rhythm of family, friendship and love. The life metaphor extends the book's appeal from children to adults.

Listeners are absorbed by the tale's magic and enchanted with the oriental drawings which grace each page. This read-aloud story deserves to be completed in a single sitting. Allot 15-20 minutes reading time.

Related Books: *The Paper Crane* (Bang, 1985) in the RAL.

BEAUTY AND THE BEAST

by Marianna Mayer   illustrated by Mercer Mayer
New York: Macmillan (Aladdin Books), 1978, 1987   44 pages

Grades: 4-8   **ESL Level:** intermediate, advanced
Genre: picture book—fairy tale

Vocabulary: animals, natural environments—forests; places in the community—rural;
   househould
Grammar: conditionals, *if-then* construction, present and past perfect tenses, questions
Patterns: literary languange, complex sentences

This is an eloquent retelling of a classic fairy tale. Through Beauty's love of an ugly but kind
beast, she breaks the powerful spell which had transformed the handsome prince. For her kindness,
she is rewarded by love, marriage and a kingdom. Her jealous sisters don't fare so well.

This version appeals to older elementary and middle school students because of the full
retelling of the story and the development of its sophisticated themes. Also, the protagonists are
attractively drawn as teenagers and young adults. Each illustration is an expressive work of art
which is more fully appreciated by older students (and adults!). The complex syntax and sentence
patterns makes this most appropriate for advanced SL learners, but with the numerous and fully
detailed illustrations as aids, it can be understood by intermediates as well. This is an absolutely
exquisite book!

Related Book: *Mufaro's Beautiful Daughters* (Steptoe, 1987)

THE VELVETEEN RABBIT, OR HOW TOYS BECOME REAL

by Margery Williams   illustrated by Ilse Plume
New York: Harcourt, Brace Jovanovich (Julian Messner), 1983, 1987   36 pages

Grades: 2-5, 4-8   **ESL Level:** advanced
Genre: fiction—short novel, modern fantasy

Vocabulary: household, animals, garden
Grammar: adjectives, exclamatory sentences
Patterns: dialogues

"Real isn't how you're made" said the skin horse to the rabbit. "When a child loves you, then
you become Real." With this philosophical talk of love and reality smoothly integrated into the
touching story of a young boy and his stuffed bunny, this classic appeals to older children and to
adults. Most children still want to believe in magic and this book will preserve that faith. It will also
help restore it for the adults who are lucky enough to share this literary gem with children. It is
most popular during springtime, especially at Easter.

This book has more text, longer sentences and fewer illustrations than a picture book, but it is
worth the challenge! This edition is particularly useful for classroom use. The page sizes have been
increased to 8½ x 11 and the number of pages expanded to accommodate larger and more
numerous illustrations.

A color film strip kit (Miller Brody) and a cassette/record narrated by Meryl Streep (Windham
Hill, 1985) provide other media support.

CHARLIE AND THE CHOCOLATE FACTORY

by Roald Dahl   illustrated by Joseph Schindelman
New York: Knopf, 1964, 1988   160 pages

Grades: 2-5   **ESL Level:** intermediate, advanced
Genre: fiction—long novel, modern fantasy

Vocabulary: food—candy; places in the community—small town; extended family
Grammar: adjectives, exclamatory sentences
Patterns: rhyming, dialogue

Once in a wonderful while, a book captures your imagination and fully absorbs your spirit. You are reluctant to turn the last page, because, then, alas, its special world will end. This book created this treasured experience for me and for every audience with whom I have had the pleasure to share it. I cannot recommend it highly enough.

It tells the rags to riches tale of little Charlie Bucket, who wins one of the five golden tickets in the whole world and thus earns the chance to vist Mr. Willy Wonka's secret Chocolate Factory. You cheer for Charlie throughout his adventures. Good guys don't always finish last! The 30 short chapters, from five to ten pages each, provide convenient breaking points, although it is hard to stop reading! The occasional black and white line drawings offer pleasant visual stimuli, but most of the imagination takes places in the listener's own head.

An excellent, full length musical also exists (available in video as well), but the book is even better. Enjoy!

Related Books by the Same Author: *Charlie and the Great Glass Elevator* (1972). This sequel is good, but not as exciting as the original.

Books By the Same Author: *James and the Giant Peach* (1961) and *Fantastic Mr. Fox* (1970)

THE WIZARD OF OZ

by L. Frank Baum   illustrated by Michael Hague
New York: Holt, Rinehart and Winston, 1982   219 pages

Grades: 2-5   **ESL Level:** advanced
Genre: fiction—long novel, modern fantasy

Vocabulary: places in the community—rural; natural environments, magical, animals
Grammar: interrogative and exclamatory sentences, adverbial clauses
Patterns: dialogue

This is America's popular fairy tale, about Dorothy, her dog Toto and their adventures in the Land of Oz. Children easily relate to this fantasy world, where munchkins, witches and wizards still thrive. No childhood should be without this magic!

Written at the beginning of the 20th century, this tale has been cherished throughout it. The 1939 movie with actress Judy Garland, filled with catchy songs and dances, has insured the book's longevity. In fact, this is one instance when one could argue that the movie is better than the book. It is certainly easier.

Reading the book aloud does require time commitment. This new edition with glossy, large pages, big, bold print, short chapters and lavish illustrations encourages us to do so. It can be creatively developed into a thematic unit, integrated with language, reading, art and drama.

Related Books by Same Author: Baum wrote many other sequels to this orginal, but none are as good, nor worth the class time. You may want to recommend them to advanced students for independent reading.

WHERE THE SIDEWALK ENDS

by Shel Silverstein
New York: Harper & Row, 1974   170 pages

Grades: 2-5, 4-8   **ESL Level:** intermediate, advanced
Genre: poetry

Patterns: rhyming, repeated refrains, metaphoric language

Shel Silverstein's first major collection of 127 of his own poems is both outrageously funny and deeply profound. Through the humor he gently tugs at our dreams and values, stimulating reflection. Written from a child's perspective, he captures the modern American experience affirming life and love.

The poems, which vary in length from four lines to two pages, are no child's play, however. Silverstein masterfully uses a variety of poetic devices, but none are overused or heavy handed. He reminds me of Dr. Seuss. His poems, like Seuss's books, are easy and fun to read. His black and white line drawings also evoke humor with their cartoon style characters. This is a delightful volume of modern poetry for children and for the child in all of us. Like all poems, they are best enjoyed read-aloud.

Related Book by Same Author: *A Light in the Attic* (1981), his second volume of poetry.

Book by Same Author: *The Giving Tree* (1964) in the RAL.

THE LITTLE PRINCE

by Antoine de Saint-Exupery
New York: Harcourt, Brace Jovanovich, 1943, 1982   93 pages

Grades: 4-8   **ESL Level:** intermediate
Genre: fiction—short novel, modern fantasy
Ethnic Identity: European—French

Vocabulary: natural environments—desert, planets; transportation—airplane, numbers— ordinals
Grammar: imperative, interrogative and exclamatory sentences, first person pronoun—subject and possessive
Patterns: informal language, dialogue

An airplane pilot is trying to repair his plane in the Sahara Desert, when he is approached by a little man from another planet. He listens to his story and helps him return home. Although accurate, this simple plot summary fails to capture the magic of this story. That lies within the characters and their symbolism.

Written orginally in French, this book has been traditionally read in high school intermediate French classes. That is because the language is at the proficiency level and the themes are best appreciated by adolescents. The two characters—the pilot and the little prince—represent adult and youth, their different values and priorities. When read-aloud to older students, the book is very thought-provoking. It easily stimulates class discussions and writing assignments that encourage students to examine their own identity.

Anthologies

TOMIE DEPAOLA'S MOTHER GOOSE

by Tomie dePaola
New York: Putnam Publishing Group, 1985   127 pages

Grades: K-3, 2-5   **ESL Level:** beginner, intermediate
Genre: nursery rhymes, anthology

Vocabulary: animals

There are many excellent annotations of Mother Goose from which to choose. I recommend this one for many reasons. First, it is a large size, which allows for easy classroom viewing. Second, it is a comprehensive collection. Third, despite its size, it feels uncluttered. That is because dePaola generously spreads out the text on each page. Fourth, each and every rhyme is individually illustrated with large, bright pictures. When there are two or more rhymes on a page, they are separated by borders, so that it is clear which illustration goes with which rhyme. In addition, dePaola's neo-primitive style provides a unifying character to the artwork.

This is an attractively designed anthology which appeals to both adults and children. This may explain its popularity and why it has sold so consistently since its publication. It makes a wonderful gift for a special occasion.

Related Book: *Richard Scarry's Best Mother Goose Ever* (1970), very popular with kids, is unfortunately out of print, but worth looking for in your local library.

Related Book By Same Author: *Tomie dePaola's Nursery Tales* (1986), a companion volume.

Books by the Same Author: See *Mary Had a Little Lamb* (1984) in the RAL.

IF YOU'RE HAPPY AND YOU KNOW IT

by Nicki Weiss
New York: Greenwillow Books, 1987   40 pages

Grades: K-3, 2-5   **ESL Level:** beginner, intermediate
Genre: singable book, anthology
Ethnic Identity: multiethnic

Patterns: rhyming, repeated sentences, work patterns and refrains

You and your students will be happy and you will know it as you sing along with one of these eighteen, illustrated "story songs." In addition to the title song, this collection includes such childhood favorites as "This Old Man," "Roll Over," "Kookaburra" and "There's a Hole in the Bucket."

It is useful as a read-aloud because each song receives its own two page spread, which is further broken down into individual pictures. These smaller drawings clearly explain the song, line-by line. Through a clever use of numbering and arrows, students are also able to follow along on their own. Although most of the tunes are widely known, the full musical notation and chord symbols are included. In addition, a page of notes about the origins of the songs are included at the end. Enjoy!

Related Book: *Roll Over. A Counting Song* (Peek, 1981) in the RAL.

THE FAIRY TALE TREASURY

by Virginia Haviland   illustrated by Raymond Briggs
New York: Putnam Publishing Group
(Coward, McCann & Geoghegan), 1972, 1980; Dell, 1986   192 pages

Grades: K-3, 2-5   **ESL Level:** intermediate
Genre: fairy tales, anthology

Vocabulary: animals, household, family, royalty

There are numerous excellent collections of fairy tales. I recommend this one for many reasons. First, it includes the most popular stories. Second, its large number of selections (33) gives it breadth and diversity. Third, each tale is clearly and briefly told, averaging about six pages of text each. The author, a fairy tale expert, has also maintained as much of the original language as possible. Fourth, this edition is large (9 x 11), so its illustrations can be clearly seen by big groups. Fifth, the illustrations themselves are dramatic and detailed, as well as large. They cleverly fill the wide margins, as well as entire pages. Often, a series of small pictures helps to reinforce a sequence of events. This is helpful for young listeners.

In sum, this is a handsome edition, intended for reading aloud and still successful, after 15 years.

Related Books: Many of the fairy tales here are included in the RAL as separate picture books. They are *Little Red Riding Hood* (Hyman, 1983), *The Elves and the Shoemaker* (Galdone, 1984), *The Little Red Hen* (Galdone, 1973) *The Gingerbread Boy* (Galdone, 1975), *The Ugly Duckling* (Andersen, 1979), *Henny Penny* (Galdone, 1968), and *The Three Billy Goats Gruff* (Galdone, 1973).

SIDE BY SIDE, POEMS TO READ TOGETHER

collected by Lee Bennett Hopkins   illustrated by Hilary Knight
New York: Simon & Schuster, 1988   80 pages

Grades: K-3   **ESL Level:** beginner-advanced
Genre: poetry, anthology
Ethnic Identity: multiethnic

This appealing collection of 57 poems is a delightful potpourri of classic, contemporary and newly written gems. According to the award-winner poet in his introduction, "These poems are meant to be read-aloud, spoken, shouted, sung and enjoyed!" The poetry selection, the happy illustrations and uncluttered design enhance these objectives. The selections cover a number of school-related topics—seasons, holidays, the animal world, alphabet and counting rhymes. The book concludes with three indexes—author, title and first line.

This is not a comprehensive collection of children's poetry, nor one whose illustrations allow it to reach beyond the third grade. Nevertheless, its large size, limited number of poems and soft illustrations make it just right for younger listeners!

Related Books: Three of the classics from this collection are annotated elsewhere in the RAL as single volumes—*This is the House that Jack Built* (Underhill, 1987), *Over the River and Through the Woods* (Child, 1974) and *Twas the Night Before Christmas* (Moore/Marshall, 1985).

THE RANDOM HOUSE BOOK OF POETRY

by Jack Prelutsky
New York: Random House, 1983

illustrated by Arnold Lobel
248 pages

Grades: K-8   **ESL Level:** intermediate, advanced
Genre: poetry, anthology
Ethnic Identity: multiethnic

This is a stunning, comprehensive anthology of 572 children's poems that spans both the past and present. Arranged in 14 thematic sections, this volume includes poems for every occasion throughout the year, every stage of growing up, and every childhood mood, passion or complaint. The subject area index, in addition to the title, author and first line indexes, makes the anthology very useful for locating appropriate poems to complement teaching topics.

The volume is enhanced by the catchy and humorous illustrations of Caldecott Award winner, Arnold Lobel, which illustrate not only each page but also most poems. In addition, the attractive design of each page creates an overall inviting effect. This is a wonderful volume to own and is also reasonably priced for its size.

Books by the Same Author: *It's Halloween* (1977) in the RAL and *The New Kid on the Block* (1984).

THE DAY IT SNOWED TORTILLAS

retold by Joe Hayes
Santa Fe, NM: Mariposa Publishing, 1982

illustrated by Lucy Jelinek-Thompson
67 pages

Grades: 4-8   **ESL Level:** intermediate
Genre: folk tales, anthology, short stories
Ethnic Identity: Hispanic—Mexican American

This is a small collection of nine Mexican American folktales. These "cuentas" have been compiled by a professional storyteller and come alive, even on the page. They easily transform to role playing, dramatization and short performance pieces. They borrow both from numerous European tales and also have their own distinct flavor, peppered with Spanish language and the Mexican American culture of the Southwest. Each is short, between four and eight pages and can easily be completed within 15 minutes. Each is also warmly illustrated with one or two brown-lined drawings. These tales cover many basic vocabulary topics and themes. Ultimately, though, they teach us about life itself.

Book By the Same Author: *Coyote E* (1985), a collection of Native American folktales.

FAVORITE FOLKTALES FROM AROUND THE WORLD

edited by Jane Yolen
New York: Random House, 1986

498 pages

Grades: 4-8   **ESL Level:** intermediate, advanced
Genre: folk tales, anthology
Ethnic Identity: multiethnic

Patterns: dialogue

International storyteller and author Jane Yolen has made a major contribution with this compendium of over 160 folktales from over 40 different cultures.

This volume offers many attributes as a read-aloud. First, because the selections come from the oral tradition of story telling, they transform easily into dramatic read-alouds, even without the

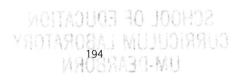

pictures. Second, each story is short, about one to three pages of small print. All can be read within a five to fifteen minute time period. Third, the text reads easily, with lots of straightforward action and dialect. Most of the syntax is appropriate for the intermediate level SL learners. Fourth, Yolen conveniently organizes the folktales into thirteen thematic topics (e.g. True Loves and False, Heroes: Likely and Unlikely). Fifth, Yolen's introduction is stimulating. It entices the adult into the fascinating world of storytelling, imagination and folktales. And sixth, at the end, Yolen also provides a brief description of each of the 160 tales. This is very helpful when perusing the collection for just the right story.

This is a real treasure chest. Be warned, however, that there is not a single illustration included. It thus works best with older, more advanced students.

Related Book By Same Author: *The Emperor and the Kite* (1988)

MORE CLASSICS TO READ ALOUD TO YOUR CHILDREN

by William Russell
New York: Crown, 1986   264 pages

Grades: K-3, 4-8   **ESL Level:** intermediate, advanced
Genre: short stories, anthology

Patterns: repeated format

William Russell has done a great service for reading parents and teachers in compiling this rich read-aloud resource. He has carefully gathered short sections from a wide range of classic literature and presented them in three different listening levels: ages 5 and up, 8 and up and 11 and up. Altogether there are 42 pieces. They include folktales, stories, plays, novels, poems and speeches from authors such as Hans Christian Anderson, Lewis Carroll, Robert Louis Stevenson, Edgar Allen Poe, Shakespeare, O. Henry and Martin Luther King.

Although there are no illustrations, each piece *is* preceded with notes about the story, approximate reading time and a vocabulary and pronunciation guide. Russell has also written an excellent introduction about the concept of reading aloud and the teachable moment. Armed with all this information, all we have to do is read and enjoy with our students and/or children.

Related Books By Same Author: *Classic Myths to Read Aloud* (1989) and *Classics to Read Aloud to Your Children* (1984). Both of these follow the same format as *More Classics*, annotated above.

REFERENCES

Children's Literature and Second Language Learners _____

Appleberry, M.H. & Rodriguez, E.A. (1988). Literary books make the difference in teaching the ESL student. *Reading Horizons, 28(2)*, 112-116.

Appolt, J.E. (1985). Not just for little kids: the picture book in ESL classes. *TESL Canada Journal, 2(2)*, 87-88.

Bird, L. B., Alvarez, L. P. (1987). Beyond comprehension: the power of literature study for language minority students. *Elementary ESOL Education News, 10(1)*, 1-3.

Elley, W.B. & Mangubhai, F. (1983). The impact of reading on second language learning. *Reading Research Quarterly 19*, 53-67.

Fritz, G. (1987). What works: using materials for different skill levels. *WATESOL (Washington Area Teachers of English to Speakers of Other Languages) News, 18(2)*, 9.

Hough, R.A & Nurss, J.R. & Enright, D.S. (1986). Story reading with limited English speaking children in the regular classroom. *The Reading Teacher, 38(6)*, 510-514.

McConochie, J. (1979). Cottleston, cottleston, cottleston pie: poetry and verse for young learners. *English Teaching Forum, 17(4)*, 6-12.

Moustafa, M. (1980). Picture books for oral language development for non-English speaking children: a bibliography. *The Reading Teacher, 33(8)*, 914-919.

Radenich, M.C. (1985). Books that promote positive attitudes toward second language learning. *The Reading Teacher, 37(2)*, 528-30.

Smallwood, B.A. (1988). Children's literature for limited English proficient speakers, ages 9-14. *WATESOL Working Papers 4*, 67-87.

_____ (1987). Literature criteria for ESL students. *WATESOL News 17(5)*, 1, 10.

Strickland, D.S. (Ed.) (1981). *The role of literature in reading instruction: cross-cultural views*. Newark, DE: International Reading Association.

Zarillo, J. (1987). *Literature-centered reading and language minority students*. Paper prepared for The Institute on Literacy and Learning Language Minority Project, University of California at Santa Barbara. ERIC Document Reproduction Service No. ED 299 541.

Children's Literature/Reading/Writing and First Language Learners _____

Anderson, R.C. & Hiebert, E. H. & Scott, J.A. & Wilkinson, I.A.(1985). *Becoming a nation of readers: The report of the Commission on Reading*. Washington, DC: The National Institute of Education.

Association of Library Services to Children (ALSC). (1989) *ALSC's notable films/videos, filmstrips and recordings*. Chicago, IL: ALSC.

Calkins, L.M. (1986). *The art of teaching writing*. Portsmouth, NH: Heinemann.

Cascardi, A.E. (1988). *The parent's guide to video and audio cassette for children*. New York: Warner Books.

_____ (1985). *Good books to grow on*. New York: Warner Books, Inc.

Chomsky, C. (1972). Stages in language development and reading exposure. *Harvard Educational Review 42*, 1-33.

Cohen, D. H. (1968). The effect of literature on vocabulary and reading achievement. *Elementary English 45*, 200-213, 217.

Cullinan, B. & Carmichael, C. (Eds.). (1977). *Literature and young children*. Urbana, IL: National Council of Teachers of English.

Davis, J. E. & Davis, H. K. (Eds.). (1988). *Your reading: a booklist for junior high and middle school students*. Urbana, IL: National Council of Teachers of English.

Elley, W. (1989). Vocabulary acquisition from listening to stories. *Reading Research Quarterly 14(2)*, 174-188.

Feitelson, D., Kita, B. & Goldstein, Z. (1986). Effects of listening to series stories on first graders comprehension and use of language. *Research in the Teaching of English 20*, 339-356.

Glazer, J. (1986). *Literature for young children*. Columbus, OH: Bell & Howell.

Hancy, D. (1989). *Reading aloud to others: factors contributing to its value and effectiveness in the classroom*. Masters Thesis. Indiana University at South Bend. ERIC Document Reproduction Service No. ED 2198 438.

Herzing, M. (1989). Children's literature in secondary school. *Journal of Reading*, (April), 650-651.

Kagan, S. (1985). *Cooperative learning resources for teachers*. Riverside, CA: University of California, Riverside, Printing and Reprographics.

Kimmel, M.M. & Segal, E. (1983). *For reading out loud. A guide to sharing books with children*. New York: Delacorte Press.

Lamme, L.L. (1985). *Highlights for children: growing up reading*. Washington, D.C.: Acropolis Books, Ltd.

Lindskoog, J. & Lindskoog, K. (1989). *How to grow a young reader. A parent's guide to books for kids*. Wheaton, IL: Harold Shaw Publishers.

McCormick, S. (1977). Should you read aloud *to* your children? *Language Arts*, 54, 139-143, 163.

Monson, D. (Ed.). (1985). *Adventuring with books*. Urbana, IL: National Council of the Teachers of English.

Moss, J.F. (1984). *Focus units in literature: a handbook for elementary school teachers*. Urbana, IL: National Council of Teachers of English.

Radenich, M.C. and Bohning, G. (1989). Informational action books: a curriculum resource for science and social studies. *The Journal of Reading* Feb., 434-439.

Raimes, S.C. & Canady, R.J. (1989). *Story s-t-r-e-t-c-h-e-r-s. Activities to expand children's favorite books*. Mt. Ranier, MD: Gryphon House.

Rudman, M.K. & Pearce, A.M. (1988). *For love of reading*. Mount Vernon, NY: Consumers Union.

Topping, K. (Ed.) (1986, 1985, 1984). *National paired reading conference proceedings* (1st, 2nd and 3rd, Drewsbury, West Yorkshire, England). ERIC Document Reproduction Service #ED285 126, ED 285 125 and ED 285 124.

Trelease J. (1989, 1985). *The read-aloud handbook*. New York: Penguin Books.

Zarillo, J. (1988). *Literature-centered reading programs in elementary classrooms*. Unpublished doctoral dissertation, Claremont University, CA.

Reading and Second Language Learners (K–8)

Feeley, J. T. (1983). Help for the reading teacher working with LEP children in the elementary classroom. *The Reading Teacher, 36(7)*, 650-55.

Gibson, R. (1975). The strip story: a catalyst for communication. *TESOL Quarterly* (June), 149-53.

Goodman, K. and Goodman, Y. and Flores, B. (1979). *Reading in the bilingual classroom: literacy and biliteracy*. Silver Spring, MD: Clearinghouse for Bilingual Education.

Moustafa, M. and Penrose, J. (1985). Comprehensible input PLUS the language experience approach: reading instruction for limited English speaking students. *The Reading Teacher 38(3)*, 640-47.

Sutton, C. (1989). Helping the nonnative English speaker with reading. *The Reading Teacher, 42(9)*, 684-88.

Urzua, C. (1985). How do you evaluate your own elementary program? Look to kids. In P. Larson, E.L. Judd and D.S. Messerchmitt (Eds.), *On TESOL '84: A brave, new world for TESOL* (pp. 219-32). Washington, DC: Teachers of English to Speakers of Other Languages.

General Sources on Second Language Learners

Celce-Murcia, M. & Larsen-Freeman, D. (1983). *The grammar book. An ESL/EFL teacher's course*. Rowley, MA: Newbury House.

Clark, R.C., Moran, P.R. & Burrows, A.A. (1981). *The ESL miscellany*. Brattleboro, VT: Pro Lingua Associates, 1981.

Cohen, A.D. (1980). *Testing language ability in the classroom*. Rowley, MA: Newbury House.

Collier, V.P. (1987). Age and rate of acquisition of second language for academic purposes. *TESOL Quarterly*, 21 (4), 617–642.

Cummins, J. (1981). The role of primary language development in promoting educational success for language minority students. In *Schooling and Language Minority Students: A Theoretical Framework* (pp. 3-49). Los Angeles: California State University, National Evaluation, Dissemination and Assessment Center.

Enright, D. S. and Riggs, P. (1986). *Children and ESL: Integrating perspectives*. Washington, D.C.: Teachers of English to Speakers of Other Languages (TESOL).

Enright, D. S. and McCloskey, M. L. (1988). *Integrating English. Developing English language and literacy in the multilingual classroom*. Reading, MA: Addison-Wesley.

_____ (1988). Yes, talking! Organizing the classroom to promote second language acquisition. *TESOL Quarterly, 19(3)*, 431-453.

Heald-Taylor, G. (1987). *Whole language strategies for ESL students.* New York: Dormac.

Jacob, E. & Mattson, B. (1987). *Cooperative learning with limited-English-proficient students.* Q & A Series. Washington, DC: ERIC Clearinghouse on Languages and Linguistics.

Krashen, S.D. (1985). *The input hypothesis: issues and implications.* New York: Longman.

_____ (1984). *Writing research, theory and applications.* New York: Pergamon

_____ (1978). On the acquisition of planned discourse: written English as a second dialect. In M. Douglas (Ed.) *Claremont Reading Conference: 42nd Yearbook.* Claremont, CA Claremont Graduate School, pp. 173-185.

Oller, J. (1979). *Language tests at schools.* New York: Longman.

O'Malley et al. (1988). Learning strategies used by beginning and intermediate ESL students. *Language Learning 35(1)*, 21-45.

Oxford, R. & Pol, L. & Lopez, D & Stupp, P. & Gendell, M. & Peng, S. (1981). Projections of non-English language background (NELB) and limited English proficient (LEP) persons in the United States to the year 2000: Educational planning in the demographic context. *National Association of Bilingual Education (NABE) Journal 5(3)*, 1-29.

Tiedt, P.L. & Tiedt, I.M. (1986). *Multicultural teaching. A handbook of activities, information and resources.* Boston, MA: Allyn & Bacon.

Literature and Secondary/Adult Second Language Learners _____

Applebee, A. (1978). Teaching high-achievement students: a survey of the winner of the 1977 NCTE achievement awards in writing. *Research in the Teaching of English 1*, 41-53.

Brown, D.S. (1988). *A world of books: An annotated reading list for ESL/EFL students.* Washington, DC: Teachers of English to Speakers of Other Languages

Gajdusek, L. (1988). Towards wider use of literature in ESL: why and how. *TESOL Quarterly, 23(2)*, 227-257.

Johnson, P. (1982). Effects on reading comprehension of building background knowledge. *TESOL Quarterly, 16(4)*, 503-516

_____ (1981). Effects on reading comprehension of language complexity and cultural background of a text. *TESOL Quarterly, 15(2)*, 169-181.

Marckwardt, A.H. (1978). *The place of literature in the teaching of English as a second or foreign language.* Honolulu, HI: University of Hawaii.

McKay, S. (1982). Literature in the ESL classroom. *TESOL Quarterly, 16*, 529-536.

Pugh, S. (1989). Literature, culture and ESL: a natural convergence. *Journal of Reading* (Jan.), 320-329.

Oster, J. (1989). Seeing with different eyes: another view of literature in the ESL class. *TESOL Quarterly, 23(1)*, 85-103.

Spack, R. (1985). Literature, reading, writing and ESL: bridging the gaps. *TESOL Quarterly 19(4)*, 703-725.

Journals and Professional Associations _____

Language Arts. A peer-reviewed journal for those interested in language arts in the elementary school, K-8. Of special interest is the regular column "Bookwatching: Notes on Children's Books" in each issue. Published eight times a year by the National Council of Teachers of English, 1111 Kenyon Road, Urbana, IL 61801. Subscription/membership $35 per year.

The Reading Teacher. A peer-reviewed journal for those interested in the teaching of reading at the preschool and elementary level. Published nine times a year by the International Reading Association, 800 Barksdale Road, P.O. Box 8139, Newark, DE 19714-8139. Subscription/membership $30 per year.

School Library Journal. "The magazine of children's, young adult and school libraries." Published monthly by SLJ, P.O. Box 1978, Marion, OH 43305-1978. Subscription $59 per year.

TESOL Quarterly. A peer-reviewed journal for those interested in the teaching of English as a second or foreign language and of standard English as a second dialect. Published four times a year by TESOL (Teachers of English to Speakers of Other Languages), 1600 Cameron St., Suite 300, Alexandria, VA 22314. Subscription/membership $42 per year. Membership also includes 6 issues of *TESOL Newsletter.*

MULTICULTURAL INDEX

Outline of Index

AMERICAN ETHNIC GROUPS
Asian American
Black American
Jewish American
Hispanic American
Native American

MAJOR UNITED STATES IMMIGRANT CULTURES
Asian
Hispanic

OTHER INTERNATIONAL CULTURES
African
European
Russian
Other Countries

CROSS CULTURAL

MULTICULTURAL

Notes:
1. This **Multicultural Index** includes those books which represent a major United States ethnic group, an international or immigrant culture, a cross–cultural relationship or a multiethnic representation. In compiling the Read-Aloud Library every attempt was made to seek out this children's literature, which would meet both the broad and more specific goals of multicultural education. However, the books had to also meet the criteria for read-alouds, as outlined in Chapter 3 of the Read-Aloud Guidelines. Finding quality selections which were both multicultural, good read-alouds **and still in print** was a real challenge. (Many ethnic books go out of print within 4–5 years, after one printing.) In addition, some ethnic groups historically have contributed more to published children's literature.

In summary, this **Multicultural Index** reflects an attempt to be as inclusive and broad as possible within the established guidelines. I am pleased that it includes over 50% of all the books in the Read-Aloud Library. My hope is that in time its size will grow.

2. For fairness, all groups are listed alphabetically.

AMERICAN ETHNIC GROUPS _____

ASIAN AMERICAN
My Best Friend, Duc Tran, 83
My Friend Leslie. The Story of a Handicapped Child, 92
Gung Hay Fat Choy, 114
How My Parents Learned to Eat, 127
In the Year of the Boar and Jackie Robinson, 154
A Jar of Dreams, 155
A Long Way from Home, 156

BLACK AMERICAN
The Patchwork Quilt, 66
The Stories Julian Tells, 79
Jamaica's Find, 81
A Letter to Amy, 82
Sam, 86
The Toothpaste Millionaire, 101
Martin Luther King, 113
The Grey Lady and the Strawberry Snatcher, 124
Corduroy, 132
John Henry, An American Legend, 140
The Story of Jackie Robinson, Bravest Man in Baseball, 143
Wagon Wheels, 147
How Many Days to America? A Thanksgiving Story, 153
The Knee-High Man and Other Tales, 172
The Snowy Day, 174
The Boy Who Didn't Believe in Spring, 174

HISPANIC AMERICAN
I Speak English for My Mom, 94
Yagua Days, 138
Sports Star, Fernando Valenzuela, 142
The Pride of Puerto Rico, The Life of Roberto Clemente, 143
Lupita Mañana, 156
Gilberto and the Wind, 175
The Day It Snowed Tortillas, 193

JEWISH AMERICAN
I Love Passover, 115
Molly's Pilgrim, 152
The Night Journey, 157

NATIVE AMERICAN
Knots on a Counting Rope, 74
The Courage of Sarah Noble, 84
Indian in the Cupboard, 85
Stone Fox, 90
Thanksgiving Day, 119
Wagon Wheels, 147
Where Do You Think You're Going, Christopher Columbus?, 152
Gift of the Sacred Dog, 167
The Girl Who Loved Wild Horses, 168

MAJOR IMMIGRANT CULTURES __

ASIAN

Chinese
Tikki Tikki Tembo, 68
Yeh-Shen, 69
The Spring of Butterflies and Other Folktales of China's Minority Peoples, 70
Gung Hay Fat Choy, 114
A Family in China, 150
In the Year of the Boar and Jackie Robinson, 154

Indochinese
The Brocaded Slipper and Other Vietnamese Folktales, 71
My Best Friend, Duc Tran, 83
Angel Child, Dragon Child, 93
The Land I Lost, Adventures of a Boy in Vietnam, 151
A Boat to Nowhere, 155
A Long Way from Home, 156
Toad is the Uncle of Heaven, 175

Japanese
Crow Boy, 93
Journey to the Bright Kingdom, 116
The Paper Crane, 127
How My Parents Learned to Eat, 127
A Jar of Dreams, 155
The Perfect Crane, 187

Other
The Master Chess Player (Mongolian), 94
A Crocodile Tale (Philippine), 167
India (My Country Series) (Indian), 151

HISPANIC

Mexican
I Speak English for My Mom, 94
Sports Star, Fernando Valenzuela, 142
Lupita Mañana, 156
The Day It Snowed Tortillas, 193

Puerto Rican
Yagua Days, 137
The Pride of Puerto Rico, The Life of Roberto Clemente, 143

OTHER INTERNATIONAL CULTURES

AFRICAN
Mufaro's Beautiful Daughters, 69
Take a Trip to Nigeria, 150
The Elephant's Child, 168
Abiyoyo, 187

EUROPEAN

British
Indian in the Cupboard, 85
St. George and the Dragon, 141
Robin Hood. His Life and Legend, 142

French
Little Red Riding Hood, 67
Stone Soup, 125
The Red Balloon, 132
Beauty and the Beast, 188
The Little Prince, 190

German
Hansel and Gretel, 126
Millions of Cats, 163
A Day on the River, 176

Spanish
Esteban and the Ghost, 119
Where Do You Think You're Going, Christopher Columbus? (also Italian), 152
The Story of Ferdinand, 172
The Seaside, 176

Other
Rapunzel, 70
A Hole in the Dike (Dutch), 87
Greek Gods and Heroes (Greek), 141
When I First Came to this Land, 146
The Witch of Fourth Street and Other Stories, 154
The Long Way to a New Land (Swedish), 156

RUSSIAN
It Could Always Be Worse, 88
Caps for Sale, 111
The Night Journey, 157

OTHER COUNTRIES
Where the Forest Meets the Sea (Australian), 148
How Many Days to America? A Thanksgiving Story (Caribbean), 156
Owls in the Family (Canadian), 157

CROSS-CULTURAL

(These books involve cross-cultural experiences. Many include interracial friendships. Others confront prejudice as experienced by young people.)

The Tooth Fairy, 73
Jamaica's Find, 81
My Best Friends, Duc Tran, 83
The Courage of Sarah Noble, 84
Free to be..You and Me, 89
Stone Fox, 90
My Friend Leslie. The Story of a Handicapped Child, 92
Angel Child, Dragon Child, 93
The Toothpaste Millionaire, 101
Corduroy, 132
Strange but True Basketball Stories, 138
The Story of Jackie Robinson, Bravest Man in Baseball, 143
The Pride of Puerto Rico, The Life of Roberto Clemente, 143
Molly's Pilgrim, 152
The Witch of Fourth Street and Other Stories, 154
In the Year of the Boar and Jackie Robinson, 154
A Jar of Dreams, 155
A Long Way from Home, 156
The Boy Who Didn't Believe in Spring, 174

MULTIETHNIC

(The illustrations in these picture books include diverse ethnic groups, making them visually multiethnic. In this way, all children can identify with the story.)

Happy Birthday to Me, 81
Nobody's Perfect, Not Even My Mother, 86
Count and See, 100
Brown Bear, Brown Bear, What Do You See?, 104
Bee My Valentine!, 114
Poems for Father, 118
The Supermarket, 121
Let's Eat, 123
The Paper Crane, 127
The Milk Makers, 128
Nutrition, 128
Playgrounds, 130
Fill it Up! All About Service Stations, 131
A Chair for My Mother, 134
Department Store, 134
School Bus, 135

We're Taking an Airplane Trip, 136
I Can be a Doctor, 144
Weather Forecasting, 145
Maps and Globes, 149
Zoo, 170
Oh, A Hunting We Will Go, 171

The Emergency Room, 181
The Magic School Bus Inside the Earth, 185
If You're Happy and You Know It, 191
Side by Side. Poems to Read Together, 192
The Random House Book of Poetry, 193
Favorite Folktales from Around the World, 193

LITERARY GENRE INDEX

Outline of Index

PICTURE BOOKS
    Wordless picture books
    Nursery rhymes
    Fairy tales
    Folk tales
    Singable books
    Fables
    Myths and legends
    Concept books
    General

EASY READERS
    Beginner level
    Intermediate level

POETRY
    Individual/narrative poems
    Collections

FICTION
    Short stories
      individual (under 50 pages), collections
    Short novels (50–100 pages)
    Long novels (over 100 pages)
    Historical fiction
    Modern fantasy
    Contemporary realistic fiction
    Mysteries/Suspense
    Science Fiction

NON-FICTION
    Picture book non-fiction
    General non-fiction
    Biography/autobiography

ANTHOLOGIES
Note: Some books fit equally well under two categories and thus appear twice in this index.

PICTURE BOOKS _____

WORDLESS PICTURE BOOKS
A, B, See, 99
Deep in the Forest, 106
Is it Rough? Is it Smooth? Is it Shiny?, 107
Peter Spier's Christmas, 120
Pancakes for Breakfast, 124
The Grey Lady and the Strawberry Snatcher, 124
I Read Symbols, 136

NURSERY RHYMES
This is the House that Jack Built, 77
Mary Had a Little Lamb, 91
Counting Rhymes, 99
The Farmer in the Dell, 158
Tomie dePaola's MOTHER GOOSE, 191

FAIRY TALES
(mostly of European origin)
Little Red Riding Hood, 67
Rapunzel, 70
The Elves and the Shoemaker, 112
The Little Red Hen, 123
The Gingerbread Boy, 123
Hansel and Gretel, 126
Henny Penny, 160
The Ugly Duckling, 158
The Three Billy Goats Gruff, 186
Beauty and the Beast, 188
The Fairy Tale Treasury, 192

FOLK TALES
(multicultural and international)
Tikki Tikki Tembo (Chinese), 68
Yeh-Shen (Chinese), 69
Mufaro's Beautiful Daughters (African), 69
The Spring of Butterflies and Other Folktales of China's Minority Peoples (Minority Chinese), 70
The Brocaded Slipper and Other Vietnamese Folktales (Vietnamese), 71
The Master Chess Player (Mongolian), 94
Journey to the Bright Kingdom (Japanese), 116
Esteban and the Ghost (Spanish), 119
Stone Soup (French), 125
The Paper Crane (Japanese), 127
A Crocodile Tale (Philippine), 167
The Elephant's Child (British–African), 168
The Knee-High Man and Other Tales (Black American), 172
Toad is the Uncle of Heaven (Vietnamese), 175

Abiyoyo (African), 187
The Perfect Crane (Japanese), 187
The Day It Snowed Tortillas (Mexican American), 193
Favorite Folktales from Around the World (international), 193

SINGABLE BOOKS
This is the House that Jack Built, 77
Mary Had a Little Lamb, 91
Roll Over: A Counting Book, 99
The Star-Spangled Banner, 118
Over the River and Through the Woods, 120
John Henry, An American Legend, 140
When I First Came to this Land, 146
The Erie Canal, 146
The Farmer in the Dell, 158
Old MacDonald Had a Farm, 160
The Fox Went Out on a Chilly Night, 161
Oh, A Hunting We Will Go, 171
If You're Happy and You Know It, 191

FABLES
Leo the Late Bloomer, 85
Frederick's Fables, 87
It Could Always Be Worse, 88
Aesop's Fables, 88
Fables, 89

MYTHS AND LEGENDS
Stone Fox, 90
John Henry, An American Legend, 140
Saint George and the Dragon, 141
Greek Gods and Heroes, 141
Robin Hood, His Life and Legend, 142
The Gift of the Sacred Dog, 167
The Girl Who Loved Wild Horses, 168

CONCEPT BOOKS
(These have a pedagogical intent, either grammatical, basic skill or cognitive. However, they are still set in a fictional context. They are usually intended for younger children, Pre K—3.)

The Tenth Good Thing About Barney, 72
The Tooth Fairy, 73
In a People House, 77
Where is My Friend?, 80
Happy Birthday to Me, 81
What Do You Say, Dear?, 82
Alexander and the Terrible, Horrible, No Good, Very Bad Day, 86
Nobody's Perfect, Not Even my Mother, 86
The School, 91

Alphabet Block Book, 95
A, B, See, 96
Q is for Duck, 96
On Market Street, 97
I Unpacked My Grandmother's Trunk, 97
Bears on Wheels, 98
One Bear All Alone. A Counting Book, 98
One, Two, Three. An Animal Counting Book, 100
Count and See, 100
A Year of Beasts, 102
Around the Clock with Harriet, 103
Bear Child's Book of Hours, 103
Do You Know Colors?, 104
Brown Bear, Brown Bear, What Do You See?, 104
Beside the Bay, 105
Shapes, 105
Is it Rough? Is it Smooth? Is it Shiny?, 107
Quick as a Cricket, 108
Fast-Slow High-Low, 108
Old Hat, New Hat, 110
The Supermarket, 121
Let's Eat, 122
How My Parents Learned to Eat, 127
Odd One Out, 129
Bears in the Night, 129
Playgrounds, 130
School Bus, 135
Traffic: A Book of Opposites, 135
I Read Symbols, 136
Where the Forest Meets the Sea, 148
The Seasons of Arnold's Apple Tree, 173
Summer Is, 173
The Seaside, 176
My Doctor, 181
The Emergency Room, 181

GENERAL

Whose Mouse Are You?, 65
The Patchwork Quilt, 66
The Napping House, 66
Sisters, 68
The Giving Tree, 73
Knots on a Counting Rope, 74
Amelia Bedelia, 78
Friends, 80
Jamaica's Find, 81
A Letter to Amy, 82
Sam, 86
Timothy Goes to School, 91
Miss Nelson is Missing, 92
Crow Boy, 93
Caps for Sale, 111
You'll Soon Grow into Them, Titch, 111

Bee My Valentine!, 114
The Mother's Day Mice, 116
Just Like Daddy, 117
The Little House, 131
Corduroy, 132
A Chair For My Mother, 134
Curious George Rides a Bike, 137
Yagua Days, 137
Three Days on a River in a Red Canoe, 138
Our Animal Friends at Maple Farm, 161
Where is It?, 162
A Bag Full of Pups, 163
Millions of Cats, 163
Dear Zoo, 169
A Rhinoceros Wakes Me Up in the Morning, 171
The Story of Ferdinand, 172
The Snowy Day, 174
The Boy Who Didn't Believe in Spring, 174
Gilberto and the Wind, 175
A Day on the River, 176
The Carrot Seed, 179
The Very Hungry Caterpillar, 179
The Lady and the Spider, 180
Curious George Goes to the Hospital, 182
Rain Makes Applesauce, 186

EASY READERS

(This list represents the books in the Read-Aloud Library that are written to encourage beginning readers. Many others books in the RAL also work well for this purpose. Most of these are also picture books, either fiction or non–fiction.)

BEGINNER LEVEL

Hop on Pop, 76
In a People House, 77
Bears on Wheels, 98
One fish, two fish, red fish, blue fish, 106
Old Hat, New Hat, 110
Hand, Hand, Finger, Thumb, 110
Are You My Mother?, 115
Green Eggs and Ham, 122
Bears in the Night, 129
Rosie's Walk, 159
Where's Spot?, 162

INTERMEDIATE LEVEL

The Stories Julian Tells, 79
Little Bear, 112
Martin Luther King, Jr, 113
It's Halloween, 118

Stone Soup, 125
Nutrition, 128
Play Ball, Amelia Bedelia, 137
Sports Star, Fernando Valenzuela, 142
Amelia Bedelia's Family Album, 144
Deborah Sampson Goes to War, 147
Wagon Wheels, 147
The Long Way to a New Land, 156
Dinosaur Time, 164
Danny and the Dinosaur, 164
Oh, A Hunting We Will Go, 171
Sunshine Makes the Seasons, 178
Your Heart and Blood, 182
Space Colonies, 184

POETRY

INDIVIDUAL/NARRATIVE POEMS

Beside the Bay, 105
The Night Before Christmas, 121
Casey at the Bat, 139
Stopping by Woods on a Snowy Evening, 177

COLLECTIONS OF POEMS

Best Friends, 83
Chicken Soup with Rice, 101
Hailstones and Halibut Bones, 107
Poems for Father, 117
It's Halloween, 118
Poem Stew, 126
Tyrannosaurus Was a Beast, 165
Where the Sidewalk Ends, 190
Side by Side. Poems to Read Together, 192
The Random House Book of Poetry, 193

FICTION

SHORT STORIES

Individual Stories

(under 50 pages)
My Best Friend, Duc Tran, 83
A Hole in the Dike, 87
The One in the Middle is the Green Kangaroo, 95
Journey to the Bright Kingdom, 116
The Red Balloon, 132
The Perfect Crane, 187
The Velveteen Rabbit, 188

Collections of Short Stories

The Spring of Butterflies and Other Folktales of China's Minority Peoples, 70
The Brocaded Slipper and Other Vietnamese Folktales, 71
The Stories Julian Tells, 79
Encyclopedia Brown, Boy Detective, 132
The Witch of Fourth Street and Other Stories, 156
The Knee-High Man and Other Tales, 172
The Day It Snowed Tortillas, 193
More Classics to Read Aloud to Your Children, 194

Short Novels

(50–100 pages)
A Taste of Blackberries, 75
Sarah, Plain and Tall, 76
The Courage of Sarah Noble, 84
Stone Fox, 90
The Toothpaste Millionaire, 101
Owls in the Family, 157
The Little Prince, 190

LONG NOVELS

(over 100 pages)
Tales of a Fourth Grade Nothing, 71
Summer of the Swan, 72
Charlotte's Web, 74
Ramona Forever, 75
Bridge to Terabithia, 84
Indian in the Cupboard, 85
In the Year of the Boar and Jackie Robinson, 154
A Jar of Dreams, 155
A Boat to Nowhere, 155
A Long Way From Home, 156
Lupita Mañana, 156
The Night Journey, 157
Top Secret, 185
Charlie and the Chocolate Factory, 189
The Wizard of Oz, 189

HISTORICAL FICTION

I Go With My Family to Grandma's, 67
Sarah, Plain and Tall, 76
The Courage of Sarah Noble, 84
The Ox-Cart Man, 133
When I First Came to this Land, 146
The Erie Canal, 146
Wagon Wheels, 147
Molly's Pilgrim, 152
The Long Way to a New Land, 153
In the Year of the Boar and Jackie Robinson, 154
A Jar of Dreams, 155
The Night Journey, 157

MODERN FANTASY

Charlotte's Web, 74
Bored-Nothing to Do, 78

Indian in the Cupboard, 85
One Monday Morning, 102
Fortunately, 109
Cloudy with a Chance of Meatballs, 125
The Paper Crane, 127
The Red Balloon, 132
The Perfect Crane, 187
The Velveteen Rabbit, 188
Charlie and the Chocolate Factory, 189
The Wizard of Oz, 189
The Little Prince, 190

CONTEMPORARY REALISTIC FICTION

Tales of a Fourth Grade Nothing, 71
The Summer of the Swans, 72
A Taste of Blackberries, 75
Ramona Forever, 75
Bridge to Terabithia, 84
Angel Child, Dragon Child, 93
I Speak English for My Mom, 94
The One in the Middle is the Green Kangaroo, 95
How Many Days to America? A Thanksgiving Story, 153
A Boat to Nowhere, 155
A Long Way from Home, 156
Lupita Mañana, 156

MYSTERIES/SUSPENSE

A Dark Dark Tale, 77
It's Halloween, 118
Esteban and the Ghost, 119
The Grey Lady and the Strawberry Snatcher, 124
Encyclopedia Brown, Boy Detective, 132
The Witch of Fourth Street and Other Stories, 154
Abiyoyo, 187

SCIENCE FICTION

The Magic School Bus Inside the Earth, 185
Top Secret, 185

NON-FICTION

PICTURE BOOK NON-FICTION

(This new category, popularized by Gail Gibbons, links concept books and pictureless non-fiction. Its focus is the content and it is generally geared for the elementary range of grades 2–6. Pictures either predominate over text or are equal in importance.)

My Friend Leslie. The Story of a Handicapped Child, 92
Think About Smelling, 109
Gung Hay Fat Choy, 114
I Love Passover, 115
Thanksgiving Day, 119
Think About Tasting, 124
The Milk Makers, 128
Nutrition, 128
The Fire-Station Book, 130
Fill It Up! All About Service Stations, 131
Department Store, 134
We're Taking an Airplane Ride, 136
I Can Be a Carpenter, 144
I Can Be a Doctor, 145
Weather Forecasting, 145
Maps and Globes, 149
Take a Trip to Nigeria, 150
A Family in China, 150
India (My Country Series), 151
Baby Farm Animals, 158
Dinosaur Time, 164
Strange Creatures that Really Lived, 165
Humphrey, the Lost Whale, 166
A Children's Zoo, 169
Zoo, 170
Koko's Kitten, 170
Flash, Crash, Rumble and Roll, 177
Sunshine Makes the Seasons, 178
Weather Experiments, 178
A Chick Hatches, 180
Your Heart and Blood, 182
The Planets in Our Solar System, 183
I Can Be an Astronaut, 183
Space Colonies, 184
The Magic School Bus Inside the Earth, 185

GENERAL NON-FICTION

(text predominates over pictures)

How and Why. A Kid's Book About the Body, 113
Strange but True Basketball Stories, 138
Shh! We're Writing the Constitution, 148
The Monsters Who Died. A Mystery About Dinosaurs, 166
Astronomy Today, 184

BIOGRAPHY/AUTOBIOGRAPHY

Martin Luther King, Jr., 113
Amelia Earhart, Adventure in the Sky, 140
Sports Star, Fernando Valenzuela, 142
The Story of Jackie Robinson, Bravest Man in Baseball, 143
The Pride of Puerto Rico, The Life of Roberto Clemente, 143
Deborah Sampson Goes to War, 147
And Then What Happened, Paul Revere?, 148

The Land I Lost, Adventures of a Boy in Vietnam, 151
Where Do You Think You're Going, Christopher Columbus?, 152

ANTHOLOGIES _____

Frederick's Fables, 87
Aesop's Fables, 88

Free to Be You and Me, 89
Greek Gods and Heroes, 141
Tomie dePaola's Mother Goose, 191
If You're Happy and You Know It, 191
The Fairy Tale Treasury, 192
Side by Side. Poems to Read Together, 192
The Random House Book of Poetry, 193
Favorite Folktales from Around the World, 193
More Classics to Read Aloud to Your Children, 193

BOOK TITLE INDEX

A, B, See, 96
Abiyoyo, 187
Aesop's Fables, 88
Alexander and the Terrible, Horrible, No Good,
    Very Bad Day, 86
Alphabet Block Book, 95
Amelia Bedelia, 78
Amelia Bedelia's Family Album, 144
Amelia Earhart, Adventure in the Sky, 140
And Then What Happened, Paul Revere?, 148
Angel Child, Dragon Child, 93
Are You My Mother?, 115
Around the Clock with Harriet, 103
Astronomy Today, 184

Baby Farm Animals, 159
Bag Full of Pups, A, 163
Bear Child's Book of Hours, 103
Bears on Wheels, 98
Bears in the Night, 129
Beauty and the Beast, 188
Bee My Valentine!, 114
Beside the Bay, 105
Best Friends, 83
Boat to Nowhere, A, 155
Bored–Nothing to Do!, 78
Boy Who Didn't Believe in Spring, The, 174
Bridge to Terabithia, 84
Brocaded Slipper and Other Vietnamese Tales,
    The, 71
Brown Bear, Brown Bear, What Do You See?,
    104

Caps for Sale, 111
Carrot Seed, The, 179
Casey at the Bat, 139
Chair for my Mother, A, 134

Charlie and the Chocolate Factory, 189
Charlotte's Web, 74
Chick Hatches, A, 180
Chicken Soup with Rice, 101
Children's Zoo, A, 169
Cloudy with a Chance of Meatballs, 125
Corduroy, 133
Count and See, 100
Counting Rhymes, 99
Courage of Sarah Noble, The, 84
Crocodile's Tale, A, 167
Crow Boy, 93
Curious George Goes to the Hospital, 182
Curious George Rides a Bike, 137

Danny and the Dinosaur, 164
Dark, Dark Tale, A, 77
Day on the River, A, 176
Day it Snowed Tortillas, The, 193
Dear Zoo, 169
Deborah Sampson Goes to War, 147
Deep in the Forest, 106
Department Store, 134
Dinosaur Time, 164
Do You Know Colors?, 104

Elephant's Child, The, 168
Elves and the Shoemaker, The, 112
Emergency Room, 181
Encyclopedia Brown, Boy Detective, 132
Erie Canal, The, 146
Esteban and the Ghost, 119

Fables, 89
Fairy Tale Treasury, The, 192
Family in China, A, 150
Farmer in the Dell, The, 158

Fast–Slow, High–Low, 108
Favorite Folktales From Around the World, 193
Fill it Up! All About Service Stations, 131
Fire Station Book, The, 130
Flash, Crash, Rumble and Roll, 177
Fortunately, 109
Fox Went Out on a Chilly Night, The, 161
Frederick's Fables, 87
Free to Be You and Me, 89
Friends, 80

Gift of the Sacred Dog, 167
Gilberto and the Wind, 175
Gingerbread Boy, The, 123
Girl Who Loved Wild Horses, The, 168
Giving Tree, The, 73
Greek Gods and Heroes, 141
Green Eggs and Ham, 122
Grey Lady and the Strawberry Snatcher, The, 124
Gung Hay Fat Choy, 114

Hailstones and Halibut Bones, 107
Hand, Hand, Finger, Thumb, 110
Hansel and Gretel, 126
Happy Birthday to Me, 81
Henny Penny, 160
Hole in the Dike, A, 87
Hop on Pop, 76
How and Why. A Kid's Book about the Body, 113
How Many Days to America? A Thanksgiving Story, 153
How My Parents Learned to Eat, 127
Humphrey, the Lost Whale, 166

I Can Be a Carpenter, 144
I Can Be a Doctor, 145
I Can Be an Astronaut, 183
I Go with My Family to Grandma's, 67
I Love Passover, 115
I Read Symbols, 136
I Speak English for My Mom, 94
I Unpacked my Grandmother's Trunk, 97
If You're Happy and You Know It, 191
In a People House, 77
In the Year of the Boar and Jackie Robinson, 154
India (My Country Series), 151
Indian in the Cupboard, 85
Is it Rough? Is it Smooth? Is it Shiny?, 107
It Could Always Be Worse, 88
It's Halloween, 118

Jamaica's Find, 81
Jar of Dreams, A, 155
John Henry, An American Legend, 140
Journey to the Bright Kingdom, 116
Just Like Daddy, 117

Knee–High Man, The, 172
Knots on a Counting Rope, 74
Koko's Kitten, 170

Lady and the Spider, The, 180
Land I Lost. Adventures of a Boy in Vietnam, The, 151
Leo the Late Bloomer, 85
Let's Eat, 122
Letter to Amy, A, 82
Little Bear, 112
Little House, The, 131
Little Prince, The, 190
Little Red Hen, The, 123
Little Red Riding Hood, 67
Long Way from Home, A, 156
Long Way to a New Land, The, 153
Lupita Mañana, 156

Magic School Bus Inside the Earth, The, 185
Maps and Globes, 149
Martin Luther King, Jr., 113
Mary Had a Little Lamb, 91
Master Chess Player, The, 94
Milk Makers, The, 128
Millions of Cats, 163
Miss Nelson is Missing, 92
Molly's Pilgrim, 152
Monsters Who Died. A Mystery About Dinosaurs, The, 166
More Classics to Read Aloud to Your Children, 194
Mother's Day Mice, The, 116
Mufaro's Beautiful Daughters, 69
Music, Music for Everyone, 134
My Doctor, 181
My Friend Leslie. The Story of a Handicapped Child, 92
My Best Friend Duc Tran. Meeting a Vietnamese–American Family, 83

Napping House, The, 66
Night Journey, The, 157
Night Before Christmas, The, 121
Nobody's Perfect, Not Even My Mother, 86
Nutrition, 128

Odd One Out, 129
Oh, A Hunting We Will Go, 171
Old MacDonald Had a Farm, 160
Old Hat, New Hat, 110
On Market Street, 97
One fish, two fish, red fish, blue fish, 106
One in the Middle is the Green Kangaroo, The, 95
One Bear All Alone, 98
One Two Three: An Animal Counting Book, 100
One Monday Morning, 102
Our Animal Friends at Maple Hill Farm, 161
Over the River and Through the Woods, 120
Owls in the Family, 157
Ox-Cart Man, 133

Pancakes for Breakfast, 124
Paper Crane, The, 127
Patchwork Quilt, The, 65
Perfect Crane, The, 187
Peter Spier's Christmas!, 120
Planets in our Solar System, The, 183
Play Ball, Amelia Bedelia, 137
Playgrounds, 130
Poem Stew, 126
Poems for Father, 117
Pride of Puerto Rico, The Life of Roberto Clemente, 143

Q is for Ducks, 96
Quick as a Cricket, 108

Rain Makes Applesauce, 186
Ramona Forever, 75
Random House Book of Poetry, The, 193
Rapunzel, 70
Red Balloon, The, 132
Rhinoceros Wakes Me Up in the Morning, A, 171
Robin Hood, His Life and Legends, 142
Roll Over: A Counting Song, 99
Rosie's Walk, 159

Saint George and the Dragon, 141
Sam, 86
Sarah, Plain and Tall, 76
School, The, 90
School Bus, 135
Seaside, The, 176
Seasons of Arnold's Apple Tree, The, 173
Shapes, 105
Shh! We're Writing the Constitution, 148

Side by Side. Poems to Read Together, 192
Sisters, 68
Snowy Day, The, 174
Something for Me, 134
Space Colonies, 184
Sports Star, Fernando Valenzuela, 142
Spring of Butterflies and Other Folktales of China's Minority Peoples, The, 70
Star-Spangled Banner, The, 118
Stone Fox, 90
Stone Soup, 125
Stopping By Woods on a Snowy Evening, 177
Stories Julian Tells, The, 79
Story of Ferdinard, The, 172
Story of Jackie Robinson, Bravest Man in Baseball, The, 143
Strange but True Basketball Stories, 138
Strange Creatures that Really Lived, 165
Summer Is..., 173
Summer of the Swans, The, 72
Sunshine Makes the Seasons, 178
Supermarket, The, 121

Take a Trip to Nigeria, 150
Tales of a Fourth Grade Nothing, 71
Taste of Blackberries, A, 75
Tenth Good Thing About Barney, The, 72
Thanksgiving Day, 119
Think about Smelling, 109
Think about Tasting, 124
This is the House that Jack Built, 77
Three Billy Goats Gruff, The, 186
Three Days on a River in a Red Canoe, 138
Tikki Tikki Tembo, 68
Timothy Goes to School, 91
Toad is the Uncle of Heaven, 175
Tomie dePaola's Mother Goose, 191
Tooth Fairy, The, 73
Toothpaste Millionaire, The, 101
Top Secret, 185
Traffic. A Book of Opposites, 135
Tyrannosaurus Was a Beast, 165

Ugly Duckling, The, 158

Velveteen Rabbit, or How Toys Become Real, The, 188
Very Hungry Caterpillar, The, 179

Wagon Wheels, 147
We're Taking an Airplane Trip, 136
Weather Experiments, 178
Weather Forecasting, 145

AUTHOR–ILLUSTRATOR INDEX

(I) indicates illustrator

Aiqing, Pan (I), 70
Aitken, Amy (I), 95
Allard, Harry, 92
Ambrus, Victor (I), 142
Ancona, George (I), 92
Andersen, Hans Christian, 158
Archambault, John, 74
Aruego, Ariane, 167
Aruego, Jose, 65, 85, 167
Asch, Frank, 117

Baker, Jeannie, 149
Bang, Molly, 124, 127
Banks, Lynne Reid, 85
Barr, Loel (I), 113
Barrett, Judi, 125
Barrett, Ron (I), 125
Barton, Harriett (I), 149
Baum, L. Frank, 189
Beatty, Patricia, 156
Begin, Mary Jane (I), 183
Behrens, June, 114, 183
Bendis, Keith (I), 139
Berenstain, Jan, 98, 110, 129
Berenstain, Stan, 98, 110, 129
Bileck, Marvin (I), 186
Blegvad, Erik (I), 72
Blume, Judy, 71, 95
Bolognese, Don (I), 147
Boone-Jones, Margaret, 113
Bornstein, Ruth Lercher (I), 173
Bracken, Carolyn (I), 136
Brand, Oscar, 146
Branley, Franklyn M., 177, 178, 183
Brenner, Barbara, 147

Brett, Jan (I), 116
Briggs, Raymond (I), 192
Brown, Marc, 100
Brown, Ruth, 77
Bucknall, Caroline, 98
Bundt, Nancy, 130
Bunting, Eve, 116, 158
Burchard, S.H., 142
Burn, Doris (I), 146
Burningham, John, 90
Burton, Virginia Lee, 131
Byars, Betsy, 72

Cameron, Ann, 79
Campbell, Rod, 169
Carle, Eric (I), 87, 104, 179
Casilla, Robert (I), 117
Cauley, Lorinda Bryan, 158, 168
Charlip, Remy, 109
Chek, Chia Hearn, 94
Child, Lydia Maria, 120
Cleary, Beverly, 75
Clifton, Lucille, 174
Cobb, Vicki, 166
CoConis, Ted (I), 72
Cohen, Barbara, 152
Cohen, Miriam, 114
Cohn, Ronald (I), 170
Cole, Brock (I), 85
Cole, Joanna, 180, 185
Cole, William, 126
Coleman, Winfield (I), 73
Cooney, Barbara (I), 133
Cooper, Floyd (I), 143
Crews, Donald, 135
Cruz, Ray (I), 86

Dahl, Roald, 189
Dalgliesh, Alice, 84
Davidson, Margaret, 143
de Saint-Exupery, Antoine, 190
Degen, Bruce (I), 185
dePaola, Tomie, 91, 124, 148, 191
Deraney, Michael J. (I), 152
Dewey, Jennifer (I), 165
Diamond, Donna (I), 84
Doty, Roy (I), 71

Eastman, P.D., 115
Elting, Mary, 96
Emberly, Barbara (I), 177
Emberly, Ed (I), 177
Ets, Marie Hall, 175

Fairclough, Chris (I), 124, 151
Flourney, Valerie, 66
Folsom, Michael, 96
Fradin, Dennis B., 184
Frankenberg, Robert (I), 157
Freeman, Don, 132
Freeman, Dorothy, 83
Freshman, Shelley (I), 178
Friedman, Ina R., 127
Friedman, Judith (I), 94
Fritz, Jean, 148, 152
Frost, Robert, 177
Fujikawa, Gyo, 122

Gackenbach, Dick, 163
Gag, Wanda, 163
Galdone, Paul, 112, 123, 160, 186
Gardiner, John Reynolds, 90, 185
Gibbons, Gail, 119, 128, 130, 131, 134,
    145, 170, 173
Goble, Paul, 167, 168
Goode, Diane (I), 67
Goodspeed, Peter, 171
Green, Norma, 87
Gregor, Elinor, 73
Grimm, The Brothers, 126
Gurney, Eric (I), 110

Hafner, Marylin (I), 118
Hague, Michael (I), 88, 189
Hale, Sara Josepha, 91
Hall, Donald, 133
Hall, Richard, 166
Hancock, Sibyl, 119
Hankin, Rebecca, 145
Haviland, Virginia, 192
Havill, Juanita, 81

Hayes, Joe, 193
Hays, Michael (I), 187
Heine, Helme, 80
Hill, Eric, 162
Hill, Florence (I), 147
Hirsh, Marilyn, 115
Hoban, Lillian (I), 114
Hoban, Tana, 96, 100, 107, 136, 162, 169
Hodges, Margaret, 141
Hoff, Syd, 164
Hoguet, Susan Ramsay, 97
Hopkins, Lee Bennett, 83, 192
Howard, Katherine, 104
Hutchins, Pat, 111, 159
Hyman, Trina Schart (I), 67, 70, 141, 157

Jacobsen, Peter Otto, 150
Jeffers, Susan (I), 126, 177
Jelinek-Thompson, Lucy (I), 193
Johnson, Crockett (I), 179
Joslin, Sesyle, 82

Keats, Ezra Jack, 82, 140, 174
Kent, Jack (I), 96
Kightley, Rosalinda, 105
Kipling, Rudyard, 168
Knight, Hillary (I), 192
Knowlton, Jack, 149
Kraus, Robert, 65, 85
Krauss, Ruth, 179
Kristensen, Preben Sejer, 150

Lamorisse, Albert, 132
Langstaff, John, 171
Lasky, Kathryn, 157
Laurin, Anne, 187
Lawson, Robert (I), 172
Leaf, Munro, 172
Leder, Dora (I), 86
Lee, Jeanne M., 175
LeMaster, Leslie Jean, 128, 182
Lent, Blair (I), 68
LeSieg, Theo, 77
Lester, Julius, 172
Levinson, Riki, 67
Levoy, Myron, 154
Lillegard, Dee, 144
Lionni, Leo, 87
Lisowski, Gabriel (I), 154
Liss, Howard, 138
Livingston, Myra Cohn, 117
Liyi, He, 70
Lobel, Anita (I), 97
Lobel, Arnold (I), 89, 97, 164, 165, 193

Lord, Bette Bao, 154
Louie, Ai–Ling, 69
Low, Alice, 141
Lye, Keith, 150

MacLachlan, Patricia, 76
MacMillan, Diane, 83
Madden, Don (I), 183
Maestro, Betsy, 80, 103, 135
Maestro, Giulio, 80, 103, 135
Mai, Vo–Dinh (I), 71, 93, 151
Marshall, Bob (I), 180
Marshall, James (I), 92, 121
Martel, Cruz, 138
Martin Jr., Bill, 74, 104
Mayer, Marianna, 188
Mayer, Mercer (I), 188
McGovern, Ann, 125
McKie, Roy, 77, 95
McNulty, Faith, 180
McPhail, David, 68
Mei, Kwan Shan (I), 94
Merrill, Jean, 101
Michl, Reinhart, 176
Mikolaycak, Charles (I), 116, 187
Miles, Bernard, 142
Miller, J.P., 104
Milone, Karen (I), 140
Minarik, Else Holmelund, 112
Moche, Dinah L., 136, 184
Moon, Bernice, 151
Moon, Cliff, 151
Moore, Clement, 121
Mosel, Arlene, 68
Mowat, Farley, 157

Naught, Harry (I), 184
Nhuong, Huynh Quang, 151

O'Brien, Anne Sibley (I), 81
O'Neill, Catherine, 113
O'Neill, Mary, 106

Palmer, Jan (I), 101
Panek, Dennis (I), 171
Parish, Peggy, 78, 137, 144, 164
Parker, Nancy Winslow (I), 171
Parramon, J.M., 176
Paterson, Katherine, 84
Patterson, Francine, 170
Pearson, Tracey Campbell, 160
Peck, Beth (I), 153
Peck, Merle (I), 99
Pels, Winslow (I), 125

Peppe, Rodney, 129
Perkins, Al, 110
Pinkney, Jerry (I), 66, 138
Pinto, Ralph (I), 172
Pluckrose, Henry, 109, 124
Plume, Ilse (I), 188
Pogrebin, Letty Cottin, 89
Prelutsky, Jack, 118, 165, 193
Provensen, Alice, 161
Provensen, Martin, 161

Rand, Ted (I), 74
Rey, H.A., 137, 182
Rey, Margaret, 182
Robinson, Charles (I), 75
Rockwell, Anne, 81, 103, 121
Rockwell, Harlow, 81, 121, 181
Rogasky, Barbara, 70
Rosenberg, Maxine B., 92
Ruis, Maria, 176
Russell, William, 194

Sabin, Francene, 140
Samton, Sheila White, 105
Sandlin, Joan, 153
Say, Allen (I), 127
Scheer, Julian, 186
Schindelman, Joseph (I), 189
Scott, Ann Herbert, 86
Scott, Rozel (I), 113
Seeger, Pete, 187
Selsam, Millicent, 165
Sendak, Maurice (I), 82, 101, 112
Seuss, Dr., 76, 106, 122
Sewall, Marcia (I), 90
Shimin, Symeon (I), 86
Shortall, Leonard (I), 132
Shulevitz, Uri, 102
Siebel, Fritz (I), 78
Silverstein, Shel, 73, 190
Simon, Nora, 86
Simont, Marc (I), 154, 185
Slobodkina, Esphyr, 111
Smith, Doris Buchanan, 75
Sobol, Donald, 132
Spier, Peter, 78, 108, 118, 120, 146, 161
Stanek, Muriel, 94
Steinem, Gloria, 89
Steptoe, John, 69
Stevens, Bryna, 147
Stewart, Arvis (I), 141
Strugnell, Ann (I), 79
Surat, Michele Maria, 93
Sweat, Lynn (I), 144

Teicher, Dick (I), 155
Thayer, Ernest, 139
Thomas, Marlo, 89
Tiegreen, Alan (I), 75
Tokuda, Wendy, 166
Tomes, Margot (I), 148, 152
Tripp, Wallace (I), 137
Turkle, Brinton (I), 106, 120, 174

Uchida, Yoshiko, 155
Underhill, Liz, 77

Viorst, Judith, 72, 86
Vuong, Lynette Dyer, 71

Wakiyama, Hanako (I), 166
Walker, Paul Robert, 143
Wartski, Maureen Crane, 155, 156
Watt, James (I), 83
Webster, Vera, 178
Weinhaus, Karen Ann (I), 126
Weisgard, Leonard (I), 84, 107
Weiss, Nicki, 191

Wells, Rosemary, 91
Wenzel, Greg (I), 166
Wexler, Jerome (I), 180
White, E.B., 74
Williams, Garth (I), 74
Williams, Margery, 188
Williams, Vera B., 134, 138
Windsor, Merrill, 159
Winthrop, Elizabeth, 116
Wolff, Ashley, 102
Wood, Audrey, 66, 108
Wood, Don (I), 66, 108

Yashima, Taro, 93
Yolen, Jane, 193
Young, Ed (I), 69

Zemach, Margot, 88
Zhoa, Li (I), 70
Zimmer, Dirk (I), 119
Zolotow, Charlotte, 173
Zuromskis, Diane Stanley (I), 158